[英国]查尔斯·福斯特 著　刘文戈 译

牛津通识读本·

医事法
Medical Law
A Very Short Introduction

译林出版社

图书在版编目（CIP）数据

医事法／（英）查尔斯·福斯特（Charles Foster）著；刘文戈译.
—南京：译林出版社，2020.8（2021.11重印）
（牛津通识读本）
书名原文：Medical Law: A Very Short Introduction
ISBN 978-7-5447-8257-9

I.①医… II.①查… ②刘… III.①卫生法－研究 IV.①D912.160.4

中国版本图书馆CIP数据核字（2020）第069929号

Copyright © Charles Foster 2013
Medical Law was originally published in English in 2013.
This Bilingual Edition is published by arrangement with Oxford University Press and is for sale in the People's Republic of China only, excluding Hong Kong SAR, Macau SAR and Taiwan, and may not be bought for export therefrom.
Chinese and English edition copyright © 2020 by Yilin Press, Ltd

著作权合同登记号　图字：10-2019-340 号

医事法　［英国］查尔斯·福斯特／著　刘文戈／译

责任编辑　许　丹　何本国
装帧设计　景秋萍
校　　对　戴小娥
责任印制　董　虎

原文出版　Oxford University Press，2013
出版发行　译林出版社
地　　址　南京市湖南路1号A楼
邮　　箱　yilin@yilin.com
网　　址　www.yilin.com
市场热线　025-86633278
排　　版　南京展望文化发展有限公司
印　　刷　江苏扬中印刷有限公司
开　　本　635毫米×889毫米　1/16
印　　张　18.5
插　　页　4
版　　次　2020年8月第1版
印　　次　2021年11月第2次印刷
书　　号　ISBN 978-7-5447-8257-9
定　　价　39.00元

版权所有·侵权必究

译林版图书若有印装错误可向出版社调换　质量热线：025-83658316

序 言
王 岳

回溯医学发展的历史,可以发现其最早起源于宗教帮助,起源于人类对同族的怜悯之心,从医学诞生之初就一直带有浓厚的人文情怀,从来不仅仅是简单的治病救人。然而由于科学技术的发展,医者从以"精神支持"为主的帮助者变为以"治病救人"为主的帮助者。在一次次医学技术的突飞猛进中,医者越发获得成功的惊喜与战胜病魔的自信,而其专断地位也越发明显。医疗服务有别于一般的民商事服务,主要在于医师对患者拥有一种"专家权力"。美国学者约翰·弗伦奇认为,"权力"就是让别人听你的话,所以除了我们熟知的国家机器拥有的公权力,还有另外四种权力,其中专家群体拥有的便是"专家权力"。法律往往会更关注弱势一方,这样才可能最终实现公平目标。正是由于医方所处的专家优势地位,使得法律制度的设计与实施都往往会将天平更向患者一方倾斜。

一直以来医疗行业堪比一个独立王国,自己制定自己的游戏规则。法律很少介入医疗行业事务,法官也自然都很尊敬医师。医师等医务人员都是尊重艺术、科学,拥有重要技能的专业人员。一般来讲,公众十分信任这一学科,医师对患者也怀着老师般的尊重,这就自然意味着医务人员不是昂贵和具有潜在破坏性的诉讼的对象。所以法官也一直在很大程度上允许医师们设置自己的行业标准,进行集体专业评估,只要标准能被同伴广泛接受。这样的方式也许不能使标准设在很高的水平上,可能仅仅是可以容忍的最低程度。然而,巨大利益诱惑下的医疗行为,其固有的侵袭性让公众越发明白那些传统的医学伦理原则似乎已经靠不住了,转而诉诸后果更为严肃和实用的法律问责和赔偿救济。公众希望那些医疗行为施于自己时,作为基本权利的生命健康能得到妥当安排与保障,各种医疗专断行为都能受到法律的管控,更为重要的是一旦受到伤害可以获得法律救济和赔偿。医事法由此在世界范围内开始兴起,但法律的介入并不意味着医疗活动理应变得冷漠无情,医学的温情绝不应当远离。恰恰相反,医事法带给医学界的是比伦理规则更为明显的"触动",一个个判例倒逼着封闭的医学界反思、改进,从另外一个维度捍卫了医学应有的人文关怀与利他精神。

  在本书的第一章,作者在介绍医事法的"起源与变迁"时就告诉读者,欧美医事法的发展总体上呈现出从传统医学主导立场向司法主导立场的转变。医事法诞生之前的医疗行业领域一直被行业自律规则所支配,那时的医师是被神圣化了的,人们对这一行业十分信任。即便是在法院之上,法官也会因为自身与医疗服务行业从业者之间所具有的专业知识鸿沟,因为医生职业定位的神圣化,抑或是因为某些法官对自己职业的"居安思危"的多虑,而表现出"畏首畏尾"的情绪。这一点在欧美国家一直持续到法院面对医疗纠纷被"博勒姆标准"所支配的时代。然而,这样的事实恰恰违反了法学最基本的原则:任何人不能做自己案件的法官。医事法诞生之后,"博勒姆标准"带给法院的影响依然存在,只不过经历了"后撤"和回到本应属于它的正确位置的过程。

相比国外,我国医事法研究起步较晚,特别是过去很长一段时间,我国传统医学教育忽视了人文社会科学素养的培养,无论是对病患的人文关怀还是最基础的法律意识都显得如此淡薄。随着医患冲突日趋尖锐,越来越多的学者将研究视野从传统法学、医学领域中分离出来,转向人文医学以及医事法领域潜心耕耘,对相关问题进行广泛而深入的探究,从而激起了医学与法学更加深度的融合。我国医事法领域尚处于创始阶段,国内医事法学领域专著大多以教材为主,相关译著也较为稀缺。

"牛津通识读本"向来被誉为真正的"大家小书",本书作为其中之一,对学者进行比较法研究、读者扩展医事法知识具有重要价值。全书讨论了医事法的基本原理以及长期以来备受学者关注的核心问题,如医事法的起源与变迁、生育权利、堕胎争议、胚胎及胎儿的法律地位、病患隐私权与知情同意权的保护、医疗过失、人体试验、医疗资源的分配等。除此之外,本书还涉及一些颇具争议的医事法前沿问题,如脑死亡标准、预立医疗指示、器官移植、安乐死、基因技术等问题。借助译者深厚的语言功底,中文版将医事法领域原本晦涩的专业问题论述得深入浅出,语言生动平实,举重若轻。无论是医事法初学者还是理论研究者,甚至包括医务工作者在内的广大读者,都值得一读。全书虽然篇幅不大,却引用大量英美法上的经典判例辅助论证,打破了医事法理论与实践的壁垒，成为此书最大的亮点之一，为学者从事实证研究提供新思路、新方法，也为我们今后研究相关问题储备了大量案例素材。

　　医事法的未来会如何？作者在最后一章中，既提出了对医事法循序渐进发展的乐观心态，也对医学界在未来被"技术宅"所支配表示出一定的担忧，并寄希望于培养不会被复杂的医学专业知识所吓倒的专业法官，来解决"博勒姆标准"的滥用问题。医事法的未来毫无疑问仍要面对无边无际的新问题，所要解决的事项也会随着医学的发展而变化，然而不变的是医事法要不断地面对关于医学生命价值的争议，所讨论的问题永远不过是"人类的尊严"，这也是医事法最根本的价值取向。因此，如作者所说，让医事法循序渐进地发展也未尝不可，"新问题不过是老问题的变种"。不过，无论在我国还是在欧美国家，医事法对医疗行业的监管都没有达到理想状态，或者说医事法的实证发展一直没有追上医学发展的脚步，如何提高医事法发展效率也是医事法学人需要思考的问题。特别将此书推荐给那些从事医事法研究与教学的人士，读后定会有所裨益。

2020年5月5日

目 录

致谢 1

第 一 章　起源与变迁　1
第 二 章　医事法的实施　9
第 三 章　生命起始之前　18
第 四 章　保密与隐私　32
第 五 章　同意权　45
第 六 章　医疗过失　61
第 七 章　人体研究　80
第 八 章　医疗资源分配　90
第 九 章　生命的终止　96
第 十 章　器官捐献与人体部位的所有权　114
第十一章　医事法的未来　125

本书探讨的案例　129

索引　134

英文原文　141

致　谢

作为他人观点的马赛克拼图，每一本书都可谓是"剽窃"作品。这种情况在法律著作中尤为常见。作者的贡献无非是用新颖的形式重排既有的观点，并适当加工。通常情况下，观点的来源无从追溯，它们可能来自研讨会上某人扬起的眉头，也可能来自某句发言中耐人寻味的语气。可以说，任何一份致谢名单都无法涵盖所有需要被感谢的人，从而有失公平。尽管如此，以下我仍打算感谢一些给予我大力支持的人。

他们包括：乔纳森·赫林、托尼·霍普、迈克·帕克、朱利安·瑟武列斯库、理查德·阿什克罗夫特、罗杰·布朗斯沃德、阿哈龙·巴拉克、米凯伊·邓恩、马克·希恩、多姆·威尔金森、约翰·基翁、约翰·廷格尔和简·凯伊，还有那一众曾经温和而又气势汹汹地指出本人谬误的出庭律师和牛津大学出版社的匿名审稿人，以及牛津大学格林坦普顿学院的院长、研究员们和学生们。

我不明白为何作者们总是觉得有必要以"所有文责概由笔者承担"作为致谢的结尾。一直以来,我都被教导要少说废话。因此,本人的致谢就此打住。

查尔斯·福斯特
2012年4月,于牛津大学格林坦普顿学院

第一章

起源与变迁

医事法是一个新兴的独立专业领域,对医疗行业的管理则历史悠久。通过侵入人体获得报酬是一种引人注目的特权,这也伴随着特殊的责任。长久以来,众所周知的是,医学与其他行当有所不同(即使这一点正在被迅速地遗忘)。也许整形外科医生与木匠拥有同样的技能,但自古以来骨骼和肌肉都被认为是由重要的甚至是神秘的物质组成,它们与松木或胶合板是不一样的。骨骼和血肉是灵魂的容器。假如容器陷入混乱,那么灵魂会遭受侵扰。以上种种,让包括内科和外科在内的所有医生获得了大祭司般的权威,令人敬畏。

医学权威的可问责性

祭司是一个独立存在的阶层,在人们的期望中,他们应当比芸芸众生表现得更好。所有的祭司都在神殿里侍奉神明,对神明负责。同样地,那些在人类灵魂的物质神殿中侍奉(无论是开胸探查,还是将水蛭置于残肢)的祭司们(医生),应当对躯体的主人或是代表着他们的社会负责。然而，这种可问责性面临着一个问题：如果这个祭司的地位至高无上，而这种工作的专业性远远超过问责者的智识，那么问责该如何实现呢？

医生们说服大家，为了公众的利益，医界必须自律。作为最佳例证的"希波克拉底誓词"出现于公元前5世纪（也许是希波克拉底学派从一些神秘的毕达哥拉斯学派前辈那里借用而来）。这项行为准则由医生起草，以医生为对象，也主要由医生实施。

在这之后两千五百年岁月的大部分时间里，"希波克拉底誓词"，或者说它的诸多变体中的某一个，形成了医学界的法律规范。需要指出的是，这些"准则"并非通常意义上的法律。它们由伦理规范组成，是一个非常专业的职业群体的内部规则。医学的圣地由穿着白大褂、身上血迹斑斑的执刀祭司们主宰。除非自律明显失效，或者法律获得罕有的自信，抑或出现质疑神秘精英自治的政治必要性，否则法律很难认为踏足医学的圣地是必要或恰当的。

总体观察，欧陆国家对医疗界的管理走在英国、英联邦国家及美国的前面，这背后的原因很难概而论之。例如，法国和德国对医生的保密义务设定法律责任远早于英国，但各国如此设定的动机却不一样。天主教传统的法国也许受到忏悔和告解室中类似保密义务的影响。如果的确如此，法国的医疗保密义务可能就源自告解的神圣性，而非对患者的人权保障。与此不同，德国则比很多国家更热衷于为了监管而监管。然而，直到20世纪中叶，几乎世界各地的医疗从业者在享有优越的社会地位的同时，还拥有近乎豁免的法律地位，这令人难以接受。

纳粹德国改变了这一状况。纳粹德国医生们的所作所为表

图1 希波克拉底(约公元前460—约前370),"西方医学之父",被认为(可能是误认)是"希波克拉底誓词"的作者。作为一篇关于医学伦理原则的宣言,"希波克拉底誓词"衍生出后世诸多医学管理规范

明,专业的资质并不必然意味着体面与良知。

这种认识发端于法国大革命和第一次世界大战期间,血淋淋的事实全面打破了上层社会不犯错的神话。然而,人们能认清留着一字胡、拥有头衔的将军的愚蠢本质,并不意味着会承认一位保证用专业能力治病救人、措辞严谨地探讨生死问题的医生有可能是无能或彻头彻尾邪恶的。纳粹德国医生门格尔的暴行让全世界明白一件事,那就是不能将希望完全寄托于医疗界的自律。此时此刻,法律之治尤为重要。

世界各国迅速吸取教训。第二次世界大战刚刚落幕,一大批国际宣言和职业守则就纷纷面世,其中包括1947年的《日内瓦宣言》(1968年、1983年修订)和1949年世界医学会的《国际医学伦理守则》(1968年、1983年修订)。①

这种对时代思潮(zeitgeist)的变革,由职业守则具体形塑,为职业守则所体现,在对不当医疗行为的监管方面相当有效(尽管如此,如后文将探讨的,医学研究仍不断出现糟糕的问题,特别是在某些不愿意实施这些新颁布的、本就缺乏强制力的国际宣言的国家或地区)。某些技术操作不当的医疗行为系出于善意,涉及它们的司法政策则更难变革。法官们仍旧倾向于认为,判决临床行为构成医疗过失意味着造反,是马克思主义革命的危险苗头。毕竟,法官和医生曾在同样的学校学习,喝着同样的陈酿红酒。如果容许医生的专业判断被质疑,这种对于专业的质疑会如何蔓延?法律职业也许就是下一个遭受抨击的。这导致了"博勒姆标准"的滥用,本书第六章将具体探讨这个问题,该标准是

---

① 《日内瓦宣言》于1968年、1983年、1994年、2005年、2006年五次修订,世界医学会的《国际医学伦理守则》于1968年、1983年、2006年三次修订。——译者

法院最常用的判断医生是否违背义务的裁判规则。按照"博勒姆标准",如果医生的行为被令人信赖的相关专业意见所认可,则该医生的行为不构成医疗过失。尽管该标准的滥用在逐渐减少,但滥用的情形仍在发生。评判医生行为的标准应该由法律而非医生自己来设定,这是不言而喻的道理。宪法诉讼律师会这样假设,社会大众也这样希望,然而,并非世界上所有的法官都认为这是不言而喻的。英国的法官接受这种新观念的进程尤为缓慢。

一套新的医事法工具

当姗姗来迟的法律开始处理医疗专业领域问题时,它借用了为其他领域的问题设计的工具。这些工具,或是为规范羊毛交易而确立的契约性法律概念,或是为预防遗嘱执行人舞弊而建立的信托法律关系,或是用于在姜汁啤酒瓶中出现蜗牛尸体时使生产商有所认知的法律责任观念。这些法理并不一定适合照搬至手术室。法律人(出庭律师、事务律师和法官)熟悉的是土地产权转让、"禁止永久权规则"、提单的解释或是牛津-剑桥赛艇对抗赛,但他们对血液循环或胆管的解剖结构一无所知。靠法律人来推动医疗领域的法制发展(事实正是如此),法律成功适应医疗实际状况的可能性并不会增加。

出人意料的是,在法律人的推动下,医事法取得了长足进展。在有可能谈论医事法的体系之前很久,医事法专业律师群体尚未形成,那时凭借对商业案件和自然人之间侵权案件法理的粗糙类推,以及在板球赛场上磨炼出的关于公平竞争的本能,法院在为数不多的医事案件中的确趋近了正义。

各级法院所处理的医事案件数量并无确切的统计数据,其中一个原因当然是定义的模糊,即何谓"医事案件"。无论医事案件应如何定义,它们的数量在第二次世界大战以后持续增加。特别是在1970年代,医事案件的增量出现井喷。医事案件数量激增的同时,将医事法视为独立法律部门的认知也在不断提升。医事法和医事案件相互促进:医事案件越多,医事法越发达;医事法的发达增进社会大众和专业人士对提起医疗诉讼可能性的认知,从而促使越来越多案件产生。

律师们蜂拥而至,在美国情况尤其如此。追求利益的初衷并不总是有助于案件的精耕细作,但即便是贪婪的律师有时也充满智慧和富有想象力。律师们对胜诉和提升声誉的渴望,为法官通过大量判例建立独特的医事法体系创造了机会。律师们如愿以偿。

十年后,美国社会对医事诉讼的热情逐渐冷却,而英国不出所料地步了美国的后尘。显而易见,英国(以及英联邦国家)的医事法继受了美国医事法的部分核心理念。医事法领域比其他法律部门更为国际化和普世化。所有人都希望借鉴他人的经验。相比其他案件,在医事案件中,法院援引外国法院的见解无须那么多解释,也不会引起尴尬。这也许因为,医事法处理的是人类最基本的问题。美国人交易土地产权的方式可能不同于越南人,但他们面临的出生或死亡的问题是相似的。此外,也许因为与生物学和形而上学交织,这些基本问题极为棘手。这就意味着,法官们欢迎所能获得的任何帮助。不管怎样,混乱的法律"交融"(愤世嫉俗者会称之为"交叉感染")一直存在着,产出了一些令人激动、充满活力的法律混合体。

医事法学的产业

另一个类似"鸡生蛋,蛋生鸡"的重要问题与法学家们的角色有关。医事法学课程已开设多年,但在近十年才真正如雨后春笋般蓬勃发展。修过医事法学课程的学生毕业后,不仅推动着医事案件数量的增长,也使医事诉讼所涉及的法律见解越来越精细,这又反过来使得老师们拥有更多研究素材,从而催生出更多医事法学教科书和医事法学课程。这种互相促进尽管并非无限循环,至少使医事法学被公认为既是一个学术领域,又是一门专业的分支学科。在某种意义上,这也带来了某种遗憾:社会认可度提高的同时,医事法学逐渐僵化。20年前的医事法学研究神气活现,富有草莽气息。当今的医事法学研究却大腹便便、衣冠楚楚,显得暮气沉沉。曾经的百家争鸣正被逐渐增长中的"通说"取代,而"通说"的盛行往往夹杂着对所谓"异端邪说"的"火刑"。

医事法与医学伦理:紧张而多产的结合

无论是作为课程名称还是教科书标题,医事法常常有一个伙伴:医学伦理。二者伙伴关系的本质既模糊,又复杂。医学伦理旨在规范医生的行为;医事法在规范医生行为的同时,也涉及**其他事项**。但事情并不是那么简单。作为伦理法院的职业惩戒机构长着令人畏惧的牙齿。

英国上诉法院法官霍夫曼在"艾尔代尔国民医疗服务信托诉布兰德案"(1993)的判词中写道:"我期待医学伦理由法律形塑,而非相反的状况。"乍看上去,他的观点仿佛存在谬误。"博勒姆标准"影响深远,在多数司法管辖区的法院,医疗责任的认定取决于医学专业同行评议。如果临床医师的行为方式获得令人信赖的相关专业医生团体认可,就不会被法院判定为构成医疗过失。通常情况下(例如涉及同意权和保密的法律问题),对医疗行为有责性的法律评价明显带有医学伦理的色彩。相关监管机构制定的医学伦理规范会被判决引用,专家们会围绕专业操守是否会导致与被告同样的结果发表鉴定意见。医学伦理似乎主导着法律的实践。

事实是否的确如此?究竟是谁在起草伦理规范?通常,法律人会参与相关委员会,将他们的聪明才智和愚蠢想法一并塞入伦理规范草案。而法律人提出的意见往往未经证明为正当就得到尊重。通过制定伦理规范和参加晚餐会谈,法律人有意无意间影响了外科医生、护士以及职业治疗师们的专业操守。霍夫曼法官没想到法律竟以此种方式发挥影响,但他本有可能加以矫正的。

然而,从事实务的法律人并不倾向于作哲学层面的思考,也没有这方面的兴趣。即便有这种倾向,他们往往也无暇顾及"经验法则""个案思维"这些实用主义以外的问题。在契约法领域,这种行为模式已让人气馁;在医事法领域,这种行为模式会使医事法成为一潭死水。每一个经过检视的问题都会变成《圣经·诗篇》所云:"人算什么,你竟顾念他?"若医事法完全由法律人主导,它将变得沉闷而死板。恰如其分地对待医事法的奇特主体(即人类),需要超乎寻常的深沉、博学以及多元的思维,无论就现状还是就以往的实际情形来说。这并不是一件容易的事。只有依靠哲学家的帮助,医事法才能少一些极端,多一些融贯。

第二章

医事法的实施

如果被人指控犯错,医务人员也许会身陷囹圄、穷困潦倒或蒙受羞辱,或是同时遭遇以上不幸。本章将探讨相关情形。

通往牢狱之路:刑事司法

医务人员不难发现,在行医过程中稍有不轨,穿着白大褂的他们就会被警察盯上。理论上,患者可能遭受来自医务人员的性侵犯。这类案件也真实发生过,尤以全科医生、家庭医生或者心理医生为甚。毫无疑问,相关医疗领域的特殊性为不法活动提供了机会,而不是这些特殊的医疗行为吸引了大量的性犯罪者。他们或以并不存在的临床需要为借口检查患者的乳房和阴部,或使用药物及催眠的方式使者丧失反抗能力,抑或是滥用临床摄影设备。

医务人员可能会参与各式各样的医疗诈骗活动,这类案件也真实发生过。医疗诈骗的形式既包括浮报医疗费用或是虚构为并不存在的患者所作的治疗,又包括在健康的牙齿上钻孔和填充的行为。

关于医疗诈骗的法律与非医疗领域诈骗的法律别无二致。任何刑法教科书都包含相同的法律原则。本书在第五章介绍同意权时，会探讨性侵犯或其他侵犯人身犯罪在医疗领域的特殊问题。医生和护士致人死亡的法律问题相当特别，引人入胜，且充满争议。

本书在第九章探讨生命的终止时，会探讨医疗活动中的谋杀与非预谋杀人问题。当清醒且具备行为能力的患者请求医生协助自杀时，国家能否对医生故意但出于同情的"舒缓死亡"行为提起公诉？这一问题无疑存在巨大而激烈的争论。

法律如何处理意外致人死亡的情形？刑事法的大枪口是否会瞄准那些因为小错酿成致命后果的医生？

以下举两个例子说明。

在一项重大腹腔手术过程中，患者突发大出血。外科医生对此既不知情，也无从预料。出血导致患者的血压骤降，如果注意到这个情况，麻醉师应该能迅速解决。然而，麻醉师没能察觉。为了打发漫长手术过程带来的倦意，麻醉师正在做填字游戏。最终，患者死于心脏骤停。

另一名患者的身体置入了硬膜外导管以进行麻醉，她大喊大叫着请求增加麻醉药的剂量。一位护士在压力之下顺手拿起药剂，没有查对药名就进行注射。该药剂实际上是一种剧毒的癌症化疗药，患者随后死亡。

警方介入了两起案件的处置。两起案件的受害者家庭都主张遭受到难以弥补的侵权损害。两起案件的当事医务人员都可能被送交相关的行业监管机构，也许还面临终生禁业的后果。

刑事诉讼程序会带来什么样的后果？

按照通常观念，致人死亡是重大事项，理应由国家严肃处置，而不是仅交由那些与事件有千丝万缕联系的人来处理。国家的建立旨在保护每个人的安全，刑事诉讼中的检察官正是国家保护义务的部分体现，而起诉行为本身就昭示着人类生命神圣性的一些重要价值（在司法鉴定结论与被告的过错不成比例时，也许**更是**如此）。

然而，关于国家责任的范围存在一些争论。国家有责任调查公民的死因（例如，《欧洲人权公约》第2条所规定的责任）。原因在于，调查既包含了健康的情感宣泄，又可以让悲剧的教训能被吸取。对于未来事故的预防，重要性还体现在另一方面，即刑事诉讼过程的剧场化效果会使其他潜在犯错者更加小心翼翼。

尽管如此，也有许多其他更恰当的途径来表明生命的重要性，彰显国家的作为。在大多数现代国家，死因裁判庭或其他死因调查程序发挥着刑事审判的揭示真相和（一定程度上）宣泄情感的功能。职业惩戒程序确保作为个体的医生能获得自我负罪感所不能给予的教训，让整个职业群体同上一堂防范风险的公开课。在刑事诉讼程序基础上增设一种程序，不过是消耗了本可用于改善医疗的经费，延宕了悲伤反应的开始，还迎合了黄色小报的趣味。

然而，患者家属们往往选择刑事诉讼程序。复仇是一种古老而根深蒂固的本能。

通往贫穷之路：民事侵权索偿

相比被提起公诉，医生们更容易成为民事诉讼的被告。原告们的主张通常如出一辙："被告不应该做此行为。这种行为给我造成损害。我请求赔偿。"典型案由包括医疗过失（参见第六章）、侵犯同意权（参见第五章）或是违背保密义务及侵犯隐私（参见第四章）。

在大多数司法管辖区，这类诉讼由职业法官独立审理。这些法官不一定掌握医事案件所需的专业知识，而世界范围内的趋势是司法专门化。

在某些司法管辖区（特别是美国），民事诉讼通常仍由非法律专业的陪审员审理。被告及其保险公司对此闻风丧胆。假如你是一名会计师，你会希望一群对资产负债表一窍不通的陪审员来评判你编制资产负债表的能力吗？主审法官很难让陪审员们紧扣主线。陪审员们很容易就被自己的喜好或情感左右，而不是关注案件事实。

在某些地方（正如英国的普遍情形），医疗服务由公共机构提供，通常公共机构而非个体的医生是医疗民事诉讼的被告。但即使在英国，大量由国家付费的医疗服务也是通过私人医生或是家庭医生（即全科医生）提供的，他们虽然最终由国家付酬，却具有独立的被告资格。假如私人医生或全科医生投保并足额缴纳保险费，且相关医疗事故纠纷属于保险条款覆盖范围（不端性行为等一般不在保险范围内），则保险公司会为医生提供保障并支付诉讼费用，包括败诉后承担的原告律师费。因此，一般而言，只要医生持续缴纳保险费，并且被诉行为"限于"过失的话，他还不至于流离失所。

医事诉讼是一个大产业，催生了职业责任保险。医疗事故保险费构成任何医生执业成本的主要部分，在高诉讼风险科别

（例如外科的各个分支）以及诉讼标的巨大的科别（例如产科，因为脑瘫婴儿的赔偿金额高企），这种情况尤为突出。

2011年的一项对美国医生的研究指出，75%的"低风险"科别医生和几乎所有"高风险"科别医生，在职业生涯的某个时候都会面临医疗事故的诉讼。但这并不意味着医生一定会败诉。大多数诉讼并没有给原告带来赔偿，这种结果在美国和世界其他地方相差无几。由于具体赔偿金额取决于不同司法管辖区的具体赔偿制度，更详细的统计数据几乎毫无意义。

在美国的许多州，强烈的改革呼声此起彼伏。部分改革已经付诸实施。改革方案通常包括，建立审理医疗事故诉讼的专门法院（假定专门法院能更高效地审理案件，从而能降低成本，且不容易被雄辩的律师愚弄）、缩短原告的起诉时效，以及为伤痛及生活不便的赔偿金额设定上限（这类赔偿主张无法通过科学的方法计算，陪审员们有时会以过分同情而全然不合理的方式判定赔偿金额）。

通往蒙羞和失业之路：惩戒和监督程序

直面职业惩戒裁判庭的聆讯是许多医务人员最害怕的事。除非道德败坏、极端大意或是非常不走运，医务人员通常不会进入刑事法院。尽管针对伤害的民事索偿麻烦而丢人，但相关诉讼通常由保险公司来兜底。监管部门审理的医疗投诉事件则几乎肯定被公之于众，会给医生带来与刑事诉讼相当的恶名。此外，由于投诉事件有可能会导致停止执业的处罚，对于医生的个人财务也是毁灭性的打击。

大多数司法管辖区都建立了某种行业自律制度，职业惩戒的程序可以被称为"准刑事诉讼"程序，包括根据标准流程展开的调查、"控方"向"被告"开示所有证据材料、详细的指控、类似刑事法院内进行的询问与交叉询问以及"判刑"环节，甚至还包括关于做证和其他减轻处罚的规定。

监管部门的裁判庭必然涉及公众对行业的信任。暂停执业或吊销执业登记证等处罚的实施，可能仅仅是为了平息公众的不满。这就使得监管部门的裁判庭有可能沦为暴民私刑的复杂形式，它重视媒体对"一磅肉"[①]的呼声，却忽略了程序规则与基本公平的要求。裁判庭的许多决定之所以被当事人提交到负责公法诉讼的法院进行司法审查，此即原因之一。

公法诉讼

医事法领域很多重要判决是关于公共机构（通常是地方或国家层面的医疗保障提供者）行为的合法性问题，诸如对某种特定类型诊疗项目资助的决定、审批人类胚胎研究的决定，以及在国家层级治疗操作守则中设定用于判断撤除生命维持治疗的标准的决定。

这类问题的诉讼方式很大程度上取决于不同司法管辖区的特殊体制。比如，在美国、德国和南非，有可能会激活宪法诉讼；而在以色列，则会处理基本法问题。英国则规定了广泛的对行政行为的司法审查。在包括英国在内的《欧洲人权公约》缔约国，法律及其实施措施可以基于违反《欧洲人权公约》的理由被

---

① 莎士比亚作品《威尼斯商人》中，夏洛克借给商人安东尼奥一笔钱。安东尼奥承诺，如果不还钱，就割下自己身上的一磅肉给他作为惩罚。该典故用来形容合乎法律但不合情理的要求。——译者

法院审查，相关案件最终可上诉到位于斯特拉斯堡的欧洲人权法院。欧洲人权法院的很多案件涉及医疗问题。在其他很多司法管辖区也存在类似的制度。

人权话语在医事法领域颇为常见，这不足为怪。医事诉讼常常引起关于人类的终极追问，不仅包括人与自己身体的关系，也包括人与他人身体的关系。人类汇成了社会洪流，而每个人都在社会洪流中畅游。

缺乏行为能力患者的诉讼问题

由法院为缺乏行为能力的当事人作决定，是医事法领域最具有法律难度、容易造成群情激奋而导致政治冲突的问题，例如涉及儿童以及永久或暂时丧失行为能力的成年人的情形。法官们常常判决对心智不全的患者实施强制绝育，允许医生将挣扎中的"耶和华见证人"儿童信徒绑在操作台上，实施挽救生命的输血，哪怕她父母认为输血使她永远被抛入火湖。法官们有时还让医生撤除对失去知觉患者提供的人工营养支持（通常伴随着患者家属的强烈抗议），使患者因此而死亡。

决定治疗措施的案件是极端而富有戏剧性的例子，显示了众所周知的充满仁慈的家长式司法。每一天，在世界各地，成千上万的家事法官们都要决定，与母亲或父亲生活是否符合儿童的最佳利益；而依照同样或类似的标准，相同或类似的法官们要决定孩子是生还是死符合其最佳利益。法官们经常要决定丧失行为能力成年人的医疗照顾者是否可以从患者的银行账户取得报酬；而遵循相似的司法过程，法官们要决定是否允许医生从这样的患者的骨盆中取出卵巢。

解决医事法纠纷的一站式商店?

各类医事争讼/纠纷解决机制既重复,又浪费。假设一位医生在手术中夹错了血管而导致患者死亡,单单由于这个过错,他可能既要面临重大过失致人死亡的刑事起诉,又要被患者家属和财产继承人提起民事索偿诉讼,同时还要应付死因裁判庭,以及在监管部门的裁判庭为保住自己的执业资格而辩护。以上种种还不包括来自医院的内部调查,这些调查结果可能会导致他的工作合约接受审查。如果他在辩护中主张医院人力资源不足危及医疗安全,有关医疗资源配置的问题就很可能被处理公法诉讼的法院加以司法审查。

除了律师,没人喜欢这种错综复杂的法律程序。医生可能需要就同一证据反复做证五六次,患者家属将被迫一遍又一遍地听到同一个令人悲伤痛苦的故事(被迫搁置悲伤反应,直到律师们完成案情的厘清),许多收费不菲的独立专家可能被邀请就同一组事实提供鉴定意见。有可能,不同的裁判主体会得出截然相反的结论。民事诉讼的法官可能认为医生行为堪称模范、完全不存在过失,而职业惩戒调查组却判定医生的行为存在严重过失,应该终生禁止执业。

考虑到不菲的律师费、医生承受的压力以及患者家属面临的悲痛,能否用一个程序处理所有问题?

答案是"不能"。尽管始于同一医疗事实,每种纠纷解决机制却都有其独特的目标和相应的程序,不同纠纷解决机制的目标和程序间并不总是兼容。例如,刑事诉讼与民事诉讼对于"过失"的定义不同,刑事诉讼要求的证明标准更高。民事索赔的损害赔偿评估程序烦琐,相关证据与各司法管辖区鲜明的本地特色密不可分。为了吸取教训、预防类似不幸事件重演,死因裁判庭会比其他法院更深入地调查造成事件的背景原因。

当然,纠纷解决机制的差异性并不绝对排斥一定程度的整合。在欧洲的一些司法管辖区,某种程度上法院可以在同一程序中处理刑事诉讼和民事索赔。相关经验有一定借鉴意义。但遗憾的是,只要我们认可各种不同目标存在的正当性,绝大多数律师将继续以此为业。

第三章

生命起始之前

尽管可以被B超或其他更具侵入性的医疗设备探查，子宫仍是一个神秘的器官。从生理学角度看，子宫内部的活动充满谜团。妊娠的过程可以通过人体解剖学的研究初步呈现，一些表层的机理也可以得到解释，但相关过程的本质和驱动器官运作的详细机制仍有待澄清。

法律一直满足于不顾形而上学的争议，专注于讨论子宫内的相关问题。法律倾向于使用"权利-义务"的理论工具在"出生前"这一灰色地带游刃，拒绝陷入关于早期胚胎法律地位的哲学争论。在运用"权利-义务"工具的过程中，法律恪守适当而恭敬的谨慎。

生育的权利与义务

一般而言，在世界上大多数地方，如果你想成为父母，遵循自然规律你就可以达成心愿。你的配子可以和几乎任何人的配子融合。如果不想生儿育女，那么你没有义务这么做。

不足为奇,法律保障生育的权利,至少不给人们的生育过程制造过多障碍。繁育后代是人类最根本的本能,但优生学的阴影仍自然而然地引起恐慌。

法律很少对生育的权利设定限制。为了避免明显的遗传缺陷,许多国家都禁止乱伦。出于类似考虑,法律不允许在人工生殖中使用(比如)父母和子女或兄弟姐妹之间的配子制造胚胎。在大多数地方,通过融合人类的配子和其他物种的配子来制作(或制作和繁育)胚胎被法律禁止。国家也立法规范年轻人的婚育,要求人达到适当的年龄方可合法地交媾或结婚。假如遵守伦常、达到法定年龄且不涉及人兽混交的问题,人便可以自由繁衍。

《欧洲人权公约》第12条的规定体现了这一国际共识:"达到结婚年龄的男女享有结婚和成立家庭的权利,各国制定结婚和成立家庭的法律。"该条后半句的规定存在掏空前半句权利的可能,但实际上任何国家都不会这么做。

以上规定并不意味着人们有权获得公共资助以实施体外受精。这也不意味着在服刑过程中,因犯有权请求当局在任意时间安排其配偶入狱进行"夫妻访问"[参见"ELH和PBH诉联合王国案"(1998)]。不过在配偶存在罹患不孕症风险时,前述情况可以有例外处理[参见"梅勒诉内政大臣案"(2002)]。

主张生育属于权利是稀松平常的,主张生育不属于**义务**则极为平常,以至于主张生育属于义务会被视为另类。事实上,主张生育属于义务完全具备充分的理由,法庭上也常常探讨这个理由。

黛安娜·布拉德的丈夫在世时,曾储存精子。黛安娜·布拉德希望使用这些精子受孕。法院拒绝了她的请求,判决的理据非常充分:这是为了让该男子的灵魂免于面对那未曾谋面的子女所带来的情感上或金钱上的困扰。判决对该案造成了残酷的后果,但这并不是推翻判决的理由[参见"人类授精和胚胎研究管理局诉布拉德案"(1997)]。

可能有观点认为,如果事情涉及已经植入子宫的胚胎,而不仅仅是使用精子,情况会有所不同。胚胎的利益加上母亲的生育意愿,分量应当足够胜过男人对繁殖的拒绝。然而,事与愿违,拒绝为人父的自主权利胜过所有相反的主张[参见"埃文斯诉联合王国案"(2006)]。

我们可以发现,相同的思维被用于另一些案件,即胚胎的父亲要求法院阻止妻子或女友进行人工流产的情形。在人工流产合法的情形中,男方的诉讼请求被驳回了。拒绝为人父母的权利高于为人父母的权利[参见"计划生育协会密苏里州中部分会诉丹福思案"(1976)、"C诉S案"(1988)和"佩顿诉联合王国案"(1981)]。

综上所述,我们也许可以得出结论:与其他任何权利冲突时,胚胎或胎儿的权利并不占上风。但如果以此为普遍结论,并不准确。

胚胎和胎儿的权利问题

法律的稳定性不应受到苛责,其哲学上的复杂性更不应受到指责。本书撰写时,除了极少数笃信天主教的拉美国家,人工流产在世界各国几乎都是合法的。然而,不同国家的规定千差万别:有的国家仅允许为了挽救母亲的性命而实施人工流产;

另一些国家则允许基于任何理由实施人工流产。一般情况下，社会大众的宗教信仰状况决定了该国人工流产的合法空间，这不足为奇。但是，这并不必然意味着人工流产宽松的国家，对胚胎的法律地位毫不在意。相反，这些国家的相关法理论述显示出那些反堕胎国家有时缺少的缜密思考。只是（他们会说），在审慎而痛苦地考虑过这个冲突之后，他们认为，意志坚定的成年母亲所享有的权利高于神秘的胚胎所享有的权利（如果存在）：前者是明显而可识别的，后者却是模糊且附条件的。

反堕胎运动者们会说，这些都是无稽之谈。确实，在价值权衡过程中存在两种权利：母亲的权利和胚胎的权利。母亲的生命权很少会受到威胁。假如遇到这种情形，就算是最保守的天主教徒也认为应另当别论。

通常情况下，受到威胁的是母亲避免因几个月的怀孕带来生活不适的权利，她自主选择生活道路的权利也会减损。"生命至上"①论者指出，这些权利本质上属于便利权，它们的保障一般遵照《欧洲人权公约》第8条。此外，"生命至上"论者进一步论证道，胎儿生命权的保障应当一直具有压倒性优势（比如《欧洲人权公约》第2条所规定的）。这不是显而易见的吗？从逻辑上讲，便利权必须以生命权为前提且服从于生命权。假如生命不存在，便利也就无从体验。

相关争议已有充分的讨论，稍后我们再探讨这个议题。但就当下而言，该论证足以让法学家和法官（其中许多人希望保持合法人工流产这个可能选项）对赋予胚胎任何权利持审慎态度，至

---

① 本书中"反堕胎"和"生命至上"是同义词。——译者

少是就早期胚胎的情形而言。这通常体现为拒绝承认胚胎、胎儿或未出生的婴儿拥有法律人格（每次有人鲁莽地使用"未出生的婴儿"一词，都会激起轩然大波）。在这种认知模式中，仅仅由于被移动几英寸、从子宫内拽出阴道，婴儿就神奇地变成完整的人，获得法律对人的全部保障。尽管简明清晰，这种认知模式存在着既与生理学事实不一致（例如，事实上妊娠23周以后胎儿的发育过程会变得更为复杂），又与人的感性认知不一致的缺陷。

在某些法律领域，赋予胎儿法律人格有利于法律的实施。事实上，有些制度确实是为此而设立的。例如，在英国法中，胎儿可以继承财产。但是出于其他考虑，赋予胎儿法律人格并不那么有利于法律的实施。于是，法律动动手脚，胎儿的法律人格就烟消云散。它们若隐若现，忽有忽无。

我们来看以下几个案例。

"刑事法领域无疑已经确立这种认知，和民事法领域一样……母亲腹中的胎儿并不具有人格，其消亡并不导致普通法上的金钱惩罚或其他责任。"["英格兰及威尔士总检察长1994年第3号司法解释案"（1998），英国上议院审理]

"允许未出生的胎儿起诉它的未来母亲可能导致法律中出现全新的概念；未出生的胎儿和母亲作为法律上独立的人，处于分离而对峙的关系中……"["温尼伯西北区域儿童和家庭服务机构诉G案"（1997），加拿大最高法院审理]

"毫无疑问，在英格兰和威尔士，胎儿出生前没有诉讼权，没有任何权利。"["佩顿诉英国孕期咨询服务机构理事会案"（1979），英国上诉法院审理]

这些关于胎儿法律地位的不同定位被用于不同目的。例如，在加拿大和其他很多国家，胎儿不能就生母在怀孕期间对其造成的损害提起诉讼。然而，假如医生或其他任何人导致胎儿受到伤害（例如，由于过失给怀孕的母亲使用不合适的药品），胎儿在出生后便可以起诉医生索偿。医生不可以反驳："在我犯下医疗过失的时候你还不存在，我怎么可能伤害一个不存在的人？"抑或是"你和母亲的人格不可分割，因此你的母亲，而不是你，才是适格的原告。"

有一个明显的异常之处值得注意。法律实际上告诉胎儿："如果你顺利出生，成为一个真正的人，我们将溯及既往赋予你完整的人格以确保你是法律认可的侵权适格对象。"这一理由让人听起来不那么顺耳。特别是在前面提到的溯及既往赋予完整人格被实施的情况下，关于母亲免于被诉的豁免也存在类似问题。母亲与胎儿有最明显的联系、最有可能伤害胎儿且最有能力保护胎儿，同时母亲应当（当然）被视为对未出生的婴儿负有某种监护责任的人，她又为何是唯一不用承担法律责任的人？

在另外一些情况下，为胚胎、胎儿或未出生的婴儿赋予法律**人格在一定意义上**是有用的。因此，这一观点被越来越多地提及，并不奇怪。这既是回应现实的需要，也能为达成相关目的提供必要支撑。

以下我们将举例说明。体外受精的过程会产生许多"备用"胚胎。它们应当被如何对待？直觉告诉我们，这些胚胎应受到尊重。于是胚胎被赋予足够的法律地位以体现这种尊重。大多数司法管辖区的制定法或判例法都或多或少对此进行了规定。负责胚胎/胎儿医学研究的英国波尔金霍恩委员会在1989年提出建立国际共识。它指出,胎儿具有"特殊的法律地位……在胎儿每一个发育阶段,我们会表达基于其发育成真正的人的潜质而应有的必要尊重"。

在一起涉及对怀孕母亲实施强制医疗的案件中,为了拯救胎儿,英国上诉法院判决强调:"无论被看作什么,一个36周大的胎儿显然并非无关紧要;如果能自然存活,它会有生命,而且无疑是一个活生生的人。"[参见"圣乔治国民医疗服务信托诉S案"(1998)]

欧洲人权法院持这种立场,即对胚胎、胎儿的法律地位采用这种操作便利但不太体面的不可知论态度。该立场导致了发生在里昂综合医院的不幸。

两位姓"武"(Vo)[①]的女士于同一天在里昂综合医院就诊,一位怀孕六个月,另一位是去摘除避孕环的。由于医院混淆了两位患者,医生们尝试在怀孕的武女士身上摘除不存在的避孕环,导致她的羊水膜被刺穿。武女士的怀孕被迫终止,医院实施了引产。

该案上诉到斯特拉斯堡的欧洲人权法院,主要争点是未出生的婴儿是否享有《欧洲人权公约》第2条规定的生命权。该条的表述是:"任何人的生命权应当受到法律的保护。"这里的"任何人"是否涵盖未出生的婴儿?假如答案是不加限定的"是",影响会非常深远,那些允许人工流产的法律岌岌可危。

考虑再三,法院的多数方意见选择含糊其词,其判决实际上没有做出抉择。判词指出:"在欧洲的层面……对于胚胎/胎儿

[①] 越南裔法国人姓氏。——译者

的属性和法律地位尚未达成共识……从好的方面看,或许可以认为,各国不同制度间的最大公约数是胚胎/胎儿属于人类。胚胎/胎儿因具备发育成人的可能性而受到民事法律的保护……为了人的尊严而请求法律保护并不能推导出胚胎/胎儿属于《欧洲人权公约》第2条'生命权'的主体'人'……基于前述分析,法院深信,现阶段回应未出生的婴儿是否属于《欧洲人权公约》第2条所保障的人的范围这一抽象命题,既不可取也不现实。"24[参见"武诉法国案"(2004)]从判词中不难看出,胚胎/胎儿被赋予某种法律地位,但法院无意厘清,更不愿展开演绎。

在美国,相关问题也面临类似的处境。有观点认为,胎儿不属于美国联邦宪法第十四修正案所保障的"人"[比如,参见"罗伊诉韦德案"(1973)中布莱克门大法官的意见书]。然而在一些特殊情况下(特别是达到妊娠三个月这一关键的分水岭),胎儿有权受到美国联邦宪法第十四修正案的保障。这或是基于类推,或是基于法制的微调,抑或是出于政治上的权宜考虑。

在这种环境下,法律只能通过零敲碎打的方式勉强提供各种解决方案。由于缺乏清晰且可识别的法律身份,胚胎抵御外来侵害困难重重。胚胎的地位低于真实的人,甚至也低于并不实际存在的人。胚胎只是潜在的人,这是反对为胚胎赋予人类同等权利的观点的理论基础之一。对胚胎的医学研究通常被允许(例如在英国),理由是这项研究对尚未出生的人类具有重要价值。这种观点不能说是错误的,但条理不清。

国家通常规定禁止孕育具有特定遗传特征的孩子(禁止乱伦的法律),但罕有国家强制母亲在怀孕到足月前流产。当然,也有例外。缺乏行为能力的患者如果怀孕,可以被强制实施人工流产,哪怕违背其意愿。相关判决的论述往往沿着同时保护母亲和孩子(如果想生下来的话)最佳利益的脉络推进。这是为什么呢?

关于母亲最佳利益的分析是直截了当的,强制人工流产并未真正违背母亲的意志。她并未(直接)表达相关意愿。但是关于未出生婴儿的利益呢?以下几个重点值得关注。首先,胎儿在司法辩论中获得了发言权(尽管就其他目的而言,胎儿的主体地位欠缺法律承认)。仅需表达不希望继续存在的意见后就能结束陈词,它也仅被允许作此陈述。其次,根据英国和其他许多司法管辖区的法律,儿童不能基于"假如母亲没有生我更好"的主张向母亲索偿,这种主张被认为违背公共政策[例如,参见"麦凯诉埃塞克斯区域卫生局案"(1982)]。假如公共政策禁止儿童的这种主张,那么为何允许(更不用说是邀请和基于)未出生婴儿提起这种主张?

父母提出的索赔内容往往涉及养育那些计划外出生子女的经济成本,这给公众和司法带来了一些压力。这些案例通常发生在避孕操作疏忽的情形,或是没有提示避孕措施失效风险的情形下。于是,孩子的父母要求获得孩子的抚养费。

这些诉讼请求是令人不悦的,作为案件当事人的父母不希望生育孩子。在英国,这种不适感蔓延到了上议院。上议院的判决指出,孩子的出生归根结底应被认为是一件幸事,这可以远远抵消相关的经济负担[参见"麦克法兰诉泰赛德卫生局案"(2000)]。当然,这仅仅是从政策角度来阐释,且该政策似乎并未延伸到将未出生的婴儿视为幸事。说得没错,谁说法律内部必须是一致的?这把我们带回人工流产本身。

法律上有两种路径来探讨人工流产问题。一种路径是从权利的角度论证。在怀孕的不同阶段,有些司法管辖区会认为"母亲享有实施人工流产的权利"或者"胎儿享有不被杀死的权利"。另一种路径则主张人工流产表面上看不具有合法性,但自有其合理性。第一种路径的实践以美国为代表,美国联邦最高法院的著名判决"罗伊诉韦德案"(1973)即为典型。第二种路径的实践则以英国为代表。

"罗伊诉韦德案"的多数方意见认为,按照美国联邦宪法第十四修正案保障的个人自由免受国家限制的规范内涵,"女性关于是否终止怀孕的决定权"受到宪法的保障。法院也指出,女性的这一权利并非绝对的,多数方意见就此论述道:国家"可以适度地维护一些重要利益,包括保障健康、维持医疗标准或是保护潜在的生命。在怀孕的某些时间点,这些个别的利益足以支撑国家对人工流产进行监管"。

于是,在母亲和胎儿相互竞争的权利冲突中,国家合法地扮演着裁判的角色。胎儿的权利是逐渐增加的。在妊娠的前三个月,国家侧重保障孕妇的权利。在这期间,"主治医生在征询患者意见以后,根据医学专业判断来自主决定是否终止患者的妊娠,不受国家的限制"。但是,在保障胎儿生命的问题上,国家也具备利害关系。何时介入女性连续的身体自主权是正当的?法院认为,主要标准在于胎儿是否发育到可在子宫外独立生存。此后,婴儿才能独立于母亲,拥有一个"有意义的人生"。

因此,在妊娠的前三个月,女性的自主权不受国家干涉。随着胎儿生存能力的提高,国家可以基于保护母亲健康的理由对人工流产加以限制[与母亲健康有关的因素被视为医学专业判断,参见"多伊诉博尔顿案"(1973)]。当胎儿度过子宫外独立生存期后,国家可以对人工流产加以限制,直至完全禁止(除非为保障孕妇的生命或健康而必须实施人工流产)。

这种不对称的法律保障有些不同寻常。在妊娠的前三个月,国家不能干预母亲的决定,亦即不能对胎儿提供保护。但在子宫外独立生存期,国家没有义务(虽然可以)对胎儿提供保护。国家的两种保护义务(对母亲的健康和对胎儿的生命)不是等量齐观的。

很多司法管辖区采用类似的基于权利的路径来讨论人工流产问题。通常,相关法律论证为胎儿提供的保护优于美国。许多认为胎儿生命权高于母亲自主权的国家,或基于胚胎法律地位的神学假设(在许多信奉天主教的国家和信奉伊斯兰教的国家),或基于人性尊严,来保障胎儿的权益。

在英国,和在澳大利亚的一些州一样,人工流产问题并未进入"权利"话语(尽管毫无疑问,相关论点可以运用《欧洲人权公约》第8条的话语来加强,该条极为宽泛地赋予了人们按自身意愿生活的权利——或许也包括免受计划外生育子女所困扰的权利)。相反,人工流产被认为原则上非法、例外情形下合法。然而实际上,在英国,妊娠24周以内(规则变化的分界点)均可以按需要实施人工流产。这并非将人工流产定位为权利,只是说你可以轻而易举地找到医疗机构实施人工流产,不会因此而受到刑事起诉。

具有讽刺意味的是,相较于以权利为基础的司法管辖区,英国的路径使胎儿的生存面临更大威胁。假如严谨地运用权利作为母亲安全的基础,至少存在某种可能(理论上确实如此),使胎儿的权利主张在司法过程中获得同等对待。

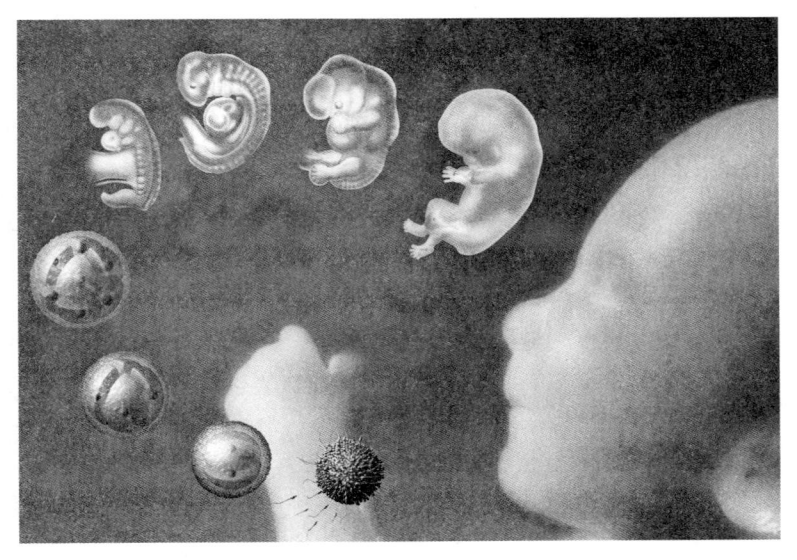

图2 发育中的胚胎/胎儿。有些观点认为，胚胎或胎儿的道德地位和/或法律地位随着它的发育而变化

克隆之辩

同卵双胞胎们互为克隆。他（她）们并不会令人恐惧，也不会必然导致功能异常。然而，对于制造克隆人的恐惧几乎影响着每个人。

涉及生殖性克隆（以胚胎足月生产为目的的克隆）的恐惧并不总是与人类胚胎的法律地位相关。不同的是，相关的恐惧关乎逾越干预自然的正当界限（"扮演上帝角色"），或是对于女性生出她自己或是她的伴侣这一想法感到恶心，同时所有克隆参与者均会蒙受心理阴影。

相关伦理问题错综复杂，相关法律问题却相对简单。几乎所有地方都将涉及人类的生殖性克隆视为非法活动。相比而言,对治疗性克隆(制作克隆胚胎用于医学研究)的管制则充斥着政治争议。例如,英国的法律规定,独立监管机构(人类授精和胚胎研究管理局)有权审批特定的申请。在美国,对克隆的监管属于各州和联邦的共同立法事项。当共和党执政时,胚胎研究的空间可能会被压缩殆尽。

在胚胎研究被定义为非法的地方,立法者对胚胎的地位作了一些评价,认为对胚胎的尊重高于医学研究可能带来的潜在好处。禁止胚胎研究的论证往往依照以下方式权衡:"从道德上看,制作和销毁胚胎所造成的恶,大于治愈运动神经元疾病所带来的善。"如果这里的"善""恶"只是与不可识别的人相关,这种权衡过程没什么困难。忽略抽象的人很容易。然而,当我们面对活生生的人时,以下说辞却是难以启齿的:"由于我相信八细胞期胚胎是不可侵犯的,你只有死路一条。"这常常是"兄姐救星"(saviour sibling)[①]案件的主要争点。

兄姐救星

三岁的扎因·哈什米患有β地中海贫血症。他最有可能生存的机会莫过于从足够匹配的兄弟姐妹那里接受脐带血干细胞。

通过自然受孕生出符合条件的弟弟妹妹的概率很低。于是他的父母寻求许可,想通过体外人工受孕方式培养胚胎。当胚胎发育到八细胞期,将从每个胚胎取出一个细胞进行测试,以确定胚胎是否能挽救扎因·哈什米的生命。英国的监管机构批准

[①] 生来就有某些特殊基因的孩子,其基因可用于治疗罹患绝症的哥哥或姐姐。——编者

了该项申请，但一个既反对销毁未使用胚胎又反对将人类生命医疗工具化的"生命至上"团体向该项批准发起诉讼，最终败诉［参见"昆塔瓦莱（代表'生殖伦理评论'组织）诉人类授精和胚胎研究管理局案"（2005）］。尽管该案主要围绕着各种技术细节，但其对原则的坚持是显而易见的。该案甚至造成"生命至上"游说者们的分裂：如果放任一个三岁的儿童死去，你还是真正的"生命至上"者吗？

早期，类似案件在很多司法管辖区曾让法官们踯躅不前。法律人倾向于采用绝对化的立场，即赋予事物明确而不可剥夺的法律地位。他们倾向于认为，采用这样的立场就能更好地解决关于生命的难题。然而，如果任何包含人类基因组的物质都具有不可分割的自然人地位，那些极度虔诚、保守的法官将被迫转向道德和法律上的相对主义，这显然会让他们感到不适。如果能抛弃成见、实事求是地观察生命，你会发现它们并不简单。正因为生命具有复杂性，法律在定义生命时才不能一概而论。

第四章

保密与隐私

　　患者会告诉医生私密的事情。公元前500年,"希波克拉底誓词"要求医生宣誓"治病救人过程中,凡我所见所闻……若属不得公之于众之事,本人绝不泄露,定将严守秘密"。至少自那时起,几乎所有人都认可,在一些情况下医生不得披露患者告知的私密事情。大多数人同意,仅在罕见的情况下医生可以泄露患者的秘密信息。然而,是否存在保密的绝对标准?如果不存在标准,为什么会这样?披露信息在什么情况下是正当的?是否存在强制披露信息的情形?这些疑问让许多平时默默无闻的法官使用异乎寻常的哲学语言来阐述自己的观点。

　　各国和国际医学伦理准则均模棱两可地承认,确立绝对标准是有害的。希波克拉底便是这种模棱两可的典型代表,他似乎承认有些事物可以符合伦理地"公之于众"。美国医学会的《医学伦理规范》则规定,"医生应该……依法保护患者的秘密",就此将真正的难题交给了法律人。2006年修订的世界医学会《国际医学伦理守则》对此做出了有意义的规定,其中一些限制条款围绕着法律上认为有必要的事项。"医生应尊重患者要求保密的权利。披露医疗秘密若要符合伦理,或以患者同意为前提;或为了患者或他人免受现实而迫在眉睫的伤害威胁,且若不违反保密义务则无法消除威胁。"英国医学总会告诉医生,"患者有权要求将就诊信息作为医生应保守的秘密。你必须对患者的信息保密,在患者去世之后亦应如此",同时又以大量细致的补充规范充分支撑起这一原则。其他专业的医务人员也有类似的伦理指导原则。

为何重视保密?

法院已经给出过很多理由,其中一些是有实际意义的。比如,常见的理由是,保守医疗秘密的法律能够促进患者安心地向医生诉说病情。假如患者觉得他们的秘密可能变成医院餐厅的八卦,他们就不太愿意把完整的故事告诉医生。这对患者和医生都不好,最终减少了患者获得必要治疗的机会。保密不仅适用于个别的医患关系,而且适用于整个医学界。假如医学职业共同体不能恪守保密责任,则患者**通常**不会那么愿意提供信息,最终造成医学界失信于公众。

另一些关于守口如瓶的原因则更为重要。众所周知,患者有**权利**要求保守医疗秘密。

对谁保密?

当然,临床医生间明智地交流患者的治疗情况是非常重要的。法律和医学伦理对此的规定都是务实的。这种务实规定建立在对患者合理预期的假设之上。假设X医生获知了某项医疗秘密,只要对治疗患者是必要的,他便可以将医疗秘密告诉Y医生。为什么会这样?因为这种信息披露在患者的合理预期范围内,所以被推定已经对此表示同意。

但这种推定的同意是有限的,而这些限制常常被扩张。教学医院满是医学生,毫无疑问,在此就诊的患者对于医疗秘密被拿来研讨有合理预期。家庭医生办公室的接待员也许和患者比邻而居、低头不见抬头见,而女性患者对于由该接待员打印人工流产转诊单是否有同样的合理预期呢?

从医学伦理到法律

若干种话语模式被用于将伦理立场转换为法律规则。

有的观点将患者的秘密视为一种知识产权。患者的秘密被传递给医生时,其用途受到严格限制。医生就像一个保管人或是受托人,采用授权以外的方式处置医疗秘密则违反信托,这就好比偷偷驾驶别人的汽车兜风。这又像是一份明示或默许的契约,医生同意会守口如瓶,却又破坏了契约。这让我们从另一角度来审视该问题,即医生的良知。拥有良知的体面医生不会像偷偷驾驶别人的汽车兜风那般行事,也不会背弃承诺。行政审判经验丰富的英国上诉法院法官西蒙·布朗总结道:

> 在我看来,正在浮现的一条清晰而稳定的主线……是这样的:吐露秘密者处于保密者的善意义务之中,这种善意义务的范围多大、是否得到了充分履行以及是否被违反的试金石是保密者的良知,不多也不少……[参见"卫生部诉信息源有限公司案"(2000)]

基于"受托"和"良知"的论证顺利地汇入了责任的概念。事实上,关于保密的法律论证多是在违反保密义务导致的侵权诉讼坩埚中炼成,在这些诉讼中,责任的概念主场作战,得心应手。

这些论证稍显笨拙。如今在很多司法管辖区,相关法律论证逐渐被人权论述的光芒所盖过。《欧洲人权公约》即是一个很好的例证,其第8条第1款规定:"人人享有使自己的私人和家庭生活、住所和通信得到尊重的权利。"这一条是《欧洲人权公约》最具弹性的条文,已经被扩张到起草者未预想到的法律领域,也必然延伸适用到医疗领域。它以患者自主权为起点,往往也以之为终点。"个人数据的保护,"欧洲人权法院在"Z诉芬兰案"(1998)中指出,"尤其是医疗数据,对于个人享有公约第8条规定的私人和家庭生活受尊重的权利至关重要。"无比正确。

人权与契约、信托、义务等论证话语有较大区别,但实质上殊途同归。正如尽职的医生通常不会违反契约,尽职的医生通常也不会侵犯患者的人权。在"坎贝尔诉《镜报》报业公司案"(2004)中,英国上议院指出,在审查违反保密义务的索偿请求时,审查标准是原告是否具有"对隐私的合理预期"。这就把普通法和《欧洲人权公约》的要求融为一体了。《欧洲人权公约》改变了律师们提出医疗保密诉讼请求的方式,但大体来说,它并没有改变这些诉讼请求带来的结果。

隐私和保密可谓水乳交融。在大多数国家,它们的融合日渐紧密。例如,英国的法官们对于过度创新感到不安,坚持认为侵犯隐私本身并不构成侵权,但滥用隐私信息构成侵权。假设一位新闻摄影师拍摄了名人的色情照片,这件事本身是没有错的,只有当他使用照片才会招致法律的制裁。在大多数实际情况下,医疗保密和尚处于起步阶段的隐私保护可以说几乎是一样的。

例如，很多医院的护理站墙上都挂着白板，通常写有患者的身份和生日，也许还载有关于患者病情的信息。任何走进病房的人都可以看到白板。这种情况下，患者的隐私是否被侵犯？当然侵犯隐私，尽管英国的律师们在承认时会带着疑惑。这种情况也违反保密义务。至少在英格兰，关于保密义务的法律和关于滥用隐私信息的侵权法都可以规范这种情形。

利益冲突的平衡：基本立场

长久以来，利益冲突都不难平衡。毋庸置疑，保密当然重要。关于保密的重要意义以及医生相应的义务，可以有诸多的表述。然而，从今往后，问题会变得复杂。患者不是孤岛，患者间存在着千丝万缕的联系。在某种意义上，除非将患者看作他们存在于其中并在很大程度上属于其成分的复杂关系的一部分，他们就无法融贯地得到考察。

被关在一所监管医院的W先生是一个非常危险的人物。他满怀信心地提交了出狱申请，邀请艾基尔医生为他做出鉴定报告，以证明继续羁押是不合情理的。艾基尔医生并没有被表面现象迷惑，其鉴定报告指出W长期对爆炸物有着病态的迷恋，释放W将对社会安全造成严重的威胁。

W的事务律师们的乐观情绪消退了，但他们的决心没有动摇。他们并没有向裁判庭提交鉴定报告。这让艾基尔医生感到不安，于是在没有获得W许可的情况下，医生披露了鉴定报告。W对此怒不可遏，并起诉艾基尔医生，要求其对违反保密义务的行为承担赔偿责任。

该案很好地呈现了大多数司法管辖区的医事法专业人士对于保密义务的看法。一系列得到广泛接受的关键问题被纳入清单。

被披露的信息是否属于应保密的范围？当然是的。在多数常规医疗环境下披露的几乎所有信息都是应保密的信息。如果你愿意，也可以说存在保密责任。如何描述保密责任并不重要，但如果选择使用责任的话语，那么你需要认识到对于患者的责任并不是绝对的，其通常被诸如"……除非……"的表述所限制。这是否意味着医生对患者以外的其他人负有相冲突的责任呢？是的，有这种可能。我们随后会探讨这一点。

信息是否被泄露了？当然，是的。假如这些信息已经存在于公共场合，那么情况会不同。一个公认的针对泄密指控的辩护理由是，该秘密已经被公之于众，甚至被置于头版头条。

那么事情告一段落了吗？W 是否由此获得胜诉？答案是否定的，他败诉了。法院认为，本案的关键问题是泄露秘密的公共利益是否高于保守秘密的**公共**利益。黑体部分是重点。保守秘密带来的利益并非 W 的个人利益，这不同于财产权。法院默示赞成保守秘密的功利主义理由。按照这种分析框架，公共利益存在于芸芸众生之中。公共利益高于本案和所有其他医疗保密案件的功利主义考量 [参见 "W 诉艾基尔案"（1990）]。

如今，如果艾基尔医生的行为代表的是公权力机构，该案的争点将是《欧洲人权公约》第 8 条的规定，价值权衡的过程也相类似。表面上看，W 受第 8 条第 1 款保障的权利是否被侵犯了？当然。但第 8 条有两款，第 2 款规定："任何公共机构不得干预上述权利（第 8 条第 1 款规定）的行使，但是，依照法律规定的干预以及基于在民主社会中出于国家安全、公共安全或者国家的经济福利的利益考虑，为了防止混乱或者犯罪，为了保护健康或者道德，为了保护他人的权利与自由而有必要进行干预的，不受此限。"W的权利受到的干预，显然可以被第8条第2款规定的全部或任意一条理由所正当化。

在何种情况下**必须**违背保密义务？

世界各地的法院几乎都在处理类似的医疗保密争议。世界各国的立法机构和法院都认为，在某些情况下医生必须披露私下获知的医疗信息。这些情形的最佳诠释是，披露信息带来的公共利益压倒一切，高过任何其他可能与之相对的考虑因素。

如果法院命令医生披露信息，他们必须照做。如果拒绝，那就是藐视法院，可能面临拘禁。在法律程序中追求真相显然是为了公共利益，但假设只能通过披露患者的秘密来发现真相，该如何是好？

在英格兰，不存在"医生-患者特权"这种允许或要求医生保持沉默的概括式规则。但在民事诉讼和刑事诉讼中，假如患者的秘密可能因为回答询问或提供文件而被泄露，法院在决定是否要求回答或文件时会将其纳入考虑范围。法院会进行当下习以为常的演绎，衡量披露秘密与否对公共利益的影响。这通常被称作"合比例性"（proportionality）。

在美国，大多数州的证据规则为患者反对医生披露秘密提供了零星的、附条件的保障。这些证据规则往往重点处理心理医生的保密问题。美国联邦最高法院将心理医生的沙发视为现代告解室，尊重其神圣价值，就心理医生的保密问题创制了可论证但较脆弱的特权，但《联邦证据规则》并未规定这种特权［参见"雅菲诉雷德蒙案"（1996）］。

不出意料，对于何种信息披露符合公共利益，不同司法管辖区存在明显不同的看法，但也存在一些共同的元素。通常认为，对社会有益的是：为了获知何人在世，可以强制披露有关出生和死亡的医疗事实；为了社会成员不受传染病的侵害，公共卫生法律要求医生披露患者患有特定传染病的隐私事实；为了让社会远离恐怖主义，在包括英国在内的很多国家和地区，关于恐怖分子的信息被要求上报，即便这些信息载于病历或是来自其他保密咨询过程。

除了这些相当清晰（通常载于制定法）的情形，法院的立场在伦理上要远为含糊，面临着法律上的困境。

假设患者告诉心理医生，他打算杀死妻子。由于恪守不可违背医疗保密义务的准则，心理医生虽然相信他的话，却没有向任何人透露。患者殴打妻子致其死亡，妻子的亲属能成功起诉心理医生吗？他们会主张："违背对患者的保密义务是你的责任。这是对患者妻子的责任。"

一些司法管辖区对这种观点持积极态度，这其中就包括美国加利福尼亚州和英格兰［参见"泰瑞索夫等人诉加利福尼亚大学校董会案"（1976）和"帕尔默诉南提斯卫生局案"（1999）］。这些案件均是侵权诉讼，其关注的问题是被告X是否对原告Y负有义务。不愿向X强加对世义务[①]是可以理解的，关联性、可预见性和合理性等审查方法被用来限缩义务的范围。

假如获知的并非对患者妻子的威胁，而是对不特定人群的

---

① 法学概念，与"对人义务"相对。——译者

威胁，但医生没有披露医疗秘密，侵权法又该如何应对这种情形呢？假如不特定人群中的一位恰好被刺中喉咙，他能否起诉心理医生，参照上例中死去的妻子的主张："你有责任为了我而违背对患者的保密义务"？

侵权法处理这一诉讼请求会更棘手，但从公共政策的角度，这个棘手的决定是否意味着法律要对心理医生课以披露医疗秘密的义务？一般法律上保密义务的公共利益问题并不能照搬到侵权索偿的私法世界，但对被刺伤的受害者作以下陈述定是令人不悦的："尽管公法和私法的协调一致很重要，但恐怕私法优于公法。你没有索偿权。"难道不该是依靠伦理而非人造的法理来快刀斩乱麻？难道不该简单地反驳："揭发患者是否真有那么合情合理，以至于心理医生没有理由不去揭发？"

在大多数司法管辖区，法律都感受到了这一问题的威力。但在几乎所有案件中，法律都不赞成披露的合理性如此明显，以至于要求医生**必须**披露信息。在大多数困扰良心的案例中，法律甘愿指出医生**可以**披露信息而不受制裁。因此，通常情况下，无论是否披露信息，医生都不会受到法律上的指责。

行业自律组织被誉为行业的良心，法律常常合情合理地从它们那里寻找灵感。例如，假设英国医学总会规定在某些情况下信息披露具有强制性，那么法律会跟随其后，行规于是被转化为法律。强制披露的例子很罕见，这表明专业界并不愿意为每一种可能的情形立法。

在何种情况下**可以**违背保密义务？

这个问题可以从两个方面讨论。一方面是秉持司法开明的信条,理解医生们在临床工作一线所面对的可怕困境。另一方面则是更多从法律的基本原则进行探讨。

其一,来自司法的同理心。医事法的领域多数是无人区,遍布着错综复杂的法律原则,满是诉讼炮弹撞出的陨石坑。关于保密的法律是一个典型的例子。在大多数实际案例中,法律人和医务人员不得不在混乱中杀出一条自己的路。他们要么从已决案件进行不那么恰当的类推,要么遵循行业自律组织制定的守则,要么追随他们自己的良知。

法律上认为,如果披露秘密的公共利益高于保守秘密的公共利益,那么违反保密义务不可诉。这种权衡往往极为困难。实践中,每一个临床医生都会进行权衡,而你无法对每一个涉及保密的问题提起诉讼。临床医生必须在既缺乏律师们详细论证的支持(理论上),又缺乏充足时间来思考(实际上)的情况下进行权衡。因此,法院友善地裁决临床医生们的决断也就不足为奇了。如果医生披露了秘密,法院会说,这是合法的,我们能理解背后的原因。如果医生未披露秘密,法院也会说,这是合法的,我们能理解背后的原因。

其二,合法而非必要地披露秘密的法律基本原则。

法律人思考这个问题的起点由专业组织设定。法律很少比同行本身对行业设定更严格的规定,法律的规定往往更宽松。然而,专业组织规模越大,伦理守则就越笼统而不实用。例如,世界医学会建议,在"患者或他人面临的真实而迫在眉睫的威胁"仅能通过违反保密义务来避免时,医生可以披露医疗秘密。这一标准对于大多数司法管辖区而言过于宽松。可能给第三方造成重大伤害的远期风险,能否成为披露秘密的正当理由?世界医学会的答案似乎是肯定的。许多其他的行业自律组织则更为谨慎。英国医学总会认为,在不披露秘密"可能使他人陷于死亡或严重伤害的风险时……如果存在可能,你应当继续寻求患者对披露秘密的同意,并且考虑到患者拒绝的任何原因……这种状况也许会存在于——例如——披露秘密有助于预防、侦查或追诉严重犯罪的情形下,特别是针对人的犯罪"。美国医学会建议:"当患者威胁要对他人或自己造成严重身体伤害,且患者存在合理的可能性实施该行为时,医生应采取合理的预防措施来保护潜在受害者,措施可以包括通知执法机构。"

这些问题在实践中呈现为何种样态?也许,医生会觉得有义务将一个掠夺成性的、潜在的斧头杀手扭送警方。但即使在今天,这也不是大多数医生的日常。更常见的情形是传染性疾病带来的风险。

一名商人到诊所就医时坦陈,在近期的泰国之行中,他与一名性工作者进行了不安全的性交。他担心自己可能感染了艾滋病毒。他有理由这样担忧,也确实很担忧。医生询问他配偶的情况。患者答道,她不知道,他也不会告诉她。此外,患者不打算停止与妻子发生性关系,也不打算使用安全套。

医生应该怎么办呢?

在大多数司法管辖区,医生可以放心大胆地告诉患者妻子,她正处于风险中。实际上,法律越来越倾向于规定医生应该这么做。在妻子同为该医生所收患者的情形中,侵权法越来越倾向于制裁医生不披露的行为。但是无论医学伦理还是关于保密的一般法律,均未要求医生提醒生命健康受到威胁的人,这涉及披露秘密的**公共**利益问题。妻子只是公众中最直接暴露于病毒的部分。

图3 有时明显泄露医疗秘密的行为被认为正当,因为披露秘密的公共利益高于保守秘密的公共(或私人)利益

儿童、缺乏行为能力的患者以及死者的秘密

关于同意权的法律与关于保密的法律形影不离。患者同意时,披露秘密是合法的;反之,则让人感到不安。但是,有一些患者无法行使同意权。幼儿欠缺必要的心智来理解披露秘密与否的利害关系。人的行为能力可能因疾病或外伤而受到影响。而众所周知,逝去的人无法表达意见。

因此,涉及儿童和缺乏行为能力的患者时,关于保密的法律遁入关于同意权的法律,这就不足为奇了。在所有的司法管辖区,情况皆是如此。因此,在英格兰,相关问题的出发点是患者的最佳利益。如果经初步认定,披露秘密有违患者的最佳利益,那么秘密被推定不得披露。但是,在其他关于保密的法律中,事情还没结束。他人的利益也将被纳入考虑范围,法官采用与其他的涉及保密义务的案件一样的方式进行权衡。

　　一个特别棘手的问题是向儿童提供避孕服务。假设一个14岁的女孩就医时提出希望长期服用避孕药，因为她和她14岁的男友有性关系。（如果男友年龄是45岁，情况会大不一样。女孩提供的信息涉及危险的性侵犯嫌疑人，会触发其他的考虑。）父母是否有权知道女儿的医疗决定？英格兰的法院认为，应当推定父母的参与是有益的［这意味着符合女孩的最佳利益，参见"阿克森诉卫生大臣案"（2006）］，但这种推定可以被推翻。美国医学会就此问题也给出了几乎相同的意见［参见《意见5.055：未成年人的医疗保密》（1996）］。不难理解向父母披露女儿的医疗秘密的推定为何很容易被推翻：如果女孩认为就医信息可能被透露给父母，她们寻求医疗帮助的念头会打消。

　　在大多数国家，死者不属于诽谤罪的对象，但死者的秘密可能例外地受到保护。专业组织（例如英国医学总会和美国医学会）要求医生在患者死亡后继续保守医疗秘密，并遵照通常的准则进行权衡。然而，家人和亲友希望了解死因的利益似乎非常重要。人们可能会认为这是在承认，揭示真相和驱散焦虑符合公共利益，但这也许有些矫揉造作。

　　在总体上赞许这些善意表达的同时，法律却倾向于坐视不管。英国的"刘易斯诉卫生大臣案"（2008）即是一个例证。该案的判决认为，保密义务是否持续到患者死亡以后**可以商榷**。

　　同意权是保密的近亲。我们接下来将拜访这位近亲。

第五章

同意权

人们往往相信自己对身体拥有绝对的控制权。实际情况却复杂得多。

一群同性间性虐恋者私下聚会,晚上活动的乐子是将彼此的生殖器钉在木板上。所有人都是成年人,所有活动都经过同意。没有人抱怨或投诉,但警方获知了相关情况。参与者们因多项意图伤害罪名被起诉。被告们回应道:"每个人都同意,同意是意图伤害的辩护理由。"英国的法院判决被告们罪名成立,而有罪判决获得了欧洲人权法院的维持[参见"女王诉布朗案"(1994)和"拉斯基、杰加德和布朗诉联合王国案"(1997)]。

无论赞成或反对定罪,法官们都是根据公共政策来判决的。没有人认为应该鼓励性虐恋活动。坦普尔曼勋爵的态度很典型,他指出:"证据表明,上诉人的行为具有不可预测的危险,危害身心健康……社会有权且必须保护自身远离对暴力行为的崇拜……"

这些判决的中心问题是国家在多大程度上被允许介入公民的私生活。一部分法官比另一部分法官更为开明,但人们在法律限制的范围内有多大的自由并不是一个新问题。事实上,人们可能将法律**定义**为对个人自由的限制。通常,限制 X 的自由之所以是正当的,是因为如果 X 不受限制,则 Y 将难以接受地受到不利影响。这种不利影响可能是直接的、针对身体的侵害(例如,这就是 X 强奸 Y 的自由受到刑法限制的原因),也可能是精神层面的困扰(这就是某些类型的暴力视频游戏受到审查的正当性基础),还可能是观念或氛围的某种潜在变化(这就是禁止协助自杀、强调人的生命价值的立法具有正当性的一个原因,尽管它会影响到个人按照自我意愿结束生命的能力)。

前述的"布朗案"有时被看作确立了个人不能对严重身体伤害行使同意权的规则。按照这种分析,国家有家长般的责任保护公民不受自己的伤害。但如果这种理解是正确的,国家的责任体系就极为缺乏一致性。拳击手可以为了奖金而严重伤害自己,当他被打得鼻梁断裂、血流满地时,围观的人群可以欢呼咆哮。滑雪和蹦极都是合法的运动,在很多国家,参与者受伤后甚至可以享受公费医疗。此外,国家有责任防止心智健全的囚犯自杀。没有人认为完全缺乏必要性的隆胸或女性生殖器整形手术违法,尽管这些手术会导致明显的身体伤害(至少在伤口愈合之前)。

关于同意权的法律是政策导向的,有时很难勾勒出法律框架的体系。政策本身是紧张关系的产物,一头连着个人自主,另一头连着社会共同利益和国家意志。

尽管如此,还是有一些法律原则获得了普遍的认可。

适格的成年人

何谓"适格的成年人"？

与做出特定决定相关的资格或行为能力，包括接受、权衡、思索和记忆有关信息的能力。这也暗含了经过思索后表达决定的能力。"与做出特定决定相关"的限定至关重要。行为能力并非"全有"或"全无"的概念。某人可能对一种决定有行为能力，但对另一种决定无行为能力。不需要过多的神经处理能力，一个人就可以充分了解褥疮的敷料包括些什么。相比之下，一个人需要更多的专业知识才能权衡癌症化疗的利弊。

行为能力的水平并非一成不变。假如喝下20品脱啤酒，一个人做出决定的能力会大为减弱。醉酒者不仅无法为自己做出医疗决定，甚至无法对任何其他事情作决定。然而到了第二天清晨，行为能力会恢复。服用药物有可能造成类似的影响，某些疾病也是如此。抑郁症会影响人的行为能力，而自然康复、以生活方式改变作为治疗或服用百忧解都有可能促进行为能力的恢复。

世界各国的法律体系都非常重视自主权，极为警惕强迫患者接受其不希望的治疗。于是，除非存在相反的证据，法律往往倾向于要求医生及其他人推定患者具备行为能力；法律也要求他们尽一切可能保证由患者亲自做出医疗决定，而不是由某个代表患者的人来作决定。例如，假设推迟一项治疗措施，在暂时性丧失行为能力的患者恢复意识之前不会危及患者的生命，那么它应该被推迟。

试想在进行盆腔粘连手术过程中，外科医生发现了卵巢肿瘤。这并不构成**急迫的**生命威胁，但外科医生认为肿瘤应该被处置。除非患者追求死亡，否则肿瘤早晚要切除。于是，医生切除了肿瘤。而患者从未对此表达明确的同意。事后，医生辩解道，由于患者处于麻醉状态而无行为能力，医生可以且必须客观地基于患者的最佳利益决定治疗方案，或是（在某些司法管辖区）依照患者的可能意愿做出决定。

法院不会认可这样的说辞。患者失去行为能力只是暂时状况。她本可以被从麻醉中唤醒，她的真实意愿本可以被确定。

适格的成年人：一般规则

至少在医院的墙壁以内，一个适格的成年人总体上可以对任何事项行使同意权，其对任何事项的拒绝都必须受到尊重。

这一原则滥觞于美国。卡多佐法官在"施伦多夫诉纽约医院协会案"（1914）的判词中指出：

> 每个已成年且心智健全的人都有权决定自己的身体接受何种处置；未经患者同意就实施手术的外科医生行为构成意图伤害，需要承担损害赔偿责任。

加拿大的法官则论述如下：

> 国家在保障适格患者的生命和健康方面的利益，必须让位于患者掌控自己生命的更大利益……在我们的社会，决定身体接受何种治疗的权利属于基本权利。这项权利内在的理念构成了自我决定和个人自主原则的基石。涉及这项权利的独立选择的自由应当……被赋予非常高的优先

级。[参见"马利特诉舒尔曼案"(1990)]

即使某个决定可能导致死亡,也并不影响它应受尊重的程度。"耶和华见证人"的适格成年信徒可以拒绝救命的输血治疗。只要能理解所作要求可能导致的后果,患者可以坚持要求医生关闭用于维持正常呼吸的人工呼吸机。基本规则是:患者自主权终身受到尊重。

当然,这并不意味着患者可以要求他人对其实施任何主动行为。通常,患者无权要求作为个体的医生或是公立医疗体制下的国家,提供医学上不利于患者最佳利益的特定治疗。患者可以要求医生停止维持生命的人工呼吸机,因为若无患者同意,继续使用人工呼吸机治疗可能被视为不当医疗行为,事实上构成意图伤害。因此,患者有权要求医生"不作为"(即拒绝治疗),但无权要求医生"作为"(即坚持获得特定治疗)。

不适格的成年人

假设某项治疗措施亟待实施,而患者本人无法自主做出决定,则需要其他人帮助患者行使同意权。让患者接受未经其同意的治疗措施,在身体和心理两方面都是残酷的,可能弊大于利。医生也许需要高大威猛的护理人员控制住患者,直到他们被麻醉。这种医疗决定不应该轻易为之,它们的实施往往是慎之又慎的。

他人如何代表患者做出医疗决定?谁能代表患者做出医疗决定?

"谁能代表患者做出医疗决定"这个问题比通常想的要更

复杂,不容易归纳。实际的答案是,要么是患者本人(患者预立有约束力的医疗决定,说明如果自己暂时失去行为能力,在治疗方面有何意愿),要么是患者在具备行为能力时委任的医疗代理人,要么是法院。

法律对患者自主权的尊重体现为,患者在具备行为能力时的意愿一经记录在案,便应该受到尊重。当患者丧失行为能力时,这些意愿中的预立医疗指示将付诸实施(关于预立医疗指示的某些难题将在本书第九章"生命的终止"中探讨)。如果预立医疗指示符合形式要件要求且被适时告知相关医疗机构,则在不存在相反的患者意见前提下,预立医疗指示理所当然应该受到充分尊重。但是,大量的"但是"存在于相关制度的实施中。

在很多司法管辖区,人们可以指定医疗代理人。当他们选择了医疗代理人且医疗代理人在授权范围内行事时,医疗代理人的决定和患者具备行为能力时的决定具有同一效力。

假如没有预立医疗指示或是医疗代理人缺位,那么将由法院做出决定。

然而实际情况往往并非如此。实践中,法院其实很少受到医疗决定问题的困扰。几乎所有代表患者做出的医疗决定都由主治医生负责,某些非医疗决定(包括生活地点、存取款或是饮食)亦可以由照护人员或家人代为决定。法院实际处理这类问题的逻辑是什么呢?

法院是法律的守护者,医生或照护人员在合法范围内的所作所为被一些国家的法院视为医疗代理人的行为。法院对此保留了最终的管辖权。任何人代表无行为能力患者做出的医疗决定,都可能被法院判决所撤销。

那么，医生或照护人员如何行事不会违法？这取决于相关的特定司法管辖区。例如，假设患者在英国，只要是为了患者最佳利益所作的决定便是合法的。与此不同的是，在美国的很多州，裁判规则的重点如下：决定者必须揣摩患者在有行为能力时对同一情形可能做出的决定。这些裁判规则将在本书第九章涉及结束生命的医疗决定背景下讨论，其时相关问题会极端化。

儿童

每个司法管辖区都出于特定法律目标对"儿童"做出了规

图4　贺加斯的组画《浪子生涯》的主人公汤姆最后被囚禁于这座被称为"混乱"（Bedlam）的伦敦精神病院。长久以来法律都认可，对处于某些精神状况下的患者进行其不会同意或无法同意的治疗措施是正当的

范的定义。在英国,医疗决定相关法制语境中的"儿童"是指任何未满18岁的人。这种定义时常导致乱象。12岁的男孩或许会被法院判决犯有杀人罪,但他无权拒绝青春痘的治疗措施。

总体而言,儿童并不具备(或者说被假定不具备)适格成年人对医疗决定后果的理解能力。但这种表述过于宽泛,无法单独作为令人信赖的造法过程的基础。按这样的逻辑,随着18岁生日午夜的钟声响起,儿童就突然拥有了一整套完整的认知能力,这种假设显然是荒谬的。许多17岁的人(还有16岁的人,甚至无疑包括某些8岁的人)拥有许多法律上适格的50岁的人也没有的成熟和老练。尽管如此,法律上应存在某种标准。

法律上的标准可能带来不公正的后果。在大多数司法管辖区,为了儿童的最佳利益,可以对未行使同意权的儿童实施治疗。但是,强迫一个具有完全理解力的成熟的17岁少年接受治疗是可怕的事。因此,法律上的标准通常需要微调。在英国,"吉利克适格"裁判规则的理念是一个典型的例子[参见"吉利克诉西诺福克和威斯贝奇区域卫生局案"(1986)]。假如儿童"具备足够的理解力和智力,使……她能完全理解提议",她就具备行为能力对治疗措施行使同意权。当然,这包括理解不接受治疗可能带来后果的能力。特定儿童是否具备这种理解力和智力,属于事实问题。

在很多法律体系中,关于儿童同意和拒绝治疗措施的法律规定是不对称的。例如,英国的制定法规定,十六七岁的未成年人与成年人拥有一样的同意权。然而,关于拒绝治疗的权利的法律规定是不一样的,该领域适用的普通法是"吉利克"规则。

乍看上去,这种规定不合逻辑。但实际上,这种制度设计是明智的。这体现了法律的推定,即医生仅会提议符合儿童最佳利益的治疗措施。相应地,法院在回应十六七岁未成年人拒绝治疗时会说:"我们仔细审视了本案以后发现,很显然医生最有权威。你将接受治疗。"

关于父母同意或拒绝的问题则较为棘手。即便是律师们也常常认为,父母(或者更准确地说应该是有为人父母责任的人)有权代表子女作医疗决定。医疗同意书如此印制,医院的内部管理制度也由这种理念主导。但以上并非相关法律的全貌。

事实是,法律上推定父母(通常无比地关心和了解子女)是子女最佳利益的最适合判断者。然而这种假设也可能被取代。关于儿童治疗措施的最终决定权总是属于法院。

以信奉"耶和华见证人"家庭的七岁儿童案例为例。这名儿童被汽车撞倒,如果不接受输血,他会死亡。虔诚的父母不同意让他接受输血。在父母看来,儿童接受输血导致的永恒后果比肉体死亡严重得多。

这种同意权案件在法院里比比皆是。几乎所有这类情形中,法院都会否决父母的意见,裁定子女的最佳利益是继续活着。例如,在美国,法院指出:

> 父母有让自己成为殉道者的自由,但这并不意味着父母有权在同样情况下让子女成为殉道者……[参见"普林斯诉马萨诸塞州案"(1944)]

当然,法院并不总是无所顾忌地否决父母。法院会仔细地考虑接受输血的儿童可能被父母厌弃、遭社群冷落的不幸事实。

相关事实被纳入最佳利益的权衡过程。我们不妨设想某种极端情形,在该情形中,前述案例中的子女幸存以后,生活质量严重受损。考虑到与世隔绝带来的影响,你可能被迫得出结论:实施救命输血并不符合儿童最佳利益。

关于最佳利益的裁判规则尚需长时间循序渐进的发展。当下,这种裁判规则仍是遥不可及的。

想象一下,假如儿童X罹患白血病。他仅有的生存机会是接受骨髓移植,供体是他八岁大的妹妹Y。移植需要使用一个大针头从Y的身体内抽取骨髓。Y拒绝这个医疗措施。她讨厌哥哥,因为哥哥偷了她的泰迪熊。事实上,当然,她的拒绝在法律上是没有意义的。她既无权同意,又无权拒绝。相较于从听话的小孩身体内提取骨髓,泰迪熊事件只是让这个过程变得更加痛苦而难忘。

关于妹妹Y能否被迫捐献骨髓的裁判规则,不过是相关决定是否符合**妹妹**的最佳利益。

在本案中,尽管从医学角度看,抽取骨髓会对Y的身体造成损害,但法院通常会认为捐献骨髓符合Y的最佳利益。而哥哥X的幸存符合Y的利益。一方面,Y可以从和哥哥X共同成长的过程中获益(尽管此时她对这一点心存犹豫);另一方面,她可以避免背负一个污点,即成为实际上杀死哥哥的刽子手。如果她对哥哥见死不救,我们很难想象她父母对她的态度会不受此事影响。

何谓不真实的同意?

在澳大利亚的维多利亚州,一个变态的医生将一件医疗器械插入女性患者的阴道。他的动机纯粹是性方面的,毫无医疗目的。女性患者同意接受这项诊疗,因为她以为这是诊断所必需。

医生被以性侵犯的罪名提起公诉。维多利亚州最高法院判决医生的罪名不成立。判决认为女患者的同意是真实有效的,医生行为的本质和特点均不构成欺诈[参见"女王诉莫比利奥案"(1991)]。

这个让许多人觉得荒诞的判决,实际上受到一个陈旧的英国判例影响,即"女王诉克拉伦斯案"(1888)。被告人克拉伦斯是淋病患者。他知悉自己的病情,妻子却不知情。妻子与他行房后,受到了感染。于是,他被提起公诉。

控方的理由是克拉伦斯对妻子的行为构成意图伤害。"胡说!"他反驳道,"同意可以作为意图伤害的辩护理由。"他的妻子是一个成年女性,完全了解她所同意的事,即性交。控方回应指出,妻子的同意并非真实有效,假如知道丈夫染病,妻子不会同意行房。上诉法院无疑担心一旦允许妻子(按照《圣经》,她和丈夫共享一个肉身)有借口拒绝丈夫的行房要求,那么会造成严重的社会后果。法院接纳了克拉伦斯的意见,即他的妻子已经对性交表示同意,同意的范围涵盖性交的"本质和特点"(nature and quality)。

在英国,"克拉伦斯案"作为判例产生了持续的影响,造成诸多不公正的结果。直到2004年,情况才发生变化。在一起涉及传播艾滋病毒的案件中,法院认为,如果性伴侣患有性传播疾病,则配偶对性行为的同意不成立[参见"女王诉迪卡案"(2004)]。在裁决性侵犯案件的责任问题时还有一条路径,即法院对被告的主观意图,而不是被害人的知情状况给予更多关注。这并不令人惊讶。

下面我们从刑事法的视角来看这个问题。医疗领域的性骚扰者比过去更容易被追究刑事责任。假如你打算触摸某人,无论是在医疗诊断还是在其他情形下,除非获得当事人的明示或默示同意,否则将触犯刑律。并且,只有当触摸的真正原因和患者的认知一致时,前述同意才是真实有效的(至少在性接触的语境下是如此)。

尽管如此,刑事法秉持无罪的倾向,必然比民事法对被告人更为宽宥。被判刑事罪行的人往往面临牢狱之灾,而因为民事过错被起诉的人最多只是金钱或名誉受损。在刑事诉讼中,让被告人出罪所需的患者同意在程度上低于民事诉讼。

整个"告知后同意"理念贯穿于医疗活动的方方面面,有时甚至造成医疗活动瘫痪。"告知后同意"本身滥觞于美国,但如同许多其他观念,它横跨大西洋,席卷欧洲和整个普通法世界。"告知后同意"血统高贵,尽管其确切发源时间存在争议,但1957年美国加利福尼亚州上诉法院的判决无疑是一个重要的节点。该判决指出:"假如医生保有任何有利于患者对治疗方案做出明智判断的信息而未告知患者,则其违背了对原告应负之职责,应承担法律责任。"[参见"萨尔戈诉里兰德·斯坦福二世大学信托董事会案"(1957)]

在"告知后同意"和其他法律原则基础上,美国法院逐渐建立起一座法律大厦来保障患者权益、规范医生行为。在具有重大影响的"坎特伯雷诉斯彭斯案"(1972)中,审理案件的美国联邦地区法院认为,医生的职责不仅包括回答问题,还包括主动提供信息。法院拒绝在同意权问题中使用英国的"博勒姆标准",认为保障患者的自我决定权在法律上至关重要,应由法律而不是医生本身来设立所需的标准。法院认为医生必须披露所有"重要风险"。重要风险的判断标准是,"一个理性的人评估个别或整体风险以决定是否接受治疗措施时,对医生所掌握的信息或站在患者立场应当知道的信息赋予的重要性"。只有当披露风险可能导致"患者心理产生严重的伤害"时,不向患者披露风险才是正当的。

加拿大的法院接受这一原则[参见"赖布尔诉休斯案"(1980)]。澳大利亚的法院后来也接受了这一原则[参见"罗杰斯诉惠特克案"(1992)]。

涉及该议题的英国法则较难归纳。"赛德威诉皇家伯利恒医院和莫兹利医院理事会案"(1985)是主要判例,但其法律见解相当复杂。

本案的五名法官给出了四个迥异的判决意见。曾经有种倾向是仅关注那些赞成"博勒姆标准"的判例(相应地,如果征询患者意见的方式受到令人信赖的医学意见认可,那么医生将免责)。但是英国的律师们渐渐转而关注和使用另外一些判例,特别是按照美国的方式处理这一问题的判例[参见"皮尔斯诉布里斯托尔医疗联合体国民医疗服务信托案"(1999)]。无论如何,专业自律守则也越来越多地使用"告知后同意"这一美国话语。在这种趋势下,很难说依照"博勒姆标准"行事的英国医生不应该感到如同置身纽约那样对患者负责。

为什么欧洲越来越多地使用美国的"告知后同意"?另一个因素发挥了作用,那就是《欧洲人权公约》。《欧洲人权公约》

第8条严格地保护着患者的自主权。即便"博勒姆标准"并不要求完全告知，第8条可能也包含这种要求——除非能在第8条第2款下辩称，这样的要求可能会造成医疗体制的混乱，从而危害社会整体利益。

事实上，这种论点并不是空穴来风。向患者完整地告知风险听起来很好，但是否可能？如果可能，它是否可行？

任何已知药物和医疗措施都存在已知或潜在的副作用，其中一些副作用非常罕见，仅载于某些鲜为人知的期刊。坦白说，不可能查明所有的风险并将它们全部告诉患者。即便能查明所有的风险，将它们全部告诉患者既是不可行的，也是不可取的。一方面，告知全部风险会挤占治疗的宝贵时间；另一方面，告知那些可怖而罕见的副作用会让患者由于过分恐惧而拒绝接受治疗，或是让患者在治疗过程中惴惴不安。因此，有必要在完全告知与合理告知之间建立适当的平衡。而适用《欧洲人权公约》第8条所要求的平衡实践也许是建立这种平衡的明智路径。

此外，还有一个非常重要的理由让我们免于因过度追求"告知后同意"而惊慌失措。这个理由就是，我们很难弄清楚到底是**何人**在真正行使同意权。自主无论如何都要被尊重，否则医疗活动是邪恶的。但我们试问："谁的自主？"假设某癌症患者正面临是否采用姑息治疗延长生命的抉择。遵从自然天性的人会尽一切努力运用各种技术来求生，恋家的人也许想拥有更多时间来陪伴孩子们成长，顾家的人为了"不成为家人的包袱"则希望早些结束生命。约翰·斯图尔特·密尔的读者们往往为自己拟就了"人生规划"，他们希望能充满尊严地生活和逝去，而不是依靠吗啡镇痛或是遭受大小便失禁之辱。虔诚的宗教信徒或许认为复杂的治疗违背了上帝的意愿。总之，人的图像林林总总。至少在面临本体论的挑战时，很少有人能坚定信念。多数人也许前一分钟是一种想法，后一分钟是另一种想法。

侵犯患者同意权的法律后果

让我们举例说明这个问题。当你看牙医时，他建议你接受一些治疗。如果不接受治疗，你的口腔健康会面临重大威胁。你签署了关于治疗措施的同意书，随后他给你的牙齿钻孔和填充。治疗措施所需费用由你支付。

刑事法上的法律后果

假如牙医明知治疗措施是不必要的，但他用欺诈方式获得了患者同意。尽管他可能会按照"克拉伦斯案"的方式进行辩护（主张你了解你所同意接受治疗的本质和特点），他很可能会败诉。除了因不诚实而导致的刑事法律责任，他还对你意图伤害，会被刑事法院单独追究责任。假如在犯罪中存在性方面的动机（假如他将你麻醉后实施猥亵），他当然会被控以额外的罪名。

民事法上的法律后果

意图伤害也是民事法上的过错。未经（充分）同意而接触某人身体构成意图伤害/实施伤害（assault / battery）。假如牙医明知道治疗措施没有必要，他可能因意图伤害造成的侵权责任被起诉。

你的牙医也许并没有不诚实。或许他只是本该更详细地向你解释治疗的风险和益处。在美国和很多其他地方，你有权获知"重要风险"。如果医生没有对此详细解释,则构成过失,你的自主权利被侵犯了。同意权纠纷案件中这类过失的法律略显复杂,本书第六章将探讨这个问题。此处仅需指明,这类过失行为的后果可能是侵权责任。

职业惩戒的法律后果

牙医要向行业自律组织负责。他有义务遵守各种职业规范。他的所作所为可能已经违反了这些义务。这导致他的执业注册资格岌岌可危,他也可能被处以其他纪律处分。

第六章

医疗过失

人非圣贤,孰能无过?医生是人,也不例外。医生的职业是与人体打交道,而人体对于人的生存、爱情或是营生都至关重要。因此,涉及人体的差错有可能影响深远、代价高昂。

但这是否意味着受害患者有权起诉善意医生的无心之过?如果答案是肯定的,医生的过错应当按照何种标准来评判?假如医生存在过错,无论远近、无论是否明确,是不是所有的侵权损害后果都由医生承受?

欢迎来到医疗过失的世界,它是一个吸引了大量眼球(特别是美国人)的法律概念。谈到医疗过失,人们心中浮现出的是那些衣着光鲜、唯利是图、漫天要价的律师们。律师的贪婪令医生和保险公司颤抖;为了赢得诉讼,他们不惜疯狂地对患者刨根问底。除了律师,医疗过失索赔是所有人的梦魇。如果可能的话,人们多么希望律师被消灭殆尽。然而,想要完全摆脱律师却不是一件容易的事。

无过错责任保险抑或侵权法？

理论上，关于医疗过失的法律产业并非不可避免。无须通过烦琐昂贵的诉讼程序，国家或保险集团就可以在无过错责任的前提下决定向医疗损害的受害人支付赔偿金。但实践中很少如此，有两个主要因素导致这种情况。其一是这样一种体系所涉及的纯粹支出。如今在英国，产科医疗事故所致的脑瘫儿可以获得大约1 000万英镑的补偿金，包括了一辈子的误工费以及一生的照护、治疗、维生设备等费用。

假设存在适中的概率（25%）免于这1 000万英镑法律责任。为了获得这样的机会，你走进赌场（也就是我们通常所称的法院）。绝大多数赌场都有入场费，这个赌场也不例外。入场费包括了律师费、专家证人费以及其他费用。即使雇用最精干的律师、聘请最出色的专家证人，仍有大约75%的概率败诉并承担原告所有费用。交纳入场费、转动轮盘、赌自己是"四里挑一"的幸运儿，人们往往觉得这些是物有所值的。

无过错责任保险在医疗过失领域不受青睐的第二个原因是因果关系难以确定。无过错责任保险通常处理的道路交通事故与医疗过失是不同的。假设A车撞击B车导致B车的车主受伤，往往不难把受伤的原因归于A车的撞击。但在医疗过失纠纷中，因果关系要模糊得多。在许多案件中，尽管法院可以认定被告没有履行职责，但原告无法证明被告的行为造成了任何损失。无过错责任保险需要推定因果关系清晰可见，而在医疗领域这是做不到的。细胞和酶不像卡车那样有规律可循。

新西兰的经验很好地表明了以上推论。新西兰建立了医疗人身损害的无过错赔偿制度,但其理赔过程要求受害人证明所受到的损害归因于"药物或手术事故"。而这一点恰恰是许多医疗过失索赔的侵权诉讼中唯一困扰人的问题。

另一些无过错责任保险则事实上走到"过错"的反面。瑞典的情形是最佳例证。该国坚持规定,过错不属于无过错责任保险的保障范围。受害人仅能由于医生"医疗上不当"的消极行为所造成的伤害而获得赔偿。然而,争论医疗行为是否由于"医疗上不当",往往就是在争论医生是否有过错。

侵权法出人意料地成为主角。

侵权法上医疗过失索赔的要件

与侵权法上任何过失索赔一样,按照侵权法成功地寻求医疗过失索赔需要证明以下事项:

——被告对原告负有注意义务;

——注意义务被违反;

——违反注意义务导致损害;

——损害属于侵权法认可的类型。

合同法上的索赔

私立医疗服务依照合同来执行。相关合同通常由患者和提供医疗服务的医生缔结。涉及医疗保险公司和私立医院时,法律关系会更复杂一些。此时的合同关系存在于保险公司和医院之间,而不是患者和医生之间。

在前述简单的情形中,即患者和医生缔结医疗合同时,合同在实践中往往不涉及侵权法的问题。很多国家(例如法国、比利时、德国、奥地利、瑞士和希腊）采用合同的方式来确立医生的法律责任。但所有的法院往往倾向于仅将医疗合同理解为一个自称具备医学专业素养的被告医生，对合理运用技术和照护患者的承诺。侵权行为法也有同样的要求。法院尤其不满的是，将医疗合同的标的看作特定医疗行为的结果，比如治愈患者的癌症，或者是将双乳整成与外科医生宣传册上一模一样的形状。这是因为法官们认识到自然界是变幻莫测的，而医生永远无法完全掌控全局。为了公平，合同不应假定医生是全知全能的。

当然，这也不是说用合同来类推完全没有启发意义。有时这种类推是有益的，特别是涉及丧失治愈机会的损害赔偿问题时。我们后面将分析这种情形。

注意义务

医事案件通常不问注意义务存在与否，总体而言不存在做一个"好撒玛利亚人"的法律责任。路旁电线杆上的天朗扩音器正在广播："周围房子里有没有医生？"医生完全可以假装没有听见广播，继续静静地坐着。在大多数（但并非所有）司法管辖区，即便这位医生违背了自己的良知，眼睁睁地看着一名本可以救回的患者死去，他的行为都不会违法。简而言之，医生通常只对他们的患者负责，医生可以决定选谁做患者。

通常显而易见的是，某人是特定医生的患者，则医生当然有责任照顾好"他们的"患者。一群医生对一名患者负责也是稀松平常的。在公立医疗体制下，适格的被告往往是法定医疗服务提供者（例如国民医疗服务信托或医院），它们雇用医生来负责直接照顾患者。

尽管如此,偶尔也会出现关于注意义务存在与否的争论。

想象一下,一位医生受雇于一家保险公司。他的工作是审查潜在被保险人的医疗记录,评估承保的风险状况。在审查X的医疗记录过程中,他发现了一个明显指征,即X正患有一种完全可治愈的癌症。显然,X自己的医生没有发现癌症。那么保险公司的这位医生应该怎么办?他是否有义务将情况告知X,让X可以获得必要的治疗?

再假设一种情形,外科医生为男孩实施输精管结扎术。由于医疗过失,手术未能成功节育,男孩实际上仍需采用避孕措施。手术后,男孩邂逅了女孩。在烛光晚餐后,男孩浪漫地向女孩保证他已经节育,于是女孩与男孩发生了没有保护措施的性行为。然而,保证是错误的,女孩后来身怀六甲。女孩能否对外科医生提起诉讼?

以上纠纷在不同司法管辖区会面临不同的解决方式。但大多数国家会采用类似英国的方案,即审查原被告之间的关系是否足够密切,审查原告遭受的损害是不是被告过失的可以预见的结果[经典判例"多诺霍诉史蒂文森案"(1932)确立起裁判标准,该案涉及姜汁啤酒瓶中的蜗牛。与其说这是关于责任的标准,毋宁说其是关于因果关系的标准],或者审查课以被告相关义务是否公平合理[参见"卡帕罗工业公开股份有限公司诉迪克曼案"(1990)]。案件审理过程中,政策考虑扮演了重要角色,特别是涉及前述第三个要件时。

前述保险公司的案例很难审判,但多数法官会认为医生的义务限于他和作为雇主的保险公司之间合同的约定范围[请对照"卡普范德诉安民银行案"（1999）]。而关于输精管结扎的案例存在真实原型：英国上诉法院判决认为，医生无法对患者所有的潜在性伴侣负有义务，因此女孩的索赔被驳回[参见"古德威尔诉英国孕期咨询服务机构案"（1996）]。

以上分析并不意味着医生对未知的第三人不会负有义务。

一名精神病患者告诉精神科医生，如果他从精神病院出院，他会杀死他见到的第一个人。精神科医生由于过失而准许该患者出院。正如患者之前所说，他在医院门前台阶上勒死了他见到的第一个路人。

受害者家属能否起诉精神科医生？答案几乎是肯定的[参见"泰瑞索夫诉加利福尼亚大学校董会案"（1976）和"帕尔默诉南提斯卫生局案"（1999）]。假如受害者是患者见到的第二个人呢？答案是极有可能。假如受害者是第二十个人呢？答案是很有可能。

为什么不能认定医生对**任何**受害者负有义务？如果这样，就会与诸如输精管结扎案例（参见"古德威尔案"）等见解相违背。但换个角度看，这实际上是为过失的医生提供豁免，只是因为患者是无心地说出他的计划。为什么患者无心的主观状态可以限缩医生的义务？这种主观状态不是使允许出院的做法过失**更大**吗？这个医生明明让一个随时随地可能造成生命威胁的危险分子回归了社会。法律该对此无动于衷吗？

答案是法律应该也确实对此做出了回应，但法律见解断断续续、前后矛盾。这个领域的法律见解处于快速演变中。未来的重要演变可能发生在以下情形中：精神病患者所致损害的法律责任认定；医生诊治的患者传播艾滋病或其他性病的法律责任认定；患者以外之人所受精神损害的法律责任认定。

这种精神损害很常见。产科医生的过失造成死产，目睹死产的父亲可能遭受精神创伤。医疗过失导致婴儿大脑受损，养育这样的婴儿的负担会让母亲患上抑郁症。对于是否对此类显然值得赔偿的索赔者进行赔偿，担忧主要在于，一旦开启闸门，海啸般的索赔请求会扑面而来。很多不能由侵权法获得赔偿的人，也许会因为医疗过失而从多个方面遭受心理影响。

很多法律工具被用来防止闸门打开，包括要求索赔者与患者有密切的关联，或是要求索赔者举证证明精神损害是医疗过失导致的"即时后果"。

违反义务

在英格兰和其他司法管辖区，判断违反义务的标准是"博勒姆标准"［参见"博勒姆诉弗莱恩医院管理委员会案"（1957）］。按照这个标准，在与相关专业领域令人信赖的意见相左时，专业人士的行为构成违反义务。"博勒姆标准"同时涉及实体法律问题和证据法则，已对专业过失法律领域全覆盖，决定着从心脏外科医生到水管工（说实话，他们之间确实有很多共同点）的所有专业人士的法律责任问题。

被告和倾向被告的法官们有时会滥用"博勒姆标准"。这些法官中有部分人将对专业同行的任何质疑视为对整个中产阶级的攻击。他们乐见过失的医生由于另一个医生的证词而被判免责。担任专家证人的通常是奇迹般地维持执业、专业上碌碌无为的医生。专家证人拿着每小时200英镑的费用，其信誓旦旦做证的内容不是来自**他本人**所采用的与被告同样的手术方式，而是来自往日他在高尔夫球俱乐部的某个令人惊讶地逃脱除名处分的球友的手术方式。

原告们理所当然地针对此弊端发起挑战。在英格兰,他们的论争导致"博勒姆标准"被修正。在"博莱索诉伦敦金融城和哈克尼卫生局案"(1998)中,法院认为某个要件已被逐渐淡忘,那就是这项老的标准所指的是**负责任的**意见。法院说,在一些判例中,尽管证据证明被告采取了通常的做法,但如果这种做法无法经受逻辑的审视,被告仍可能被判过失成立。

医生们对此变化叫苦不迭,他们担忧专业活动将被非医学专业的法官二次审查。医生们的抱怨在大众听来是在使性子。医生们实际上坚持的是有且只有医生可以对医疗行为设定评价标准。但如果你自己就是法律,那么你不是在法律之上了吗?

正是这些担忧使其他司法管辖区拒绝根据"博勒姆标准"审理,将法律标准的设定权牢牢攥在法院手中。最佳的例证来自关于同意权的法律领域,详情见后文。

"博勒姆标准"正在后撤。"博莱索案"只是让"博勒姆标准"回到适当的位置,但医学本身已经显著地弱化了"博勒姆标准"的权威性。医学正在朝着循证的方向发展。关于医疗措施适当性的评价越来越多地基于对疗效的大量统计学研究,这些研究成果也被临床操作手册所吸收。这种变化趋势逐渐限缩了专家证人鉴定意见的空间。例如,文献研究的结论指出X疗法比Y疗法更好,那么(不考虑经济因素)专家证人怎么可能**负责任地**选择Y疗法?

在医疗过失的世界里,同意权的案件占据着独特的角落。它们很常见。例如,患者也许会抱怨说她没有被充分告知手术风险,如果知道风险她就不会同意手术,也就免于手术带来的伤害了。

即便在遵循"博勒姆标准"裁判的司法管辖区,诸多权威的审判机构也认为,"博勒姆标准"并不当然是审理涉及患者同意权的过失导致法律责任的唯一标准。在著名的晦涩判例"赛德威诉皇家伯利恒医院理事会案"(1985)中,作为在英国具有引领地位的司法机构,上议院在维持"博勒姆标准"仍然适用这一总体主张的同时,小心谨慎地指出,与其他专业领域案件情况不同的是,法官们更倾向于自主判断涉案医生是否履行了必要的职责。

斯卡曼勋爵在不同意见中采用了美国判例"坎特伯雷诉斯彭斯案"(1972)的立场。在这个判例中,美国法院坚持认为应当由法院而不是医学专业组织作为仲裁者,但该案并没有否认和医疗活动有关的证据与评价照顾的适当性之间的关联性。斯卡曼勋爵的见解在很多英联邦国家得到响应。即使在保守的英格兰,他的见解也渐渐地被重新认识。自"坎特伯雷诉斯彭斯案"开始,遭受冷落的"博勒姆标准",开始在加拿大、澳大利亚和南非的涉及同意权的案件中恢复影响力[参见"赖布尔诉休斯案"(1980)、"F诉R案"(1983)和"卡斯特尔诉德·赫里夫案"(1994)]。

本书第五章已经提到,"坎特伯雷诉斯彭斯案"清楚地建立起"理性患者标准"。重要风险必须被提示,而风险重要与否的判断标准是,一个理性的人处于患者立场时对该风险的重视程度。该标准也存在例外,即"治疗特权"(therapeutic privilege)。世界各国的法官之间对此存在分歧,某些行业自律组织也对此明显心存疑惑。"治疗特权"意味着信息可以对患者保密以免造成精神损害。

变革一旦开启，就滚滚向前。如果过去难以想象的观念可以从同意权的角度来思考，那又为何止步于此？为何不在一切医疗过失案件中破除专家医学证据的宰治，改由法律来承担设定判断标准的任务（很多人觉得这是法律唯一或最主要的任务）？

这正是澳大利亚联邦最高法院法官戈德龙在"罗杰斯诉惠特克案"（1992）中的观点：

> ……在我看来，即使在诊断和治疗领域，按照"博勒姆标准"限制法律责任也缺乏法律基础……也许在一些案件中适用该标准可以为证据评价提供便利。同样地，在一些陪审团审理的案件中适用该标准是一种简便的解决方案。除此之外，这一标准并无用处……

这是一份战斗宣言。它没有被"罗杰斯诉惠特克案"的法院多数方所采纳。该案的多数方意见仅允许在医疗咨询类案件中限制适用"博勒姆标准"，判词指出："诊断治疗与为患者提供咨询信息之间存在巨大的差异……由于患者抉择的前提是医生所知而非患者本人所知的信息，如果认为医生应提供信息的量的判断标准取决于医生的单方面看法，或是医学界的看法，那是不合逻辑的。"

有很多人希望看到"博勒姆标准"被从法学教科书中完全清除，而并不止于从那些与医疗咨询相关的章节中清除。在他们看来，"博勒姆标准"充斥着医疗父爱主义的作风，意味着面对绝望的患者，把身穿白大褂的专业阶层封闭起来。

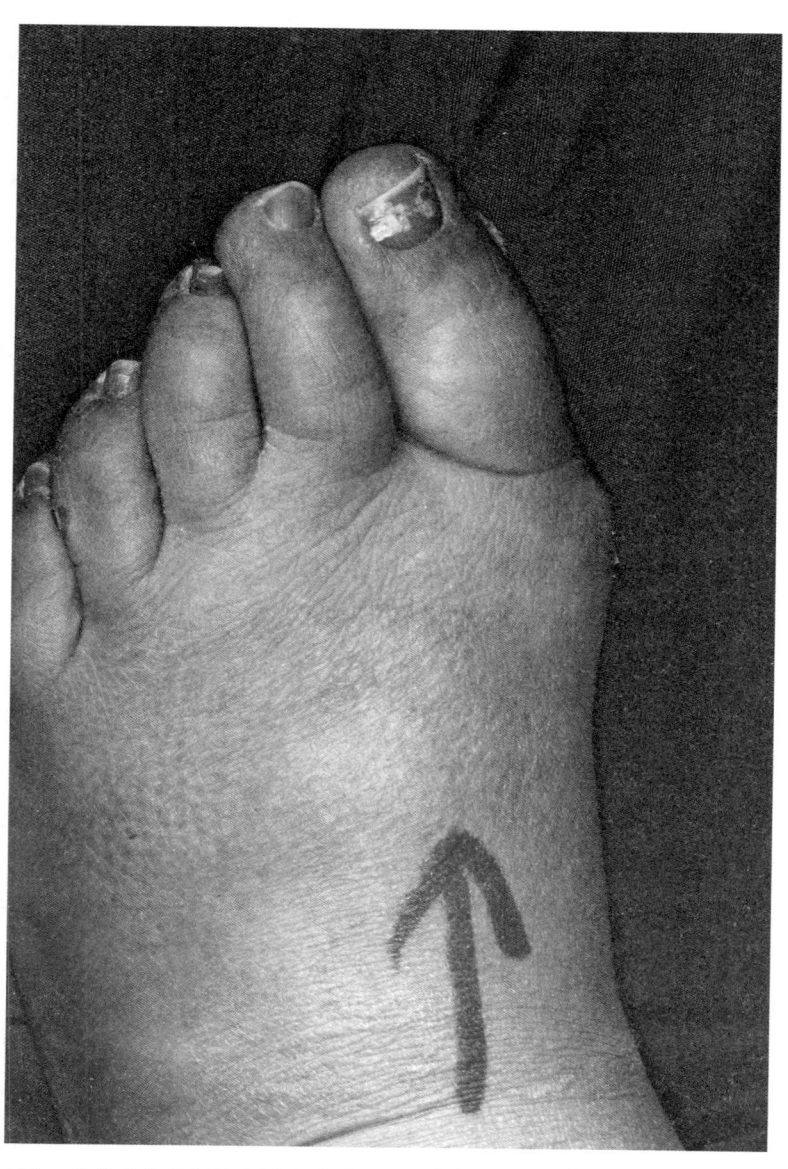

图5 手术部位标识旨在避免混淆。无论"博勒姆标准"多么宽松,任何负责任的专业意见都不会认可在错误的指头、胳膊或腿上动手术

尽管在政治、社会或是法律方面存在反对"博勒姆标准"的意见，尽管循证医学的变革导致"博勒姆标准"走下神坛，很难想象这个标准会消失得无影无踪。它不能完全消失。特别是在涉及诊断和治疗的医事案件中，法官需要"博勒姆标准"。

同意权的案件有其独特性。它们实际上关乎患者的人权，一般而言作为凡人的法官有资格来评判人权是否被侵犯。但关于诊断和治疗的医事案件在技术层面要复杂得多。与"博勒姆标准"等效的其他标准将不可避免地继续适用于这类案件，只因为法官们不具备专业知识来对案件中特定医疗活动的适当性进行评判，专家证据不可或缺。这些不可避免的外部协助必然发展为类似"博勒姆标准"的东西。正如没有专家证据的帮助法官就无法判断医疗活动是否正确，在大多数案件中法官也缺乏专业知识从两个不相容的医疗方案（原告的和被告的）中选出最适合病情的那一个。法官应该依据专家证人的西服剪裁来判断呢，还是依据专家发表的匿名审稿论文数来判断？显然两者都不是正解。因此，上诉理由往往关注何谓"一个负责任的医学意见"。尽管"博勒姆标准"地位有些动摇，但其距离完全退场时日尚远。

因果关系

基本规则："必要条件"因果关系

无论被告的过失达到何种程度，只要没有产生损害后果，原告的诉讼请求就不成立。基本的审查标准听上去符合常识：原告方需要证明，若非被告过失这一必要条件，她本可以免受事实上遭到的损害。

我们不妨举例说明。就诊时,患者告诉家庭医生自己胸部的肿块令人担忧。医生检查了肿块之后,错误地向她保证肿块是良性的。而实际上,她应该被嘱咐转诊,接受进一步检查。假如她转诊了,她所患的乳腺癌可能被诊断,而相应的治疗可以被实施。此时她的乳腺癌被完全治愈的可能性有49%。然而,由于误诊,等到她的乳腺癌被确诊时,治愈的机会已经降到5%。

这名医生承认自己违背了义务,但由于仅仅是丧失治愈机会,患者的索赔主张并不成立。从统计学角度看,首诊时患者已是在劫难逃。就因果关系而言,医生的过失与损害后果缺乏关联性。

机会丧失

以上推论可能让很多人感到困惑。医生的所作所为难道不是侵犯了患者的某种可以用来作为侵权法上索赔基础的权益?按照合同法,假如合同被违反而导致获利或者避险机会丧失,通常原告可以依法获得补偿。曾经有个古老的英国判例,一个女孩向报社支付费用以获得参加选美大赛的机会。由于报社经营不善(违反了与女孩的合同),她未能参加选美大赛,从而丧失了获胜的机会(尽管最多也就一半的概率)。最终,女孩胜诉[参见"查普林诉希克斯案"(1911)]。同理,假如一名不称职的事务律师导致客户胜诉的机会下降(比如说)三成,这名事务律师不可以对客户说:"你本来就很可能会输官司,所以你不能让我赔钱。"但这恰恰是医生推卸过失责任的说辞。

为什么会有矛盾的结果?有人也许会说,这并不矛盾。在他们看来,报社和事务律师是依照合同行事,而认为矛盾的人是将这些合同与医生治疗患者以使其有机会痊愈的合同混为一谈了。但是，许多医疗服务都是按照合同提供的，这些医疗合同难道可以用不同的方式来解释？如果这一问题成立，那么在同样情形下，相比私立医疗体系中的患者，公立医疗体系中的患者获得补偿的救济渠道被剥夺是否能接受？有人会辩称，获利的机会（前述报社和事务律师的案例）和避险的机会（前述乳腺癌的案例）有所不同。这种观点也不能成立，原因有很多，其中一个原因是将利益说成风险，或者反过来说，都是法律实务中司空见惯的小儿科。谁会告诉癌症患者，你并未完全丧失活下去和陪伴子女成长的好处，只是未能避免死亡的损害？如此玩弄概念并无任何道德根据（纵然乳腺癌的案例有很充分的道德根据）。这使得法律蒙羞。

关于这个问题的实务操作并非逻辑推导的结果，而是政策使然。如果坦率地承认这一点，法律的名声也许不会太差。事实上，政策是一个有说服力且实事求是的理由。我们已然在其他语境下见过：如果在医疗过失案件中允许对机会丧失进行补偿，那么法院将无可救药地被诉讼堵塞。许多（可能是大多数）医疗过失都会让患者丧失**从事某活动**的机会。如果原告基于机会丧失就足以获得对损害的补偿，他事实上便可以跨越所有医疗过失案件中因果关系的证明。如此一来，接下来就是判定违反义务和评估损失。这些听上去或许符合正义，但自然界是变幻莫测的，对损失进行测算往往面临困难、成本高企。是否因为某些案件的困难就让正义完全折腰，这是一个争论未决的议题。

实质诱发损害与导致损害的风险

尽管自然界有诸多不确定性，法律并不总是躲着走。法律上有时会承认，被告不应该总是躲在"这种情况相当复杂"说辞的背后,不能老套地简单运用"必要条件"标准而得到意外收获。

下面以职业病的案子为例。在为若干个雇主长年累月工作的过程中,原告吸入了有毒粉尘。某些雇主的过失导致原告吸入有毒粉尘,其他一些雇主则没有过失。原告罹患尘肺病,拟寻求赔偿。他起诉了有过失的雇主。雇主回应道:"按照'必要条件'标准判断,你无法证明我们的'有罪'粉尘是你患病的必要条件。谁确切知道这是什么造成的,或者什么时候发展到如此严重的程度? 也许是无关的粉尘导致了你的疾病。"

法院通常不会接受这样的答辩。大多数司法管辖区的法院发展出一条赔偿这类原告的路子,即认为原告的举证已充分证明被告的过失实质诱发损害[参见"贝利诉国防部案"(2009)]。法院有时会更进一步认为,在某些情况下,被告的行为实质提升了风险即需要承担责任(即便事实上是原告行为导致了最终损害后果)[参见"麦吉诉国家煤炭局案"(1973)]。

医疗损害案件的许多情形与职业病的案例类似。例如,脆弱的大脑处于缺氧的时间段既包括了过失导致的情况,也包括非由于过失导致的情况。鉴于医疗知识的现状,医学鉴定专家们也许不能断定医疗过失导致了损害,但可以查明医疗过失提升了损害的风险。政策导向的思维让法院在"机会丧失"案件中畏首畏尾,也让法院对类推适用职业病案件的法理也小心翼翼。但在许多地方,法律正逐渐接受这种类推适用。

有关同意权的案件

就确定因果关系而言,同意权案件看上去没那么困难。假设由于疏忽,外科医生未能提示计划中手术的风险。如果患者被充分告知风险,她就不会同意接受手术。手术照计划进行,在术中或术后,由于手术的原因,患者遭受了损害。

适用"必要条件"标准来处理这类案件并无问题。无论损害是否属于外科医生本该提示患者的范围,过失是损害发生的必要条件,(根据下文将讨论到的"疏远性"规则)因果关系通常能够成立。

但是不要着急,我们看看下面这个案例。案件的事实部分不算罕见。

一位患者在脊柱外科顾问医生处就诊。她需要接受椎板切除术来为脊髓减压。外科医生没有警告她的是,这种手术存在1%的风险导致尿失禁。她同意接受手术,手术也是完全成功的。不幸的是,由于1%的手术并发症概率被她遇到,她罹患尿失禁。于是,她将外科医生告到法院。法院判决认为,假如患者被充分告知,那么她可能也会同意接受手术,但至少她会在同意之前略作思考,于是不会在实际手术的那天进行手术。判决认为,由于1%的并发症风险徘徊于每个接受手术的患者身上(恰好在她实际手术的时候发生在她的身上),短暂的延迟也许能让她避免这种风险。于是,同样的外科医生进行同样的医疗咨询,在同样的手术台接受同样的手术,不同的是手术日期。她能胜诉吗?如果能,她应该胜诉吗?

如果严格适用"必要条件"标准,以上两个问题的答案都是肯定的。在一个充满争议的英国案例中,患者确实得到了这样的结果[参见"切斯特诉阿夫沙尔案"(2005)。当然,该案的结论并不只是建立在"必要条件"标准的基础上]。很多人对这个判决的结果感到愤慨。外科医生的过失和患者的损害后果之间的关联性既模糊又玄奇。

我们不妨用一种更好的路径来看待此类案件。患者确实受到了伤害,这种伤害并不是控制膀胱的神经受损,而是她充分知情的权利,亦即她的自主权利被侵犯。人权被侵犯时,即便不涉及身体伤害,按惯例也应获得赔偿。

推定的因果关系

常见的医疗过失索赔往往涉及"不作为",而非"作为"。一名医生由于过失未能照护患者,或是未能安排特定的检查项目。于是法院不得不假设在医生已经照护或是检查患者的情形下可能发生什么。一般而言,这类审查会运用"必要条件"标准,或是沿着实质诱发损害的路子来诠释这个标准。然而现实生活中的事物往往比法律上理想化的情形要来得复杂。

例如,一名儿科医生由于疏忽而未能对呼叫器的呼叫做出反应。结果,婴儿由于缺氧性脑损伤而不可逆地残障。专家证言指出,唯一能够防止损害后果的治疗措施是立即给婴儿实施气管插管。但是,儿科医生答辩指出(且为法院接受),即使她注意到了,也不会给婴儿实施气管插管。法院同时查明,负责任的儿科医生不会使用给婴儿插管的治疗方式。换句话说,如果这位儿科医生响应了呼叫器但未对患儿实施唯一可能防止损害后果的治疗措施,她的行为不构成医疗过失。

原告胜诉了吗?在英国和很多其他推崇"博勒姆标准"的地方,原告没有胜诉[参见"博莱索诉伦敦金融城和哈克尼卫生局案"(1998)]。案件的争点是若非过失,伤害是否本可以避免;而过失的认定则依照"博勒姆标准"。在本案中,过失与损害后果之间没有因果关系。即便医生勤勤恳恳地冲向病房,损害后果也不会有什么不同。

以上讨论并非分析此案的唯一视角。这位疏于照护患者的医生要想说服自己(以及法院)她不会实施唯一有效的治疗措施,压力必定是极大的。也许有人认为,为了回应社会压力,法律不妨推定医生会实施有效的治疗措施。如果是在一个不受"博勒姆标准"主导的司法管辖区,这种观点会容易被法院接纳。如果"博勒姆标准"在违背义务的法律领域占据绝对主导地位,也就很难阻止它主导因果关系的认定。

法律所认可的损害类型

医生们的过失行为林林总总,但其中只有很少一部分能成为医疗过失案件。造成这种情况有许多重要原因,其中之一是,绝大多数过失行为所导致的通常只是情感受伤、沮丧或行动不便,这些损失不属于法定应赔偿的损害类型。

一位患者住院接受角膜移植手术。术后,外科医生巡视病房时告诉患者,手术进展非常顺利,视力将逐渐恢复。然而,坏消息是医院的人体组织库刚刚告诉医生,移植的角膜供体曾在多年前罹患梅毒。不幸的是,人体组织库在事前并没有获悉这个本应被获知的情况。"但是,"外科医生继续说,"您不必担心,研究文献从没有提到过有人通过这种方式感染梅毒。"为了确保绝对安全,患者需要接受一个疗程的预防性抗生素治疗。

患者走出医院(这么多年以来首次遇到这样的麻烦),把医院告上了法院。

但患者的损失是什么?患者没有感染梅毒,未来也不会感染梅毒。他只是由于获知角膜来源的事情而受到惊吓。任何精神科医生都不会将这种"惊吓"定义为已知的心理疾病。

在大多数司法管辖区,患者的起诉都不会成功。医疗活动存在过失,过失也导致了某种**后果**,但这种后果并不属于任何一种应受赔偿的损害。

这不是因为沮丧、担忧以及类似情绪太过模糊,无法量化评价。疼痛、丧失便利或是声誉受损虽不容易用金钱衡量,但法院按惯例会将这些情形纳入考量范围。相反,这恰恰又是政策的考虑。为了不被索赔诉讼淹没,法院武断地为可受理的损害后果的严重性设定了最低门槛。

赔偿额计算

过失案件的赔偿旨在使原告回到未受被告过失行为影响的状态。典型的医疗过失索赔通常包括若干要件。

裁判指引和得到报告的案例均提到对"疼痛、遭受痛苦或是便利受损"的估价。例如,在英格兰,2013年四肢瘫痪的赔偿金通常在255 000英镑至317 500英镑之间,而单腿膝关节以下截肢的赔偿金通常在104 500英镑至177 000英镑之间。

此外,理论上而言,索赔的计算可以更加科学和量化,包括收入的损失、交通费、残疾后支持和辅助器具费用以及护理费。预期寿命(根据患者的状况个别评估,或是在患者存活到保险精算师预计的寿命情况下参考人口死亡率的数据)被用于计算未来损失所持续的时间。考虑到赔偿金投资可能的孳息,这个数字会略打折扣。计算的过程非常复杂。

也许,医疗过失诉讼律师们的律师费毕竟不是白收的。

第七章

人体研究

在目睹门格尔和其他纳粹医生们的暴行之后,国际社会纷纷呼吁"不让惨剧重演"。纳粹的所作所为(正如他们中的一些人在战后审判中所言)实际上根植于长期存在、可耻而又根深蒂固的滥用医学研究的传统。早在1840年代,J.玛丽昂·西姆斯就在未实施麻醉的女性奴隶身上反复试验手术;而到了20世纪上半叶,利奥·斯坦利则将猪、山羊和绵羊的睾丸植入囚犯的体内;在科学的幌子下,遍及许多国家、不计其数的患者被蓄意传染致命或致残的疾病。

从奥斯威辛到赫尔辛基,再到非洲丛林

作为对奥斯威辛、布痕瓦尔德以及其他集中营所暴露真相的直接回应,《纽伦堡法典》(1947)宣示了一切研究必须以参与者的同意为前提,而《日内瓦宣言》(1948)则规定了医生对患者负有医学伦理上的义务。

《纽伦堡法典》后来被世界医学会的《赫尔辛基宣言》

（1964）取代。《赫尔辛基宣言》先后作了六次修订,最新的是2008年版。《赫尔辛基宣言》本身并无法律上的约束力,却深刻地影响了世界各国和国际上关于医学研究的伦理规范和法律规范。如我们所看到的,具有权威性的医学伦理守则可以透过某些机制成为实践中或是事实上的医事法。大多数国家都认可《赫尔辛基宣言》或它的某个版本。所以,要了解国际上的法律共识,研读《赫尔辛基宣言》是最好的途径。

为扭转二战结束前的医学研究中那种不顾他人的功利主义倾向和彻头彻尾的非人道思潮,《赫尔辛基宣言》发挥了重要的作用。但这还不够。类似门格尔的医学滥权仍在继续。在美国亚拉巴马州的塔斯基吉,1932至1972年间,梅毒患者被告知正接受针对性的治疗。他们原本有机会接受真正的治疗,但实际上并没有接受。很多患者因病去世,不少儿童则由于垂直传染而罹患先天性梅毒。在纽约市的斯塔顿岛,直到1966年为止,患有精神障碍的儿童被秘密地传染肝炎病毒。而在美国得克萨斯州的圣安东尼奥,直到1971年为止,接受节育治疗的妇女在未经同意的情况下服用安慰剂,而非有效的避孕药物,很多妇女因此怀孕。在1960至1971年间,美国国防部和国防原子武器发展局资助了在未经患者同意的情况下实施的全身放射试验。1994年,一项研究发现名为"齐多夫定"的药物对减少艾滋病毒母婴传播非常有效。在后续的临床试验中,为了确保美国的患者可以获得药物,第三世界国家患者的药物被克扣。类似的悲剧一再重演。

现行的《赫尔辛基宣言》凸显了患者的自主和"告知后同意"的重要性,强调患者的利益重于社会福祉或科技进步。

《赫尔辛基宣言》的出发点是好的。它是一项诚实的努力，试图在保障人类个体权利的同时，承认科技进步的重要性，承认社群主义的视角有时是有道理的。但既然有如此雄心，便很难追求哲学意义的自洽，《赫尔辛基宣言》就不够自洽。它像是百衲被，并不是由体现同一原则的纱线毫无缝隙地编织而成的。当然，这本身并不意味着对它的否定。某些制定良好的法律也混杂着好几种哲学。但既然《赫尔辛基宣言》针对患者自主给出了明确的口惠，值得一说的是，它却在第21条规定仅当研究目标的重要性高于研究受试者承担的风险时，人体研究方可进行。这一条规定体现的是家长作风式的限制。假如制药公司支付一大笔钱让我参与新品牌洗发水的潜在危险研究，为什么不能这么做？我的身体不属于我自己吗（我参与的并不是本书第五章提到的那种捆绑性虐活动）？

　　《赫尔辛基宣言》的不同版本体现了非常显著的进化。很多版本引发了激烈而急切的争论。以下我们将分析为什么会造成这种状况。

　　想象一下，你是跨国制药公司的负责人。你的公司持有一种非常有前途的能治疗疟疾的药品的专利。消灭疟疾非常重要，因为它每年导致数百万人死亡，而几乎所有患者都身处最贫困的国家。如果药品可以用于临床，公司的股价和你的分红都将飞涨。

　　这种药品的有效性需要得到确认。这意味着要在热带贫困地区实施临床试验。

　　为了获得最有科学价值的结论（这会使药品迅速获得市场认可），临床试验会在非洲腹地某处的一大群受感染患者群体中实施。受试者全都是需要治疗的患者,被分为两组:一组受试者服用药品;另一组受试者服用不含有效成分的安慰剂。这是一场"双盲"试验,无论是患者还是分发药品/安慰剂的管理员,都不知道谁服用的是药品、谁服用的是安慰剂。

但这里存在一个问题,服用安慰剂的患者有可能会不治身亡。这是不光彩的,也是可以避免的。患者本可以服用有效的药品来避免死亡。

应该怎么办呢?

答案并不容易得出。如果临床试验未通过伦理审查,那么最终没有人能获得治疗。其中很多人都会不治身亡。无疑(如果药品确如设想那般有效),死的人比临床试验造成的死亡更多。相较于0%的可能性,潜在的受试者难道不应该更倾向于50%的生存机会吗?此外,由于不使用涉及伦理问题的其他试验方法就无法得出清楚的结论,该药品上市时间大大推迟,这就会使更多的人丧命。

假如这些基本上持功利主义的论点站得住脚,那么对于在同样一群受试者身上进行完全未经同意的医学研究,又该如何反驳呢?每个受试者也许觉得自己只是喝了一杯免费的柠檬饮料,但实际上他们服用的要么是药品,要么是安慰剂。研究方法的科学性不存在问题,而生命将因此得到拯救。问题到底出在哪儿?

笔者在此不作判断。《赫尔辛基宣言》不乐见任何一种疟疾试验的情形。除非不存在已知的有效治疗方式,或是基于"有说服力和科学性的方法上的原因"必须使用安慰剂对照方式,且服用安慰剂或不接受有效治疗的受试者不会遭受严重或不可逆伤害的风险,否则《赫尔辛基宣言》不赞成进行安慰剂对照方式的人体试验（第32条）。《赫尔辛基宣言》告诫："要特别小心，以避免此种选项被滥用。"美国食品药品监督管理局拒绝受到这些限制的约束，理由是这些限制使科学研究难有作为，并不符合世界的终极利益。

《赫尔辛基宣言》的后续修订版本努力回应这些担忧，规定仅在受试"人群或社群"有合理的可能性从研究结果中获益时，人体研究才具有正当性（第17条）。此外，第33条还规定，人体研究完成后应将有利于改善受试者状况的任何研究结论告知受试者。

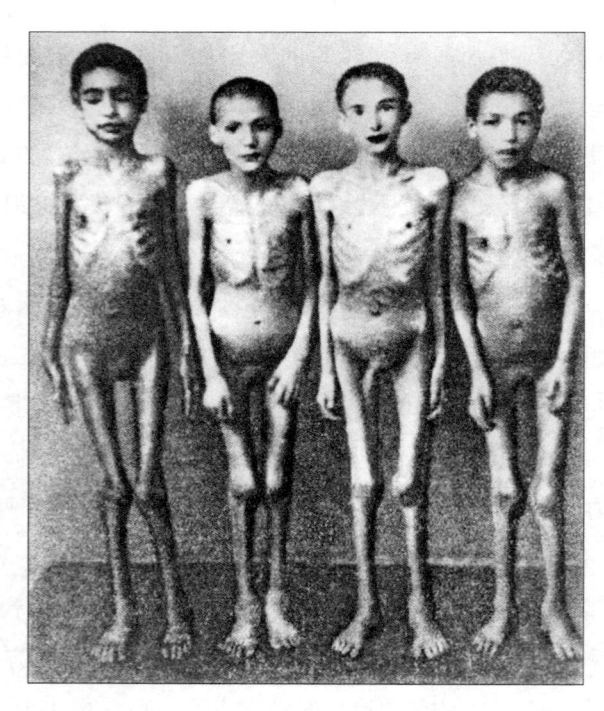

图6 被纳粹德国医生约瑟夫·门格尔用来在奥斯威辛集中营实施医学试验的双胞胎们。纳粹政权的恐怖行径对现代人体试验观的形成有深远影响

如果唯一的希望尚处于未知世界

《赫尔辛基宣言》的保守是正确的,其不断提及如何向受试者充分提示风险。通常,在新产品的临床试验启动时,已存在**一部分**证据证明它具备功效。但实际情况并非总是如此,仍有一些真正的药理学谜题等待解答。

一家制药公司常年坚持研究一种针对结肠癌的新药。这种药品已经在小白鼠的试验中展现出惊人的疗效,可以抑制小白鼠体内癌细胞的转移,将小白鼠从死亡线上救回来。但是,我们人类并非小白鼠,也不应该被看作小白鼠。下一步就是人体试验,药理学家们却忧心忡忡。新药有可能治愈患者,也可能杀死患者,或导致患者残疾。这种新药能否进入人体试验阶段?还是说,除非等到研究者们证明它致死或致残的可能性低到能让健康的志愿者放心地参与试验,否则不批准这种临床试验?

《赫尔辛基宣言》秉持着务实的精神,这也是我们所乐见的。如果在百分之百死于癌症和"五五开"治疗成败之间作选择,多数人会毫不犹豫地选择这颗也许有魔力的子弹。尽管几乎没有必要性,《赫尔辛基宣言》第35条还是专门就这种情形作了规定,允许实施这种人体试验。《赫尔辛基宣言》的另一些条文与第35条一起促成了这样的结果。将"告知后同意"与医学研究的损益权衡结合,外加"以受试者为中心",就组成了第35条。如果没有这颗有魔力的子弹,患者无论如何都逃不过死亡,那么即使这颗有魔力的子弹最终穿过受试者口腔的上颚,也并不违反《赫尔辛基宣言》。

人体试验应于何时停止？

假设你启动了有关疟疾的研究。这种灵丹妙药效果极好,以至于很快就证明它比竞争对手更好。为了能赚得盆满钵满,你急不可耐地想将它投放市场。然而,太着急显然不是一个好主意。为了能彻底赢得竞争,你想让试验再多做一阵子。如此一来,支撑产品的统计数据将变得无懈可击。

但这里再一次出现问题。在这些情况下继续实施这项研究也许会在科学上更站得住脚（你也许可以在更高概率水平上验证你的案例）,但也会导致更多的牺牲。为了完善科学的（也是商业的）研究,对照组的受试者可能死亡。这么做是否值得？

《赫尔辛基宣言》第20条要求,"发现风险高于潜在利益,或已经获得决定性证明表明结论积极而有益"时,人体研究应停止。当然,这条规定也引发许多疑问。就统计学意义而言,何时可以认为风险高于潜在利益？何时关于积极结论的证明变得具有"决定性"？《赫尔辛基宣言》并未就这些疑问给出指引。也许,假如那些受到伤害或者未能从人体试验中获益的人们将这些问题置于公堂之上时,它们会激活相关的国内法。例如,能否运用评价医疗过失的"博勒姆标准"来判断人体试验停止时间的恰当性？理论上,有关这些问题的处理规则应当在事前纳入被严格审查的试验设计。然而,事实并非总是如此。

涉及儿童和无行为能力的成年人

涉及那些无法有效行使同意权的人的试验像一个幽灵,令人恐惧。《赫尔辛基宣言》试图运用严格的管控来驱除这个幽灵。这些潜在受试者不能被用于（used，笔者用词，以激起康德主义者们的颈羽）那些可能对他们毫无益处的人体试验，除非人体试验旨在促进受试者所属人群的健康（例如为了治疗儿童或成年的唐氏综合征患者），相关研究无法通过具备行为能力的受试者完成，研究只会造成最低程度的风险和负担，并且获得相关代理人的"告知后同意"（第27条）。

然而，法律上评价代理人为患者行使同意权的标准是患者个体的"最佳利益"，如果受试者并没有获益时，会发生什么呢？这种情况比比皆是。例如，在对正常儿童展开生理学研究的过程中，一般会抽取儿童的血样。尽管抽血造成的风险极小，却会造成不适，对大喊大叫的儿童并无任何益处。承认参与这类人体试验符合儿童的最佳利益，是对"最佳利益"过于宽泛的，也是社群主义式的解读。这种结论导致大量的儿童用药难以进入临床试验。也正因为如此，很多常用的儿科药品并不是专门获批为儿童用药的。本来亟须监管者批准的医学研究，却始终被视为不符合医学伦理，或者被认为在法律上不适当。

人体试验的报酬

所有人都见过招募医学研究受试者的广告。在有的国家，广告也许会提到"报销费用"，或是更加明目张胆地声称会"慷慨地补偿你付出的时间和精力"。但所有人看后都明白这是在提供什么。以支付金钱作为诱因，人体成了试验对象。人们的确会被金钱打动。

《赫尔辛基宣言》本身并未提及有关向受试者支付金钱报酬的任何内容。它止于规定：研究者必须确保受试者的同意是真实的。很多因素会影响同意的真实性。按照普遍接受的正统观念，金钱是其中一个因素。这种正统观念体现在很多地方性操作规范中，通常要求报酬仅限于报销费用和补偿误工费。然而，人们无视这些操作规范。法律则关注更严重的强迫行为，对此问题也置若罔闻。向受试者提供报酬的做法遍及全世界。假如不支付报酬，对健康志愿者的人体试验将难以为继。仅仅为了对科学的热爱和对他人的博爱，就愿意牺牲一个下午的时间、献出血液，能如此愉快地接受人体试验的真正利他主义者太少了。

以上这种实用主义观点并无不妥。金钱和志愿行为之间的关系太复杂，很难在法典中用一条或多条来归纳。大多数人没有报酬是不会去工作的，但极少有人提议制定法律禁止他们工作。从事危险职业的工人往往能获得更高的报酬，同样极少人主张对高风险的补偿有违公共政策。

研究计划的审查和非法研究的取缔

外行的、随心所欲"边走边瞧"的独行侠们已死，或至少是没多少活路。《赫尔辛基宣言》无疑尽全力封杀这种非法研究。为了捍卫自己的各种原则，《赫尔辛基宣言》要求人体研究必须系统地、深思熟虑地展开，对所涉及的伦理问题保持应有的关注。《赫尔辛基宣言》捍卫原则的主要工具是研究伦理委员会，它有权审查研究计划，有权批准研究计划，还有权对研究的全过程进行监督。

世界各国都采用大体相似的方式来设置这种监管机构。然而，通常这些旨在监督随心所欲者和外行者的警察们自己就是随心所欲和外行的。他们或不了解自己监管领域的科学，或对伦理问题太过漫不经心。也许真正的问题在于身份认同危机，即他们不知道自己存在的意义。他们是公众的眼睛和良心吗？还是人体研究受试者权利的守护者？这些职责间有没有区别？研究者和潜在受益者的利益由谁来代表？伦理审查委员会遵循审慎、透明、一致的程序，是否就履行了职能，还是说它所面对的每个问题都存在理想的"正确答案"？各国内部对于这些关键问题都缺乏共识，更遑论在世界各国间寻求共识。学者和政治观察家们没有被委员会传出的热烈掌声所迷惑，这并不奇怪。

也许最富争议的伦理审查委员会就是美国的机构审查委员会。对机构审查委员会最有杀伤力的批评是针对利益冲突的。委员会的主要精力被用于与大型制药企业和医疗器材制造商同流合污，造成一些棘手的伦理病症。一份2006年的研究指出，大学医学中心的机构审查委员会成员中超过三分之一的人很少或从不披露与其他机构审查委员会成员间的利益冲突，而超过三分之一的机构审查委员会成员与关联企业之间有财务往来。美国政府承诺整肃机构审查委员会，但整肃的成效有待观察。

第八章

医疗资源分配

　　世上的病痛无穷无尽，拯救病患的医疗资源却是有限的。我们怎样决定谁应该得到何种医疗资源？这种两难困境折磨着我们。治疗某人就意味着拒绝治疗另一个人。X被拯救的同时Y却受到惩罚。

　　医学创新使以上问题变得越发严重。假如今天的医生所拥有的治疗选项还是一百年以前的水平，我们就有合理的机会为每个患者提供治疗。然而，今天我们能做的比一百年以前多得多。医学上每一项新进步都伴随着新的伦理困境。

　　这些伦理困境具有政治上的轰动效应。各种新的拯救生命和改善生活质量的治疗措施都需要支付高额的费用，只有富人才能享受得起，这合理吗？假如身处公立医疗服务制度下，政府坦率地告诉你："我们提供基本医疗服务。如果想要尖端医疗服务，你最好去私立医院。"这么说合适吗？或者，政府换一套说辞："我们没有能力为所有人提供免费的服务，但为了证明我们真的是民主主义者，我们将为一部分患者提供世界一流的前沿治疗措施。"这么说就合适了吗？如果以上假设付诸实践，那么这"一部分"患者包括哪些人？如果国家的责任限于提供基本医疗服务，"基本"的范围有多大？

我们往往用完全西方的，至少是狭隘的民族视角来审视这个问题。如今，每天有大约40 000名儿童死于饥饿。另有数万人死于疟疾或是其他经饮用水传染的疾病。几乎所有这些死亡本来是可以避免的。西方国家几台老年人的心脏移植手术的费用，就足以让以上所有人免受死亡威胁。

要拯救这些人，需要靠谁？不是法官。他们已经很明确地表达了自己的立场。无论在世界何处有人站出来指控医疗资源被非法地使用，总有一股浓浓的司法气息扑鼻而来，随之是一阵彼拉多洗手式①的喧闹。当法院被迫就他们不介入这些争议给出理由时，法院坚称干预医疗资源分配问题必然会侵犯立法权的范围。如果问题具体化为该将特定治疗提供给A还是B，法院则会说干预具体治疗措施是不合适的，这属于医学专业决定的范畴。

当然，司法也并不总是对立法俯首帖耳。立法决议常常被司法审查叫停或推翻，法院这么做的依据无外乎是宪法或一系列人权原则。在很多司法管辖区，"博勒姆标准"已经消逝或被侵蚀，司法对医学专业决定不再尊让。司法拒绝对诸如是否停止维持生命治疗发表意见的原因，与其说是法律原则，毋宁说是人类对于这类决定的畏难情绪。法官们不希望为此辗转反侧，彻夜难眠。谁能怪罪他们呢？

绝望的诉讼当事人的确会怪罪法官。

---

① 指撇清责任，源于《圣经》中罗马帝国犹太行省总督本丢·彼拉多在判处耶稣死刑之后洗手，以示不负处死耶稣的责任。——译者

很少有人比十岁的"儿童B"的双亲更绝望。她正遭受白血病的折磨。医生对她病情的诊断并不乐观,但仍存在一种成功率20%的治疗方法值得尝试。医疗主管部门拒绝为此支付费用,父母就这一拒绝的决定告到英国上诉法院。然而,他们败诉了。判决认为,只有主管部门被证明在分配医疗资源时缺乏理据,司法才能介入这一问题[参见"剑桥卫生局诉B案"(1995)]。

该案折射出世界上绝大多数国家面临的状况。

"缺乏理据"是一个很难达到的标准。医疗资助领域绝大多数涉及缺乏理据的诉讼请求,不是对决定所造成后果的直接攻击(这些攻击通常是徒劳的),而是对决策过程的质疑。假设某地的医疗主管部门决定不向变性人的变性手术提供资助,而理

图7 非洲某地的诊所内坐满了排队等待治疗的患者。无论在哪个国家,医疗需求都远大于医疗资源,这让法律在处理两者关系的问题上陷入困境

由仅仅是主管部门觉得更有必要把钱花在购置肾透析设备而不是手术上,这个决定很可能是无可指摘的。但如果做出同样的决定,主管部门考虑的是出于公共政策,变性不应该受到鼓励,那么结果也许会很不一样。

差别待遇本身并不一定违法,它源自人的本能。法律只是要求差别待遇应当公开透明,有理有据。例如,在大多数司法管辖区,拒绝给吸烟者实施心脏搭桥手术是合法的,只要相关医疗决定的正当性得到了详细证明。证明过程不会太复杂。吸烟者接受心脏搭桥手术的成功率明显较低。换一种方式来分析(医院会计青睐的实用主义方式),在吸烟者身上投入资源进行手术时,每一块美金所换来的"质量调整寿命年数"比较少。手术的资金投入远大于手术的疗效。

令人惊讶的是,人权立法对医疗资源分配的法律几乎没有影响。有人也许会认为,在《欧洲人权公约》缔约国,第2条(课予国家保护生命权的立法责任)、第3条(禁止非人道或有损人格的待遇)和第8条(广泛地保障个人自主,赋予人们按个人意愿生活的权利)也许可以让医疗资助的决策更适合由法院审理。但事实并非如此。

《欧洲人权公约》第14条禁止歧视的规定看上去能比其他条文发挥更大作用,但很难找出一个案例属于国内法律无法给予救济而必须依赖第14条的。由于公共政策而被拒绝实施手术的变性人可以依据第14条来提出诉讼请求,但为何要如此大费周章?在大多数西方国家,即便没有第14条,这种行为也是缺乏理据的,应当被判定违法。当然,在某些国家情况可能不那么乐观,也许有的国家会支持一项歧视性的公共政策。即便基于第14条的上诉在欧洲人权法院胜诉,这种胜利也是代价不菲的。也许将来,对于拒绝这些手术的理由,这些执迷不悟的国家会不那么坦诚。

前面讨论的主要是政策形成的问题。在个别患者的医疗照护决定中又面临哪些问题呢?

一名处于永久植物状态的患者在病房中由鼻饲管提供营养。如果诊断结果准确,永久植物状态意味着她再也无法感受到活着的意义(尽管她的家人仍从探视中获得慰藉)。继续让她接受维持生命的治疗费用很高。她可能会继续躺上若干年。她的生存意味着很多完全可以被救治的患者死去或残疾。不夸张地说,她就像隔壁病床患者身上的致命寄生虫。隔壁病床的那位拥有4个孩子的35岁母亲所患的癌症本来完全可以治愈,医院却苦于资金短缺而无力采购必要的药品。

可以杀死永久植物状态的"寄生虫"(很多人会认为她实际上已经死亡)来换取隔壁病床母亲的性命吗?也许可以吧。但大多数司法管辖区的法律对于评判人与人之间生命价值的后果小心谨慎,答案往往是否定的。实际上,英国上议院对此做出的判决认为[参见"艾尔代尔国民医疗服务信托诉布兰德案"(1993)],在决定是否要撤除永久植物状态患者的维持生命治疗措施时,医疗资金分配给其他患者的可能性不得被纳入考虑范围。大多数国家赞成这种看法。

让我们检视这种观点。如果允许医生对具有X症状的患者实施治疗,而不许医生对具有Y症状的患者实施治疗,这种医疗政策是合法的。如果同时面对永久植物状态患者和癌症患者,医生基于临床的理由继续治疗永久植物状态患者而放弃癌症患者是合法的,医生甚至可以告诉癌症患者:"对不起,我们医院的年度预算资金已经用尽,你只能等死。"假如癌症患者在法院上说道:"医院拯救植物人,却让我陷入不幸,这不合理!"她活不了几天,因为法院不会介入。

有些法官不乐见放弃职责的做法。归根结底,法官的天职是作裁决。他们已经对撤除维持生命治疗措施做出了出色的判决;有时候(例如,涉及连体婴儿分离手术可能导致一生一死的情形),他们也在两个生命之间做出取舍(尽管他们通常会争辩说他们不是在做这样的事,让人难以信服)。医院的拨款委员会必须决定,哪位患者可以接受治疗,哪位患者不能接受治疗。委员会作决定时,并没有像法官那样在专家证人帮助下拥有充分的信息,也没有用高超的司法技艺将争论聚焦在同样的问题上。在决定治疗患者X还是患者Y的过程中,作为个体的医生无疑会将财务因素纳入考量范围,而这恰恰是现行法律要求他们否认的。如果医生可以这么做,为什么法官不可以?如果医生们被鼓励对医疗决定的理由开诚布公,这样不是更好吗?

当然,问题不仅仅在于司法缺乏能动性或是专业知识。问题也不在于,很难发展出一整套实体法律来应对这个问题。真正的问题是防洪闸这个老问题。如果挑战医疗费用决定的诉讼太容易被提出,法院就会挤满求取费用的患者和患者家属。在很多情形下,实在法是由现实考虑塑造的:医疗资源的分配就是一个经典的例子。

第九章

生命的终止

一位晚期疾病患者躺在医院的病床上。一名医生走进病房，站在了她的病床边。医生拉上了隔断帘，于是没有人能看到他在做什么。他从医用手提箱中掏出一件器具，并用它对患者做了些什么。医生的行为导致了患者的死亡。

法律应该为此做些什么？

当然，答案取决于各式各样的前提。还缺少许多关键信息。

我们需要了解这所医院坐落何处。如果这是一起安乐死或协助自杀的事件，某些司法管辖区不认为医生的行为触犯了法律。如果这是一起发生在安乐死合法地区的安乐死事件，我们需要查明医生操作的程序是否遵循安乐死法律的规定。这些程序可能包括：由独立的执业医师来判定患者是否患有属于相关法律规定范围内的晚期疾病；患者自愿提出安乐死要求之前，已经被充分告知了病情的预后和姑息治疗等事实；患者的决定未受到来自亲属或照护者的不当影响；提出安乐死要求之后，患者经过了一段时间的"冷静"期；患者的安乐死要求已经得到患者亲自签署,并经妥当见证;等等。

我们需要知道医生使用的是什么器具。如果它是一个注射器,而医生是通过注射使患者死亡的,那么我们需要知道注射器吸取了些什么。如果注射器里面装的是氯化钾,我们也许要报警。一小颗氯化钾会让人的心脏立刻停止跳动。除非将死亡当作一种治愈,否则氯化钾绝对不会被用于治疗。即便确定了注射器里的药剂是氯化钾,我们也无法立即断定医生犯有谋杀罪(这一罪名意味着杀人、意图杀人或导致他人身体重伤)。也许在注射时,医生认为注射器里面是别的无害药剂。在这种情形下,医生的行为会被认为是严重过失导致的非预谋杀人罪,我们会追问:医生是亲自用注射器吸取药剂的吗?如果是他亲自为之,他事前有没有足够仔细地检查安瓿?(听上去好像确认这些事实会存在困难。)已经装满药剂的注射器是不是护士递给医生的?如果是这样,那么医生关于护士能很好地履行职责的信任是否合法,或者说医生对职责的放任是否构成严重过失(或一般过失)?如果明知医生会给患者注射并导致其死亡,护士仍递给医生装满了氯化钾的注射器,那么**护士**是否犯有谋杀罪?

如果注射器装满了吗啡,同样的一些问题会被提出。但如果注射器中吗啡的剂量、患者的病情以及诊疗历史不一样,也许还会问一些其他问题。医生也许可以基于"双重效应"原则免于被追究法律责任。"双重效应"原则区分意图和预期。按照这一原则,如果你行为的意图是A,但知道B也可能发生,那么你不会因为B而被追究刑事责任。

在这个例子中,假如医生给患者注射吗啡的目的是减轻疼痛,即便他明白足够止疼的剂量有可能把患者送进坟墓,他的行为也不构成谋杀罪。

也许医生从医用手提箱取出的只是一把剪刀。也许他用剪刀剪开了气管造口管周围的胶布,而正是此管把患者与维持生命的呼吸机连接起来。也许医生随后移除了气管造口管,导致患者死亡。

以上事实可能引起一系列新问题,其中一些我们已经遇到过。医生的行为可能构成谋杀罪,也可能构成严重过失造成的非预谋杀人罪。然而,假如医生**没有**移除气管造口管,那么他的行为可能只构成伤害罪。有可能患者意识上具备完全行为能力,坚持要求移除气管造口管。也有可能患者不具备行为能力,但她也许已经立下有约束力的医疗指示(生前遗嘱),内容是在她处于医生走进病房那刻的状态时,她拒绝任何生命维持治疗。情况可能是,医生抽出的是饲管,让她不再"非法地"活着;也可能拔掉的是导管,不再给她注射能抵挡致命细菌的抗生素,如果清醒她也许把这些细菌看作仁慈的朋友。

简而言之,死亡是一件复杂的事。就连说清楚死亡是什么也很难。

死亡的法律定义

有时候,绞刑犯人的心脏在犯人落入活板门后仍可以继续跳动20分钟。在人体停止呼吸和供血后很长时间,某些细胞仍可以继续发挥功能。人类都是缓慢而渐渐地死去。

有些损伤可能摧毁人的大脑皮层。患者会失去痛感、快乐,失去沟通或其他知觉能力。患者家属们谈起患者时仿佛觉得他们已经死了。然而,患者的心脏仍在跳动,患者的胸膛随着自主的呼吸而起起伏伏。埋葬这样的患者有什么问题吗？

　　法律有两个宽泛的关切领域。一方面，法律要求确保在埋葬、火化或是捐献遗体的关键器官前，他们已经不可逆地死亡；另一方面，法律要求照顾家属和朋友的感受。无论从生物学上看一个人如何确定地死亡且无可挽回，遭受心理创伤的家庭显然不乐意看到铲子将泥土撒到仍在起伏的胸口上。

　　作为脑部进化意义上最古老的植物性神经，脑干包括了维持呼吸的中枢神经。如果脑干受损，不仅脑皮层的高级功能极有可能会丧失（这让很多人不情愿区分脑干死亡和全脑死亡），自主呼吸也会停止。尽管如此，患者的心脏也许会继续跳动一段时间。假如使用呼吸机维持患者的呼吸，心脏可能会继续跳动相当长的时间。

　　仅采用脑干死亡作为死亡的定义无疑具有很多优势。例如，这意味着可以在自主心跳供血的条件下从患者的身体取出器官，这也是器官移植的最佳时机。这也意味着不必浪费医疗资源用呼吸机维持某些患者的呼吸，他们已难免一死，从狭义的生物学意义上看，维持他们的呼吸心跳也没有可以想见的实益。

　　正是出于这些原因，英国和其他很多司法管辖区采用了脑干死亡作为死亡的定义。确诊死亡需要遵循的规范化操作流程受到严格控制。它们往往包括证明患者无法自主呼吸，并要求提供如脑血管造影等其他检查结果作为补充。

　　该领域立法面临困难的原因在于，立法必须涵盖所有可能的情形。我们在前文提到，借助呼吸机的作用，一名脑干死亡患者的心脏可以继续跳动很长时间。因此，立法者倾向于两边下注。例如，美国的《统一死亡判定法案》（1980）规定，"血液循环和呼吸功能"或"整个大脑的所有部分（含脑干）"不可逆地停止的人方可被判定为死者。

致命的积极行为和致命的消极行为

关于死亡的多数法律思考的核心，在于区分积极行为和消极行为。

托尼·布兰德在足球场上由于冲撞而受伤，其大脑皮层的大部分受损，进入持续性植物状态。他丧失了知觉，并且会一直如此。尽管忠诚的亲属常年都来医院的病床边陪伴，他对此全然不知。他的心脏正常跳动，他的呼吸正常，连消化系统也功能健全。但那就是他活着的全部了。为了保持生存，他通过饲管接受食物和水分。

最终，他的家人还是决定放弃。是时候承认他们深爱的托尼已经离开了。医生们也对此表示同意。他们共同决定，解决这个问题的最佳方式是取出饲管。由于不再供应食物和水分，他很快就会死亡。按照法律的定义，如果持续性植物状态的诊断是正确的，他对死亡的过程不会有什么感觉。

但是存在一个问题：如果将不再提供食物和水分视为一种积极行为，那么这是一种意图导致死亡的积极行为。假如该行为实际造成了死亡，那么医生的行为构成谋杀罪。如果按照同样的意图按压装有致命药剂注射器的活塞，而不是拔出饲管，他们一定会被判定犯有谋杀罪。二者的区别是什么？

英国上议院的判决认为[参见"艾尔代尔国民医疗服务信托诉布兰德案"（1993）]，这种区别在于，不再提供食物和水分是一种消极的行为。

这一观点让很多人眉头紧锁。将积极的行为论述成消极的行为并不需要多少法律手腕，反之亦然。假如某人拒绝提供食物导致孩子被饿死，他可以期待法院冷静地接受他的说辞，即他只是消极地没有做某事。哲学家们设计出无数种思想实验，以证明积极的行为和消极的行为之间没有实质的区别。其中最著名的假设或许是"有轨电车难题"，而最容易理解的假设是两个邪恶叔叔的故事。

如果婴儿C死亡，则叔叔A将获得一笔巨额的遗产。在主动给婴儿C洗澡时，叔叔A将他的头按在水中，致其溺水身亡。叔叔A犯了谋杀罪。

叔叔B也会从婴儿C的死亡中获得巨大的财富。他也给婴儿C洗澡。正当他准备伸出手把C的头按到水下时，C的头不慎撞到浴缸边缘，沉入水中。B本来完全不费功夫就能托起C的头，从而使C获救。但是当然，他乐见这意外之财。于是他袖手旁观，眼睁睁地看着C溺水，心中却在为即将到来的财富而摩拳擦掌。

在大多数司法管辖区，B会被判完全无罪。少数司法管辖区对于这种情形设定了救助义务，但他们认为不予救助不会构成故意杀人罪。可是，叔叔A的积极行为与叔叔B的消极行为在伦理上是完全一样的。如果不承认这一点，法律是不是有些荒谬？

当然，可能确实如此吧。但是很多人觉得，尽管脑洞大开的哲学家们可以想象出若干反常的例子，可无论从情感上还是智识上判断，积极行为和消极行为之间都存在巨大的鸿沟。其中一个标准被"布兰德案"使用，即善意的医生不会因为拒绝实施无效的治疗而身陷囹圄。

谋杀、安乐死和协助自杀

无论身处世界何处,如果你走进酒吧对某人注射致命剂量的药剂,且意图杀人或致人重伤,那么你就犯了谋杀罪。需要特别注意的是,意图并不等于动机。很多人犯下谋杀罪时带着同情的动机。最经典的例子是"仁慈的杀手",即为了让妻子少受一些痛苦,他用枕头压住妻子的面部使其窒息身亡。他的动机是爱和慈悲,但他的意图是杀人。

多年来,莉莲·博伊斯饱受类风湿性关节炎的痛苦。病情还在不断恶化。身体被触碰时,她就会痛苦地号叫。各种姑息疗法的选项已被用尽。她反复哀求内科医生考克斯让她结束痛苦。考克斯医生不断地拒绝她的这种请求。她的精神状况没有任何问题。由于她一再恳求和号叫,考克斯医生最终给她注射了能致命的药剂,并在病历上记录了这一过程。护士联络了警方,考克斯医生被控企图谋杀(注意本案是"企图"而不是"完成"谋杀,因为控方无法确切地证明注射是死亡的原因。理论上存在一种可能性,即患者在注射器活塞被推动的那一刻由于完全无关的心律失常而死亡。更有可能的是,控方意识到,由于英国法律规定谋杀罪的刑罚是唯一死刑,因此企图谋杀罪更容易被陪审团接受)。本案很难辩护,法律是清晰的。从法律的角度看,考克斯医生和用枕头杀人的丈夫别无二致,于是被妥当地定罪。考克斯医生善意的动机反映到了量刑上,其仅被判处较短的缓刑[参见"女王诉考克斯案"(1992)]。

所有人无疑都会同情莉莲·博伊斯和考克斯医生。但问题是,这种同情是否可以作为改变法律上谋杀罪的充分理由?

安乐死合法化的支持者倾向于用两组论点来证成他们的观点。其一,他们认为同情使得安乐死具有道德意义的强制性。我们不会让自己的狗带着无法治疗的痛苦尖叫多年,而会把它带到兽医那儿接受安乐死。为什么我们不能把狗所拥有的基本尊严施与人类?其二,他们强调自主。他们认为,我们的生命属于自己。我们可以决定如何处置生命。如果选择结束生命,这是我们自己能说了算的。

法律改革的反对者往往——但绝不是总是——受到对生命神圣性的信仰驱使。这种信仰通常根植于"神的形象"(Imago Dei)的观念,即人是按照上帝的形象造出来的,剥夺生命就是抹去上帝的形象。他们通常会质疑自主权的优越地位,认为这并不是唯一发挥作用的原则。他们强调,X行使自主权必然影响到Y的生命(以及Y行使自主权)。一个特别而重要的例子是,所谓的"滑坡谬误"让自愿安乐死滑向非自愿安乐死(杀死未表示同意的患者,杀死未经充分告知而同意的患者,杀死受到来自家属或照护者的种种压力而同意的患者,或是杀死仅出于认识到继续生存可能成为他人负担而同意的患者)。

无论在安乐死合法还是不合法的司法管辖区,或是在有保障机制预防极端道德风险的安乐死合法地区,"滑坡谬误"都会引发激烈的争论。在请求安乐死的患者群中,减弱行为能力的抑郁症是一种常见且容易被漏诊的情形,可能符合前面的假设。这就意味着,有理由质疑患者同意的效力。换句话说,可能是患者的抑郁症导致了其对死亡的期待。但这并不必然意味着,不能采取足够的保障措施将这些问题的风险降到最低。

安乐死的反对者认为，假如患者自主是行为的唯一判断标准，为什么要限制死于疾病晚期患者的权利（正如承认安乐死合法的司法管辖区的常见情形）？为什么不允许精疲力竭、万念俱灰的人在回家的路上停在安乐死的小摊上？他们认定，在这类争论中，将患者自主当作行为的唯一判断标准是匪夷所思的。

安乐死的支持者有三点回应。第一点，也是最激进的："为什么不呢？但令人遗憾的是，社会尚未成熟到如此开明的阶段。"第二点，常被关联到第一点上："这并不是我们现阶段需要的法律，因此不用考虑这些无关紧要的问题。"第三点，也是更让人消除疑虑的："真正的问题在于，身体健康的人提出这种要求时是否心智健全。因此，这种情况下，患者自主是存在疑问的。"

反对者们的另一个争点是医生的角色定位，因为医生将承担杀人的任务。如果为了成功的论证，我们说患者X有权在他所希望的时间、地点和环境中被杀死，那么这是否意味着X可以对Y说："无论是否愿意，你必须杀了我"？如果Y是整个社会，那么这种要求可能不那么令人反感。而如果Y是一个人，或者甚至是某种特定职业，那么情况就变得棘手。最终是某个职业群体，以及群体中的某位专业人士，不得不从事杀戮工作。

无论对于安乐死的态度是否开明，作为个体的医生通常会表达对自己从事杀戮工作的厌恶。由于担忧安乐死法律对医患关系产生的影响，很多国家的医学界对这种法律持消极态度。但这种情况也并非绝对，由于只有极少的国家有处理安乐死的经验，我们很难对整体情况进行有效归纳。

值得注意的是，在支持安乐死医生的队伍中，从事姑息治疗的医生们是缺席的。他们的主要工作是减轻濒死患者的身心痛苦。他们的立场往往是安乐死并不必要，现代姑息照护可以让所有患者的死亡过程不那么痛苦。即使在一些罕见的无法有效镇痛的个案中，患者也总是能保持安详直到失去意识，即有效麻醉患者直到其死去。

安乐死的支持者回应指出，并不是所有人都能享受良好的姑息照护。况且，声称通过致死让患者不可逆地失去意识与通过麻醉让患者不可逆地失去意识具有道德上的差别，这既荒谬，又在理智上不诚实。

于是争论仍在继续。

协助自杀是安乐死的近义词，但两者存在若干重要的区别。

现如今在大多数司法管辖区，企图自杀都不被认为是犯罪行为。这是有具备说服力的理由的。改变的压力来自医生们，他们指出，担任控方主要证人协助指控他们成功拯救的患者，不利于医生和患者间的诊疗关系。然而通常情况下（例如在英国以及美国的很多州），协助某人自杀属于犯罪行为。

当然，协助自杀涉及一系列法律上的罪行，其中一些罪大恶极。例如，一个晚近的英国案件中，被告迫使女友认为自己一无是处、恶魔附身，唯有自杀方可一了百了。最终，她相信了被告，喝下了他递来的那瓶伏特加以壮胆，并在他的鼓励下从桥上纵身一跃。某些协助自杀行为仅仅是出于同情。对协助自杀行为的某些法律管控看上去是恰当的，但检方拥有很大的裁量权也是恰当的。

图8 菲利普·尼奇克研发的"解脱仪",曾合法地用于澳大利亚的北领地。假如患者能正确回答计算机给出的一系列问题,致死剂量的巴比妥类药物会被自动注入患者体内

正如所有允许协助自杀的司法管辖区的法律所规定的那样,任何理智的法律在允许协助自杀行为时,都需要建立有效的保障机制,以确保自杀的要求是出于自愿。法律应该确保患者未受到胁迫,对有关事实完全知情且充分理解。

保持和撤除生命维持治疗措施

由于颈椎出血,B女士颈部以下的身体瘫痪。她无法自主呼吸,需要依赖人工呼吸机来维持生命。

她无法忍受自己的生活状态,于是请求主治医生关闭人工呼吸机让她死去。医生拒绝了这个请求,因为他们喜欢她,觉得她活下去是有意义的。

她把医生们告上法院,请求法院宣布继续对她使用人工呼吸机是非法行为。

法院要处理的唯一争点是,她的心智是否具备行为能力来作这样的决定,亦即她对自己的请求事项是否具备认知能力,以及她是否充分知情。她具备行为能力,因此未经同意对她使用人工呼吸机构成伤害。法院命令负责照护她的英国国民医疗服务机构(而不是那些拒绝她请求的医生们)关闭人工呼吸机,放任她死去[参见"B诉一家国民医疗服务信托案"(2002)]。

这显然不是自杀,也不属于实施安乐死的积极行为。B女士的死亡系自然死亡。杀死B女士的并非关闭人工呼吸机开关的行为,而是出血及其造成的呼吸系统瘫痪。该案提出了在所有司法管辖区都被奉行的原则,即具备行为能力的成年人有权拒绝哪怕是维持生命的治疗。该原则的否命题则意味着令人恐惧的父爱主义。美国的类似判例包括"萨茨诉珀尔马特案"(1980)、"麦凯诉贝里斯泰特案"(1990)和"佐治亚州诉麦卡菲案"(1989)。

涉及无行为能力的患者时,情况要复杂得多。

一名45岁的男性遭遇灾难性的意外。和托尼·布兰德一样,他处于持续性植物状态。他没有知觉,也不可能恢复知觉。他通常不需要接受饲管喂食之外的其他积极医疗照护。由于胸腔感染,他需要接受疗程五天的口服抗生素治疗。如果不实施治疗,他有可能死去。医生应该怎么办?

法律上应对这个问题通常有以下四种策略。

替代患者判断

在此种情形中,医疗决策者努力做出与患者在具备行为能力时一致的决定。这就需要探寻患者的意愿及价值观。

尽管在美国这是一种常见的法律分析路径，但在患者观点无法足够确定地查明的情况下，很多州转而求助于最佳利益的策略。

"替代患者判断"标准听上去很好，它的修辞直指患者自主。然而，假设性的患者观点通常难以获知，或者只能从家属或照护者们饱含偏见的目光中寻找线索，而他们往往与患者的死亡利益攸关。很少有人在考虑自己将如何死去时会头脑清醒、心如止水，几乎不会有人具备必要的医学知识来修饰自己的言论以使其与濒死时的临床状况接近。还有大量的研究文献指出，当身处我们在健康状态下最害怕的就医状态时，我们会发现自己的生命比想象的有价值得多，也能忍受得多。我怀疑，大多数人早年思考令人压抑的死亡问题时都受到文学作品的影响，而这些早年的对话恰恰是探求替代性判断的主要参考。

当然，"替代患者判断"无法帮到那些从未自己作决定或是表达过自己意愿的人（例如儿童或从未具有行为能力的人）。由于大多数人都或多或少缺乏行为能力或是不善言辞，我们的观点也缺乏可靠的记录，那种认为法律意义上缺乏行为能力的人和其他人之间存在严格的区分，应该采用完全不同标准的观点是不可思议的。

患者最佳利益

比如，英国法院使用的标准是"患者最佳利益"标准，即在符合患者最佳利益的前提下，积极行为或消极行为是合法的。"患者最佳利益"是从整体上考虑的，不限于"医学上的最佳利益"。

理论上,这一标准是客观的。某一事实要么符合患者的最佳利益,要么不符合患者的最佳利益。

在涉及持续植物状态的案件中(众所周知的"布兰德案"),法官们会纠结于质疑一个永久地、不可逆地丧失知觉的患者是否拥有任何利益。当然,患者确实拥有利益,例如他也许希望被好好地记住。处于持续植物状态的患者并不只是砧板上的一大块肉。假如提议允许医学生在处于持续植物状态的患者身上练习直肠检查,这合适吗?当然不合适,这是因为患者拥有的剩余利益(或许最适合的定义是尊严利益,在笔者看来,在欧洲这种利益受到《欧洲人权公约》第8条和/或第3条保护)会被侵犯。患者不应该因为缺乏常人的特征就受到虐待。

实践中,"替代患者判断"常常被代入判断"患者最佳利益"的过程中。例如,英国的《心智能力法案》(2005)要求医疗代理人在判断患者最佳利益时,应充分考虑患者曾经表达过的观点。因此,按照这个法律的规定,如果患者曾经表明某医疗决定会带来不快,那么该医疗决定也许不符合患者的利益。

法院常常鼓励采用"资产负债表"式的推导过程。他们扮演患者人生的审计师,在"资产负债表"的一栏列出赞成患者继续生存的理由,在另一栏列出赞成患者死亡的理由。显然,并不是所有理由都具有相等的权重,不同的理由需要抉择。而一旦理由被适当地权衡,则分别对每栏求和。得分高的一栏获胜,而司法的拇指也随之竖起或朝下。

这个标准听上去比实际中更简便、更科学。"患者最佳利益"的晦涩难懂众所周知。有时(特别是患者年幼且严重残疾,甚至无法通过发声或面部表情来展现疼痛或愉快的情形),法律上有必要进行推定。一种重要的推定是支持继续生存的推定。如果愿意，你也可以称之为对生命神圣性的基本尊重。该原则历史悠久，名声卓越。在决定如何权衡最佳利益计算过程中的各种因素时，这也是至关重要的。它通常发挥决定性作用，但也可能（且常常）被取代。

医疗代理人

有时，人们会委任某人代替自己做出医疗决定。患者一般以持续有效和永久的授权书进行委托。通常情况下（例如在美国的很多州和英国），授权书要想赋予代理人权力，去代表患者拒绝包括救生或维生治疗在内的医疗措施，就必须符合一般授权所不适用的特定形式要件。

当然，父母通常代替孩子做出决定，这也包括了治疗决定。然而，父母的视角最好被视为有助于决定何为孩子的最佳利益。他们的帮助非常有意义，以至于大多数司法管辖区假定父母的观点就是孩子的最佳利益。但这种假定并非不可推翻，法院在此问题上有最终发言权。

一般而言，成年人的医疗代理问题也是同理。所有关于永久授权书的立法，都保留了法院审查代理人决定的权力。因此，给出授权书的人的命运可能仍需要遵循（依司法管辖区的不同）"患者最佳利益"标准或"替代患者判断"来决定。

预立医疗指示

又称为"生前遗嘱"，是指人们在具备行为能力时做出的、关于自己在失去行为能力情形下愿意受到何种治疗的意见。它

图9 安德里亚·奥尔卡尼亚壁画《死亡的胜利》的细节部分，呈现盲人和残障者呼唤死亡的景象。死亡并不总是被视为不受欢迎的掠夺者

第九章 生命的终止

们可能被适用于撤除或保持生命维持治疗，但往往需要满足特定的形式要件。"预立医疗指示"的形式可以是关于临终医疗决定的若干原则的声明，也可以是具体的医疗指示，比如"如果失去知觉且大小便失禁，我不希望接受任何生命维持治疗"。

不同司法管辖区的"预立医疗指示"法律效力迥异。在有的地区，它们仅作为医疗决策的参考证据。在另一些地区，如果有效且可执行，其效力等同于患者在具备行为能力情况下对治疗措施的拒绝。

重要的是，"预立医疗指示"的内容几乎总是**拒绝**。这是因为，很少有机会能够要求医生提供其所不愿提供的积极治疗。但要求医生不实施其认为有价值的治疗措施则是不一样的。

"预立医疗指示"可能有用，但它们需要被谨慎对待。它们需要保持更新。医学在发展，患者的想法也在变化。当"预立医疗指示"开始落实时，治疗或姑息疗法的可能选项、患者的自身处境或人生哲学信念均有可能与立下"预立医疗指示"时的情形大不一样。

有时，疾病也会改变人的性格。假设患者X对阿尔茨海默氏病感到恐惧，他的"预立医疗指示"的内容是，当他罹患阿尔茨海默氏病时拒绝生命维持治疗措施。不幸的是，恐惧被应验了。他被诊断出阿尔茨海默氏病的痴呆症状。疾病让他的大脑丧失很多功能，但同时也使他的恐惧感大大减弱。他不像未生病时那样，觉得生活在地狱中。他仿佛进入一个童年般的伊甸园。他对着护士大笑，与病友们一起咯咯直笑，充满乐趣地观看最无聊的晨间档电视节目。迄今为止，任何人都可以看出他比以前生活更快乐。

然而，随后他肺部感染了。正如前文提到的45岁交通事故受害者一样，假如不接受口服抗生素治疗，他会在5天内死去。作为遗嘱上唯一的受益人，他的女儿拿出"预立医疗指示"，要求不给他服用抗生素，否则将起诉医院侵权。

医生们应该怎么办呢？看上去是不是仿佛X已然死了，现在重生为一个性情大变的患者Y？X和Y之间仅存的同一性是肉体上的，即他们共享细胞。X和Y明明从未谋面，X也未曾预见到Y的状况，为什么已经死去的X签署的文件，可以作为患者Y的死刑执行令？

尽管教科书的观点通常毋庸置疑，认为患者Y的死亡在法律上是不可避免的，但在任何司法管辖区对此问题都没有直截了当的答案。

撤除还是保留？没有区别

最后一个要点：律师和伦理学家通常断言，撤除或保留治疗之间并不存在实质的区别。理由是历历可辨的。假如二者存在区别，那么停止已经开始的治疗在法律上或伦理上会面临困局。这有可能使医生不愿意实施具有潜在价值的治疗。这种区别不符合任何一方的利益。

第十章

器官捐献与人体部位的所有权

至少如果我身处英格兰，我对自己的身体并无所有权。身体确实不能成为所有权的标的物。我甚至不能支配自己的身体[参见"女王诉本瑟姆案"（2005）]。

这看起来有些奇怪。我在感知万物和侃侃而谈时，身体仿佛是属于我的。然而，当我这样觉得和谈论身体时，在法律上却是非常草率的。我实际上想表达的是我有权利（或者至少比其他人有更多的权利）来控制可能会发生在自己身体上的事情。如果主张是这样的，法律会赞成我的观点。事实上，正如我们在审视关于同意权的法律时所看到的，法律会非常强烈地赞成这种观点——只要你是一个法律上具有行为能力的成年人，身处医院而不是在性虐恋者沙龙中。

但在法律上引入将活人身体视为财产的观念，则存在问题。确实，如果换作尸体，同样存在问题，且问题由来已久，但其实它是活人身体所涉及问题的必然延续。为何我的后裔对我的尸体具有请求权，而在世的我却无权对同样的这一大堆细胞主张权利?

法律对此的厌恶有两个根源。第一个根源是来自神学的影响。法律由宗教信徒们形塑,而在他们心目中,对自己的身体主张所有权会亵渎神明。我们并没有创造自己,因此我们没有对自己身体的所有权。这种看法(也许受到根深蒂固的本能支撑)仍然持续,但这种信念基本上已不存在。第二个根源与第一个相关,但它是康德哲学和启蒙运动的产物。这是一种对于"商品化"的憎恶。

"厌恶""本能""憎恶"这些词听起来不像是一本关于法律的书所应该包含的。但是在这一领域,也许法官凭直觉鲁莽行事的情形要多于其他任何人(他们也表达过很多感性的看法)。很难追寻始终如一的推理脉络,公共政策往往非常难以置信地被打扮成逻辑。

时隐时现的财产

然而,我们其实很难完全摆脱财产的观念。财产的思维方式和财产的话语时不时能发挥重要作用。而且,总的来看,法院并没有精心地回避。法院一直秉持实用主义来处理这些议题。在某种程度上,将人体部位视作财产有利于解决争议,法院也确实是这么做的(在判决书中撒满限制性的胡椒粉)。总体的结果是,判决有时将人体部位视为财产,有时则特别强调人体部位并非财产。

以下是一个体现这种实用主义的例子。在"女王诉凯利案"(1999)中,英国上诉法院重申了古老而基本的法则,即未经改动的人体部位不属于财产。判决随后指出:"也许……在未来某个时候……为了审理[盗窃罪]的需要,法院可以判决人体部位属于财产,只要人体部位的用途或意义已超出它们的现状,即便它们尚未获得不一样的属性。这可能发生在以下例子中,比如将人体部位用于器官移植手术,或者是用于提取DNA(脱氧核糖核酸),或者是……用作庭审的物证展示。"这个判决体现了非凡的坦诚态度。它的意思实际上是:我们未来会赋予某物任何必要的属性,以便我们能做正确的事情。这不是坏事。获得正确的结论是至关重要的,而法律学者们往往低估了这种重要性。

德国人对独立人体部位的地位,观点非同寻常地直截了当,且始终如一。在德国人看来,它们都属于财产。而大多数其他司法管辖区纷纷尝试回避"财产"这一简单明了的标签,及其可能造成的后果。

澳大利亚联邦最高法院的做法即是一个典型。在"杜德沃德诉斯彭斯案"(1908)中,尽管坚守历史传统、认为尸体不属于财产(盗墓贼会被指控盗窃裹尸布,或被指控晦涩的关于亵渎坟墓的基督教罪行),法院指出,人们在处理尸体或尸体部位的过程中,如果通过工作使它们具备"一些不同于仅仅等待下葬的尸体所具有的属性",便获得了继续占有的权利。

"杜德沃德案"让从皇家外科医学院盗窃人体部位的小偷遭到了报应。他们辩称,自己不应该被判犯有盗窃罪,因为没有财产被不法占有。英国上诉法院回应道:你们说的站不住脚。人体部位被防腐保存,而一些人力投入到了这一过程中。基于此,被偷走的人体部位当然属于"财产"[参见"女王诉凯利案"(1999)]。

在回避财产观念的情况下,关于活人人体部位或衍生物所有权的案件考验着法官们处理艰难问题的能力。

在美国加利福尼亚州最高法院审理的"穆尔诉加利福尼亚大学校董会案"（1990）中，原告患有白血病。他的脾脏和身体其他部位被切除，在未经患者同意的情况下，他的细胞被用于建立兼具经济价值和医学价值的细胞系。该细胞系被授予专利，带来了巨额的金钱收益，原告却分文未得。

原告的起诉特别强调，他的细胞属于被"转用于"其他用途的财产。法院不同意这一观点，其担忧在于，假如完全无辜的研究者基于善意目的对来源不明的细胞系进行转换，却要承担法律责任，医学研究将受到压制。原告还有其他救济途径：未取得同意就切除人体组织的医生将会承担法律责任，因为违反诚信义务以及未经患者同意而实施手术。但与细胞系所带来的数十亿美元收益相比，这些诉讼请求对应的赔偿数额微不足道。

在"海奇特诉洛杉矶县高等法院案"（1993）中，美国加利福尼亚州上诉法院认为，按照遗嘱处置的精液可以被视为财产，理由是提供精液的男子对于如何处置该精液有充分的话语权，正是这种话语权让精液变成财产。这种认定的效果在于，他的女友可以重新获得这些精液并将其用于本来的目的，也就是让她受精［在英国，类似的案例，例如"人类授精和胚胎研究管理局诉布拉德案"（1999）和"埃文斯诉阿米库斯医疗有限公司案"（2004），最好被视为关于生育自主权和制定法解释中的细节问题的案子。相关讨论见本书第三章］。

支配这两个判决的逻辑与其说是法律，毋宁说是政策。在"穆尔案"中，基于财产的分析总体而言是弊大于利的，因此这种分析被法院否定。而在"海奇特案"中，基于财产的分析则是利大于弊的,所以被法院采纳。

在英国上诉法院审理的"耶尔沃斯诉北布里斯托尔国民医疗服务信托案"(2010)中,由于疏忽,为在癌症化疗后生育子女而保存的精液遭到破坏。本案中的过错是显而易见的,但应该如何描述这种过错?法院判决认为,尽管制定法限制了男人对精液的用途安排,但这种限制并不意味着男人在追究疏忽责任的诉讼中不可以对精液"享有所有权",因此,"更不用说男人对精液拥有充分的权利,由此成为精液的财产持有者"。所有权和持有财产(照看动产)都意味着法院承认精液属于某种财产。

因此,在美国、英国以及其他国家,假如财产的定义能服务于正确的判决,人体部位和人体衍生物则被认定为财产。

法律又该如何处理涉及人体部位或人体衍生物的交易呢?例如,卖血就存在一个市场。人可不可以把自己变成"血液农场",如牲口产奶那样卖自己的血获利?卖掉一个肾脏对还清按揭贷款有很大的帮助,还能拯救他人的生命。

如果血液和肾脏都是我的财产,为什么不呢?确实,为何这些买卖的合法性变成了对"财产"概念适用范围的莫名(正如我们所看到的)而武断的质疑?即使我的肾脏不属于财产,并且如土地法专业的律师所理解的那样,我在持有它这件事上没有权利,我仍然应该拥有比其他人多得多的权利来决定那些涉及它的事情。如果我选择每天晚上喝得烂醉,让肾脏沉浸在杜松子酒里,法律不会阻止我的行为。为什么当我要做一些有利可图且有益于社会的事情,法律却要阻止我?在很多司法管辖区,妓女可以合法卖淫。为什么她不能为了生产救命的血液制品而卖血呢?

当然，从道德的角度，对这些问题不假思索的答案是防止"商品化"，这也是一个引发无尽追问的回答。是的，这些行为是"商品化"，但那又如何？一个适当的答案也许应该用上人性尊严的话语。

很多司法管辖区都禁止人体器官和人体衍生物的商业交易。关于这一点，国际共识体现为欧洲委员会制定的《欧洲人权与生物医学公约》第21条，其中规定："人体及人体部位不得被用作营利目的。"

器官捐献

对人体器官的需求量远远大于人体器官的供应量。

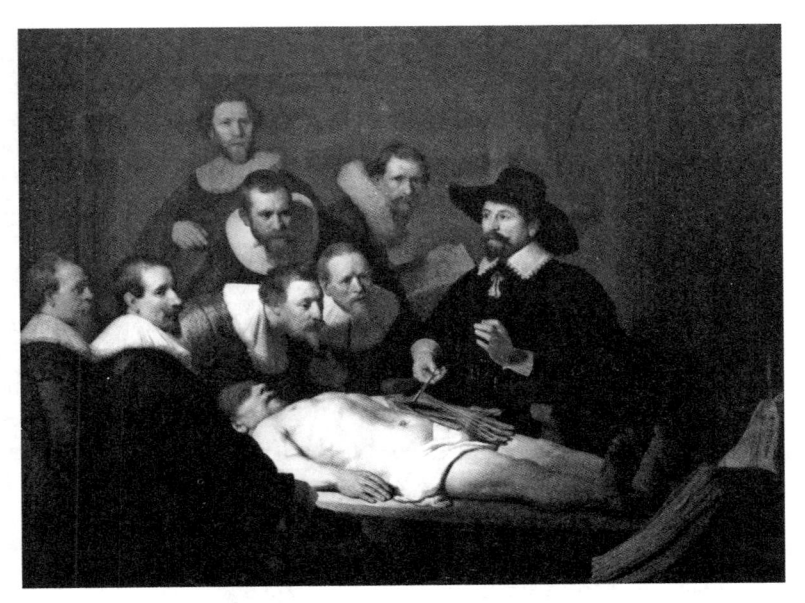

图10　伦勃朗的作品《尼古拉斯·杜尔教授的解剖学课》。人是否拥有绝对的权利来决定自己死后尸体的境遇？

一种解决思路是鼓励活体器官捐献,这主要涉及部分器官,例如肾脏。在前文中,我们已经简要讨论过这个问题。例如,在很多司法管辖区,活体捐献者无偿捐献骨髓,甚至单侧肾脏,通常都是合法的;尤其是在监管部门进行广泛的调查,确定潜在捐献者的捐献完全出于自由意志且完全了解捐献器官的全部风险后,做出捐献单侧肾脏这样重大牺牲的情形。但这显然不适用于心脏、肺以及其他器官捐献的情形。假如要移植这些器官,需要从死者的身体上摘取。

从死者的身体上摘取器官时,在法律层面有两个主要的担忧。第一个担忧事关同意,即死者或者特定情况下的死者家属是否恰当地给予了同意?第二个担忧事关死亡,即死者是否已真正地、不可逆地死亡?

在大多数国家,人们决定死后尸体处置的资格主要受到制定法的管制。这些制定法基本上都倾向于规定自主权延伸到坟墓,因此我们每个人都有资格决定自己是被土葬、火葬还是被循环利用。

若干法律机制被用于确保自主权得到尊重。在某些司法管辖区,如果你未就如何处置自己的尸体给出说明,利用你的任何器官都是违法的。因此在这些司法管辖区,捐献器官需要捐献者"选择加入"。另一些司法管辖区则规定,假如你反对捐献器官,需要明确表达自己的意见,对此保持沉默则会被推定为同意(这也被称作"选择退出"模式)。还有一些司法管辖区要求人们做出选择,例如,将其作为申领驾照的必要条件(这也被称作"强制选择"模式)。围绕以上法律选项的可接受性,伦理学家们已有相当多的辩论,政治家们和医生们则争论这些法律选项对于提高器官捐献率的效果。然而,它们在法律层面却并不那么吸引人。

在法律层面更令人感兴趣的问题包括:死亡的定义(本书第九章已经讨论过)(改变了从"有心跳捐献者"身上摘取器官的适当性),有时给出的关于从永久植物状态患者身上获得器官问题的建言(目前在全球范围内这都不合法,这就好比从一个被麻醉后实施阑尾切除术的健康人身上摘取器官是不合法的),以及从无脑畸形的儿童身上获得器官问题的建言(目前这种情形在所有国家都符合死亡判定标准,但条理清晰的证成需要快马加鞭,因为这种疾病的预后如此清晰而不幸)。

世界卫生组织制定的指南体现了关于保障措施的广泛国际共识,这些措施适用于从有心跳捐献者的身体摘取器官的情形,其中就包括禁止从事人体器官移植的医生对捐献者的死亡进行判定,这也是为了预防某些显而易见的罪恶。

知识产权

如果有观点认为一家生物技术公司有权指着一幅基因图谱,说"这是我们的,只有我能用这段基因序列赚钱",这将引起各种政治的、伦理的乃至宗教的骚动不安。

正如人们从"穆尔案"(前述)中所预期的那样,美国人对于这个问题的态度比欧洲人要更加自由放任。至少在这方面,美国人根深蒂固的自由市场倾向胜过他们的宗教保守主义。美国联邦最高法院赞成给转基因嗜油细菌授予专利,并指出立法者意图使专利法涵盖"普天之下人类制造的任何事物"。在这一语境下,"人类制造的"包括了人类对天然存在的核酸的操控[参见"戴蒙德诉查克拉巴蒂案"(1980)]。

从一只老鼠身上可以清晰看出美国与欧洲的不同。美国哈佛大学培养出一种老鼠(被称作"肿瘤鼠"),其被视为一枚生物定时炸弹。这种老鼠的DNA带有一种人类肿瘤的基因,因此会不可避免地患上癌症。哈佛大学在美国顺利地申请到专利,欧洲人对此则慎重得多。这种老鼠在欧洲最终获得了专利,但申请的过程充满了争议,两个争点分别是授予生物体专利是否违背道德准则,以及授予动物物种以专利是否违法(两项反对意见的依据都是《欧洲专利公约》)。

与美国相比,欧洲给人类基因序列授予专利的数量要少得多。但是一度,欧洲仿佛对此有所松绑。欧洲人认为DNA不是"生命",因此关于"扮演上帝角色"式的反对意见相应减少。但据说,授予这种专利可能给研究资金带来灾难性影响。然而,欧洲人在能否给人体组织授予专利的问题上,维持了固有的保守立场。如今,这种保守立场被写入欧盟1998年制定的关于生物技术领域发明保护的指令,该指令明确了未来法律和伦理辩论的战线。指令的第5条第1款规定:"处于形成和发展不同阶段的人体,以及单纯发现人体的某一要素,包括某个基因的完整或部分序列在内,不构成可授予专利的发明。"指令的第6条第1款还规定:"如果发明的商业性利用有违公共秩序或道德,该发明应被视为不可授予专利……以下各事项尤其应被视为不可授予专利:……克隆人的程序……为工业或商业目的使用人类胚胎。"在大多数司法管辖区,这些战线的总体立场是相似的。

保密问题：身体会讲故事

一位名人下榻饭店以后，女服务员从枕头上收集到他的头皮屑，并卖给一家全国性的报社。该报打算通过分析DNA来确定这位名人是不是那个引人注目的私生子的生父。这位名人能否主张头皮屑属于他的财产，而要求物归原主？头皮屑到底是不是财产？假如头皮屑属于财产，那么名人是否已经抛弃了它，从而使任何拾获它的人都有权持有它？

这个例子距离医事法的现实世界并不遥远。世界各地许多医院的储藏室中都存有人体组织，它们是从手术和解剖过程中合法地获得的，而这些人体组织的保存却未曾获得它们曾经的"所有者"的明确同意。这些人体组织同样能揭示有价值的信息，这些信息对医学研究者有价值，对保险公司也有潜在的价值。通过扫描基因，保险公司可以对作为人体组织供体的人的保险风险状况进行评估。

头皮屑案例和医院储藏室案例的情况非常相似。医院储藏室中的样本更大，而这并不应该成为以区别于头皮屑案例的方式对待它的正当理由。然而，很大可能是由于样本的大小，世界各国的律师更愿意为医院储藏室的人体样本是否属于财产以及能否被当作财产来处置而殚精竭虑，头皮屑则没有得到如此关注。

我们已经看到将人体部位视作财产可能导致的问题，而这些问题同时存在于生者和死者的情形。我们已经看到，如果有助于得到正确的答案，法律会秉持实用主义而乐见它们被称作"财产"。但在前面提到的两个案例中，确无必要着手使用财产的话语来保护那些亟须保护的利益。重要的不是人体组织本身，而是人体组织所承载的信息。最好的论理当然是关于保密或隐私的法律，而不是财产法。

很多司法管辖区的律师和立法者逐渐意识到了这一点。例如，英国的《人体组织法案》（2004）规定，未经授权而分析DNA的行为被特意确认为一种危害。这无疑是一条阳关道：为伤害后果定制救济，而不是把难题塞进那些陈旧的人造盒子（例如名叫"财产"的盒子），使法律变得复杂而扭曲。

第十一章

医事法的未来

作为一个独特的专业领域，医事法还很年轻。但从法律的角度看，年轻并不意味着强健。医学专业的发展日新月异，医事法需要紧跟医学专业发展的脚步，以胜任这种监管工作。

如何最好地适应监管的需要？我们能否声称，医事法的原则、规则和推论中充斥着维多利亚时代的契约观、义务观和信托观，将这些破碎、零散而且缺乏普适性的医事法通通撕碎？我们能否摒弃形而上学，转向根据神经科学来理解人类意志，起草出一部紧跟时代潮流的全新医事法典？

笔者的看法是，我们不妨得过且过。医事法应该循序渐进地发展，而不是另起炉灶。医事法的主题亘古不变、始终如一，那就是人类。深思熟虑的智者们为人类设计法律。我们遇到的新问题不过是各种老问题的变种。人类不可能安然地让法律彻底摒弃形而上学，因为人类自己就不可能摒弃形而上学。

当然，医事法进化的速度应当再快一些。法律人需要努力提高医学素养和伦理学素养。出色的法律论证离不开对医学实务的精通，也离不开对伦理影响的拿捏。这是一份宏大的诉状（brief）。各种医事法与医学伦理教科书和课程的发展如雨后春笋，这表明我们能够掌握它们。在本书第一章，我们审视了医事法与医学伦理之间的复杂关系。但最终，它们的关系如何定性并不重要，重要的是它们的关系既友好又亲密。在医事法与医学伦理之间保持对话始终至关重要。

医学正不断朝着技术化、循证化和"规范化操作流程驱动"（protocol-driven）的方向发展。尽管医学人文主义的捍卫者们仍在绝望地防守，谈论医学的技艺之维正变得越来越不合时宜。关于这种技艺消亡的论断逐渐成为一种自我实现的预言。医学的未来将由那些才华横溢的"技术宅"们主宰。他们的眼里只有显示屏或自己脚下，没有患者，更别提索福克勒斯的那些悲剧作品了。就算有意向和能力，"技术宅"们也没有时间思考某种新的生殖医学措施是否符合人道。即使得出结论，他们也可能认为造成非人道的影响不属于这种疗法的禁忌症。

因此极为重要的是，医事法不再像以前那样过度依赖医学专业判断。"博勒姆标准"应逐渐淡出，或至少是退避三舍。这种变化不是因为医学在明确的操作规程指引下逐渐变成追求精确的技术活（这也是"博勒姆标准"当下面临的威胁），而是因为设定法律标准的不应该是医生，而是法律。法律界有机会，也有责任来妥当地全盘考虑。医学界也有这样的责任，但他们刚刚失去设定法律标准的机会。

唯有自信的医事法律师方能胜任这种法律工作。"博勒姆标准"的某些夸张而惊人的滥用，不过是因为辩护人和法官对于医生的言论缺乏基本判断，因而决定将疑点利益归于被告。而在具备良好医事法素养的法官们的观念中,这样的疑点本来不应该出现。因此,我们需要培养专业法官。专攻医事法的法官将会更高效、更精通医学专业,并且(至少因为他们不会在午餐休庭时被医学辞典误导或恐吓)有更多机会在文献的海洋遨游。阅读文献可以帮助法官建立起更为全面、深刻而长远的医学观,而医学界却早已放弃了这种观念。

对司法的医学专业化改造也存在一些风险。这也许会让医学"技术宅"们趋之若鹜。这也许意味着医事法无法获得与某些法律部门融会贯通的机会,事实证明,这些法律部门在过去丰饶多产。如果商事法院的法官们只是戴着假发、浑浑噩噩地度日,这不会有多大影响,因为他们只要把钱的问题处理好就万事大吉。医事法专业的法官们不仅要处理人的身体、头脑和心灵,而且要处理将这些物件黏合在一起的各种奇怪胶水。有利于身体健康的决定不一定有利于心理健康。这种情形令人沮丧。然而,总体而言,值得冒险培养懂行的医事法专业法官。在很多司法管辖区,已经涌现出一大批懂行的医事法专业律师。他们都具备良好的专业素养。

法律人必须具备良好的专业素养。在医事法的前路上,他们会遇到各种需要绞尽脑汁的史诗级挑战。

人类胚胎的法律地位到底是什么?它的法律地位是否完全等同于一个成年人?如果二者不能完全等同,为什么不同?为了拯救患者Y而杀死患者X,这到底是否合法?如果这不合法,当维持永久植物状态的患者所消耗的资金能够支付拯救许多人生命的治疗措施时,你该如何处置?假设在伦敦实施一场隆胸手术所需的金钱可以拯救10 000名刚果儿童的性命,伦敦法院的法官能否判决伦敦的隆胸手术是合情合理的？按照法律的观点,生命是一种全有或全无的事物吗？在失去知觉和死亡之间的无人区徘徊时,患者是否与完全身心健康的儿童拥有同样的权利？女性是否有权使用男友和她刚刚用过的安全套里的精液来使自己受孕？如果有权,男友将面对何种后果？假如一名患者希望将自己的双腿用作浴室的展品,实施手术切除患者健康的双腿是否合法？一对听障夫妇希望生一个小孩与他们分享无声世界的亲密关系,他们通过体外人工受孕培养胚胎,并选出带有"听障"基因的胚胎植入母亲的子宫。孩子出生后,起诉那些造成她听障的医生,医生们反驳道:"如果不是听力障碍,你根本就不会来到这个世界。"假设在怀孕期间服用一种药物,孩子出生后可以终身免疫所有类型的癌症,而父母拒绝服用这种药物。长大后,孩子罹患癌症,于是将父母告上法院。一位医生正在参与培养仿生改造战士的项目,这些战士能跑得更快、跳得更高,可以在黑暗中看清物体。应该阻止这位医生吗？这种人体增强与为罹患关节疾病的老年女性置换人工髋关节之间的原则性区别是什么？医生为即将参加考试的大学生开具认知增强剂的处方,它们能帮助人更专注于复习,这种处方行为应该允许吗？假如认知增强剂价格昂贵,这样的处方意味着家境富裕的学生可以在考试中取得更好的成绩,情况又如何呢？假设有种旨在增强认知能力的基因改造可以让智商大幅提高50分,这样的基因改造有问题吗？如果有问题,是否意味着与通过倍增孩子大脑的神经元连接来提升智力具有同样效果的做法,即花巨资送孩子接受私立教育,从而具有认知上的优势,也是错误的？诸如此类的问题无穷无尽。

好一个令人兴奋的待办事件箱！

本书探讨的案例

本书正文在引用案例时标注的年份是登载该案的法律报告注释中所包含的年份。这个时间有时与案件本身判决的时间不一致。权威的法律报告的编纂出版有时会延迟很久。

第一章　起源与变迁
"博勒姆诉弗莱恩医院管理委员会案"（1957）1 WLR 583
"艾尔代尔国民医疗服务信托诉布兰德案"（1993）AC 789

第三章　生命起始之前
"ELH 和 PBH 诉联合王国案"（1998）25 EHRR CD 158
"梅勒诉内政大臣案"（2002）QB 13
"人类授精和胚胎研究管理局诉布拉德案"（1997）2 WLR 806
"埃文斯诉联合王国案"（2006）1 FCR 585
"计划生育协会密苏里州中部分会诉丹福思案"（1976）96 S Ct 2831

"C诉S案"（1988）QB 135

"佩顿诉联合王国案"（1981）3 EHRR 408

"英格兰及威尔士总检察长1994年第3号司法解释案"（1998）AC 245

"温尼伯西北区域儿童和家庭服务机构诉G案"（1997）3 BHRC 611

"佩顿诉英国孕期咨询服务机构理事会案"（1979）QB 276

"圣乔治国民医疗服务信托诉S案"（1998）3 All ER 673

"武诉法国案"（2004）2 FCR 526

"罗伊诉韦德案"（1973）410 US 113

"麦凯诉埃塞克斯区域卫生局案"（1982）QB 1166

"麦克法兰诉泰赛德卫生局案"（2000）AC 59

"多伊诉博尔顿案"（1973）410 US 179

"昆塔瓦莱（代表'生殖伦理评论'组织）诉人类授精和胚胎研究管理局案"（2005）2 AC 561

第四章 保密与隐私

"卫生部诉信息源有限公司案"（2000）Lloyd's Rep Med 76

"Z诉芬兰案"（1998）25 EHRR 371

"坎贝尔诉《镜报》报业公司案"（2004）2 AC 457

"W诉艾基尔案"（1990）1 Ch 359

"雅菲诉雷德蒙案"（1996）518 US 1

"泰瑞索夫等人诉加利福尼亚大学校董会案"（1976）17 Cal（3d）358

"帕尔默诉南提斯卫生局案"（1999）Lloyd's Rep Med 151

"阿克森诉卫生大臣案"（2006）QB 539

"刘易斯诉卫生大臣案"（2008）EWHC 2196

第五章 同意权

"女王诉布朗案"（1994）1 AC 212

"拉斯基、杰加德和布朗诉联合王国案"（1997）24 EHRR 39

"施伦多夫诉纽约医院协会案"（1914）211 NY 125

"马利特诉舒尔曼案"（1990）67 DLR（4th）321

"吉利克诉西诺福克和威斯贝奇区域卫生局案"（1986）1 AC 112

"普林斯诉马萨诸塞州案"（1944）321 US 158

"女王诉莫比利奥案"（1991）1 VR 339

"女王诉克拉伦斯案"（1888）22 QBD 23

"女王诉迪卡案"（2004）1 QB 1257

"萨尔戈诉里兰德·斯坦福二世大学信托董事会案"（1957）154 Cal App 2d 560

"坎特伯雷诉斯彭斯案"（1972）464 2d 772

"赖布尔诉休斯案"（1980）2 SCR 894

"罗杰斯诉惠特克案"（1992）175 CLR 479

"赛德威诉皇家伯利恒医院和莫兹利医院理事会案"（1985）1 AC 171

"皮尔斯诉布里斯托尔医疗联合体国民医疗服务信托案"（1999）PIQR P 53

第六章 医疗过失

"多诺霍诉史蒂文森案"（化名为"麦卡利斯特诉史蒂文森

案")(1932) AC 562
"卡帕罗工业公开股份有限公司诉迪克曼案"(1990) 2 AC 605
"卡普范德诉安民银行案"(1999) 2 Lloyd's Rep Med 48
"古德威尔诉英国孕期咨询服务机构案"(1996) 2 All ER 161
"泰瑞索夫诉加利福尼亚大学校董会案"(在前)
"帕尔默诉南提斯卫生局案"(在前)
"博勒姆诉弗莱恩医院管理委员会案"(在前)
"博莱索诉伦敦金融城和哈克尼卫生局案"(1998) AC 232
"赛德威诉皇家伯利恒医院理事会案"(在前)
"坎特伯雷诉斯彭斯案"(在前)
"赖布尔诉休斯案"(在前)
"F诉R案"(1983) 33 SASR 189(FC)
"卡斯特尔诉德·赫里夫案"(1994)(4) SA 408
"罗杰斯诉惠特克案"(在前)
"查普林诉希克斯案"(1911) 2 KB 786
"贝利诉国防部案"(2009) 1 WLR 1052
"麦吉诉国家煤炭局案"(1973) 1 WLR 1
"切斯特诉阿夫沙尔案"(2005) 1 AC 134

第八章　医疗资源分配

"剑桥卫生局诉B案"(1995) 1 WLR 898
"艾尔代尔国民医疗服务信托诉布兰德案"(在前)

第九章　生命的终止

"艾尔代尔国民医疗服务信托诉布兰德案"(在前)

"女王诉考克斯案"（1992），未载入法律报告
"B诉一家国民医疗服务信托案"（2002）2 All ER 449
"萨茨诉珀尔马特案"（1980）379 So.2d 359
"麦凯诉贝里斯泰特案"（1990）801 P. 2d 617
"佐治亚州诉麦卡菲案"（1989）259 Ga. 579（385 SE2d 651）

第十章 器官捐献与人体部位的所有权

"女王诉本瑟姆案"（2005）2 WLR 384
"女王诉凯利案"（1999）QB 621
"杜德沃德诉斯彭斯案"（1908）6 CLR 406
"穆尔诉加利福尼亚大学校董会案"（1990）793 P 2d 479
"海奇特诉洛杉矶县高等法院案"（1993）20 Cal Rptr 2d 275
"人类授精和胚胎研究管理局诉布拉德案"（在前）
"埃文斯诉阿米库斯医疗有限公司案"，见"埃文斯诉联合王国案"（在前）
"耶尔沃斯诉北布里斯托尔国民医疗服务信托案"（2010）QB 1
"戴蒙德诉查克拉巴蒂案"（1980）447 US 303

第十一章 医事法的未来

"博勒姆诉弗莱恩医院管理委员会案"（在前）

索 引

（条目后的数字为原书页码，
见本书边码）

A

Abortion 人工流产
  European Convention on Human Rights: Article 2《欧洲人权公约》：第 2 条 21, 24—25
  European Convention on Human Rights: Article 8《欧洲人权公约》：第 8 条 21
  fetal viability, relevance of 胎儿发育到可在子宫外独立生存 27—28
  generally 概述 20—29
  rights of biological father 生父的权利 20
Academic medical law 医事法学 6—7
Accidental killing 意外致人死亡 10—11 参见 Manslaughter 和 Negligence
Acts/omissions distinction 积极行为/消极行为的区分 100—102
Advance directives 预立医疗指示，见 Consent 项下 Advance Directives
American Medical Association 美国医学会 32, 42, 45
'Anatomy Lesson of Professor Nicolaes Tulp, The'(Rembrandt)《尼古拉斯·杜尔教授的解剖学课》（伦勃朗）119
Animal-human hybrids 人兽混交 19
Assault, sexual 性侵犯, 见 Sexual Assault
Assisted suicide 协助自杀, 见 Suicide, assisted
Auschwitz 奥斯威辛集中营 80, 84
Autonomy 自主权 48—52, 57—59, 60, 80—89, 103—104, 117, 120

B

Best interests test "最佳利益标准" 25—26, 51—55, 109—111
Blood, sale of 卖血 118
'Bolam test' "博勒姆标准" 4—5, 7—8, 57—58, 67—72, 77—78, 86, 125
Brain stem death 脑干死亡, 见 Death, Definition of

C

Capacity 行为能力 15—16, 25—26, 44—55, 48—55, 86—87
Causation 因果关系
  'but-for' test "必要条件标准" 72—73, 76
  consent and 相关的同意权问题 75—76
  generally 概述 72—78
  hypothetical 推定的 77—78
  loss of a chance 机会丧失 73—74
  material contribution 实质诱发损害 74—75
Children 儿童
  consent, and 与同意权问题 52—54
  research involving 参与人体试验 86—87

rights of confidentiality of 儿童的医疗保密相关权利 44—45

Chimaera 嵌合体 19

Clinical negligence 临床过失，见 Negligence Cloning 29—30

Compensation, claims for 赔偿金申索，见 Damages, claims for

Competence 适格，见 Capacity

Confidence, duty of 保密义务，见 Confidentiality

 in France 法国的 2

 in Germany 德国的 2

Confidentiality 保密

 balancing competing interests 权衡冲突的利益 36—45

 children and 涉及儿童的 44—45

 codes relating to 相关伦理守则 32—33

 dead patients and 涉及死者的 44—45, 122—123

 Federal Rules of Evidence, and (US) 涉及美国联邦证据规则 38—39

 generally 概述 32—45

 incapacitous patients and 涉及缺乏行为能力的患者 44—45

 information from body parts and 涉及人体部分承载的信息 122—123

 legal models of 法律论证模式 34—36

 privacy, relationship to 与隐私的关系 35—36

 privilege, doctor-patient "医生-患者特权" 38—39

 reasons for respecting 重视的原因 33

Consent 同意权

 advance directives 预立医疗指示 50—52, 98, 111—113

 best interests 最佳利益 51—55, 86—87, 109—111

 'Bolam test' and 涉及"博勒姆标准" 57—58

 capacity, definition 行为能力定义 48—49

 children, and 涉及儿童 52—55, 86—87, 110

 consequences of failing to obtain 侵犯患者同意权的法律后果 59—60

 generally 概述 46—60

 'Gillick competency' "吉利克适格标准" 53—54

 informed consent 告知后同意 57—59, 69—72

 negligence and 涉及医疗过失 69—72

 proxy decision-making 代理人决定 51, 86, 110—111

 research and 涉及人体试验 80—89

 sexual assault, and 涉及性侵犯 55—57

 Sado-masochism, and 涉及性虐恋行为 46—47

 sporting injuries, and 涉及运动损伤 46—47

 substituted judgment 替代患者判断 51—52, 108, 110—111

Contract 合同

 clinical negligence claims and 医

疗过失诉讼与 63—64
Convention on Human Rights and Biomedicine《欧洲人权与生物医学公约》118
Corpse, property in 尸体的财产属性 114—118

D

Damage, types recognised by the law 法律承认的损害类型 78—79
Damages, claims for 损害索赔 12—13, 61—79
　参见 Quantum, assessment of
Death, definition of 死亡的定义 98—100
Declaration of Geneva《日内瓦宣言》4, 80
Declaration of Helsinki《赫尔辛基宣言》80—88
　Article 17 第 17 条 83
　Article 20 第 20 条 86
　Article 21 第 21 条 82
　Article 27 第 27 条 86
　Article 32 第 32 条 83
　Article 33 第 33 条 83
　Article 35 第 35 条 85
'Deliverance machine' "解脱仪" 106
Dementia 痴呆症状 112—113
Dignity 人性尊严 118
Disciplinary proceedings 惩戒程序 11, 13—14
Discrimination and resource allocation 歧视与医疗资源分配 92—95
Double effect "双重效应" 原则 97

E

Embryo 胚胎 29
　Cloning 克隆，见 Cloning
　generally 概述 18—31
　legal status of 法律地位 20—31
　'spare' "备用" 23
End of life decision-making 终止生命的医疗决定 96—113（参见 Euthanasia; Suicide, Assisted; Withdrawal of Treatment）
Enforcement of medical law 医事法的实施 9—17
Ethics, medical, and law, relationship 医学伦理与医事法的关系 7—8
European Convention on Human Rights《欧洲人权公约》
　Article 2 第 2 条 11, 21, 24—25, 93
　Article 3 第 3 条 93
　Article 8 第 8 条 21, 28, 35, 38, 58—59, 93
　Article 12 第 12 条 19
　Article 14 第 14 条 93
　Generally 概述 15
Euthanasia 安乐死 96—97, 100—105

F

Federal Rules of Evidence (US) 美国联邦证据规则 39
Fetus 胎儿，见 Embryo
First World War 第一次世界大战 4

Food and Drug Administration (US) 美国食品药品监督管理局 83
Fraud 欺诈 9
French Revolution 法国大革命 4

G

Gender reassignment surgery 变性手术, 见 Transsexuals
Gene, patenting of 基因的专利保护申请 121—122
Geneva, Declaration of《日内瓦宣言》, 见 Declaration of Geneva
Germany, Constitution of 德国宪法 14
'Gillick competency' "吉利克适格标准", 见 Consent 项下的 'Gillick competency'
Great War 第一次世界大战, 见 First World War

H

Helsinki, Declaration of《赫尔辛基宣言》, 见 Declaration of Helsinki
Hippocrates 希波克拉底 3
Hippocratic Oath "希波克拉底誓词" 2, 32
HIV, transmission of 传播艾滋病病毒 43, 56, 67, 81
Human Fertilization and Embryology Authority 人类授精与胚胎研究管理局 30

I

Imago Dei 神的形象 103
Incapacity, mental 缺乏行为能力, 见 Capacity
Incest 乱伦 19
Informed consent 告知后同意, 见 Consent 项下的 Informed Consent
Inquests 死因裁判庭 11
Institutional Review Boards (IRBs) 机构审查委员会 88—89
International Code of Medical Ethics《国际医学伦理守则》32—33
In Vitro Fertilization (IVF) 体外受精, 见 Reproduction 项下的 Artificial techniques
Insurance, for medical malpractice 医疗事故保险 12—13
Intellectual property rights, genes and 基因与知识产权 121—122
Intrauterine damage, liability for 子宫内损害的赔偿责任 22—23
IRBs 机构审查委员会, 见 Institutional Review Boards
Irradiation, research on 放射试验研究 81
Israel, Basic Laws of 以色列的基本法 14

J

Jehovah's Witnesses "耶和华见证人" 15—16, 49, 54

Judicial review 司法审查 13—14, 91—93
Juries 陪审员 12

K

Killing, accidental 意外致人死亡, 见 Accidental Killing

L

Living Wills 生前遗嘱, 见 Advance Directives

M

Malaria, research into 疟疾研究 82—83
Manslaughter 非预谋杀人 97—98
Medical ethics 医学伦理, 见 Ethics, medical
Mengele, Josef 约瑟夫·门格尔 4, 80, 84
Murder 谋杀 96—97, 100—105

N

Negligence, Clinical 医疗过失
  'Bolam test' "博勒姆标准", 见 'Bolam test'
  breach of duty 违反义务 67—72
  causation and 因果关系判断, 见 Causation
  consent and 涉及同意权问题 69—72
  contract, and 涉及合同法问题 63—64
  damage, types recognised by the law 法律承认的损害类型, 见 Damage, types recognised by the law
  duty of care 注意义务 64—67
  generally 概述 12—13, 61—79
  'no-fault' schemes "无过错责任" 保险 62—63
  psychiatric injury 导致精神损害, 见 psychiatric injury
  quantum, assessment of 赔偿额计算, 见 Quantum, assessment of
  third parties, liability to 第三方责任 64—67
  tort, elements of claim in 侵权法中的医疗过失索赔要件 63
New Zealand, 'no-fault' schemes in 新西兰的"无过错责任"保险, 见 Negligence, Clinical, 'no-fault' schemes
Nitschke, Philip 菲利普·尼奇克 106
'No-fault' schemes "无过错责任"保险, 见 Negligence, Clinical, 'no-fault schemes'
Nuremberg Code 《纽伦堡法典》80

O

Omissions/acts distinction 消极行为/积极行为的区分, 见 Acts/omissions distinction
OncoMouse "肿瘤鼠" 121
Organ donation 器官捐献
  definition of death and 与死亡的定义 99, 120—121
  generally 概述 114—121

医事法

Organ sales 器官交易 118

P

Permanent Vegetative State(PVS) 永久植物状态 94, 100—101, 107, 109—110

Persistent Vegetative State 持续性植物状态, 见 Permanent Vegetative State

Polkinghorne Committee 波尔金霍恩委员会 23

Prisoners, reproductive rights of 囚犯的生育权利 19

Privacy 隐私 (参见 Confidentiality) 35—36

Proceedings, multiplicity of 程序的错综复杂 16—17

Property, body parts as 作为财产的人体部位 114—123

Proxy decision-making 代理人决定, 见 Consent 项下的 Proxy-decision-making

Psychiatric injury 精神损害 66—67

Public law 公法 14—15

PVS 永久植物状态, 见 Permanent Vegetative State

Pythagoreans 毕达哥拉斯 2

Q

Quantum, assessment of 赔偿额计算 79

R

'Rake's Progress, A' (Hogarth)《浪子生涯》(贺加思) 52

Regulatory proceedings 监督程序, 见 Disciplinary Proceedings

Reproduction 生殖
  artificial techniques 人工辅助技术 19—20, 23, 29—31
  obligation to reproduce 生育的义务 19—20
  right to reproduce 生育的权利 18—20

Research on human subjects 人体研究
  children and 涉及儿童 86—87
  Declaration of Helsinki《赫尔辛基宣言》, 见 Declaration of Helsinki
  generally 概述 80—89
  incompetent adults and 涉及不适格的成年人 86—87
  Institutional Review Boards(IRBs) 机构审查委员会, 见 Institutional Review Boards
  Nuremberg Code《纽伦堡法典》见 Nuremberg Code
  payment 报酬 87—88
  placebo-controlled trials 安慰剂对照方式的人体试验 82—83
  review of research projects 研究计划审查 88—89
  stopping a trial 停止人体试验 85—86

Resource allocation 医疗资源分配
  discrimination and 歧视与 92—95
  European Convention on Human Rights and《欧洲人权公约》与 93
  gender reassignment surgery and 涉及变性手术 92—93

139

generally 概述 90—95
individual patient care and 涉及个别患者的医疗照护 94—95
policy making 政策形成 90—94
Quality-Adjusted Life Year(QALY) 质量调整寿命年数 93
smoking and 涉及吸烟 93

S

Sado-masochism 性虐恋行为 46—47
Sanctity of life 生命的神圣性 103, 110
'Saviour siblings' "兄姐救星" 30—31
Second World War 第二次世界大战 4, 5
Semen, post-mortem use of 死亡后的精液使用 19—20, 117—118
Sexual assault 性侵犯 9, 55—57
Smoking, resource allocation and 吸烟对医疗资源分配的影响 93
South Africa, Constitution of 南非宪法 14
Staten Island, hepatitis research 斯塔顿岛,肝炎人体试验 81
Sterilization 绝育
　compulsory 强制的 15
　negligent 过失的 26, 65
Substituted judgment "替代患者决定",见 Consent 项下的 substituted judgment
Suicide, Assisted 协助自杀 105—106
Sweden, 'no-fault' schemes in 瑞典"无过错责任"保险,见 Negligence, Clinical, 'no-fault' schemes

T

Theft, body parts of 盗窃人体部位 114—118
Transsexuals 变性人 92—93
Treatment, withdrawal of 治疗措施的撤除,见 Withdrawal of Treatment
'Triumph of Death, The'(Orcagna)《死亡的胜利》(奥尔卡尼亚) 111
Tuskegee, syphilis research 塔斯基吉,梅毒研究 81
Twins, Mengele's experiments on 门格尔对双胞胎的试验 84

U

USA, Constitution of 美国宪法 14, 25

W

Withdrawal of treatment 治疗措施的撤除 97—98, 100—102, 106—113
Withholding treatment 保持治疗措施,见 Withdrawal of treatment
World Medical Association 世界医学会 4, 32, 42
　Declaration of Helsinki《赫尔辛基宣言》,见 Declaration of Helsinki
World War II 第二次世界大战,见 Second World War

Charles Foster

MEDICAL LAW

A Very Short Introduction

Contents

Acknowledgements i

List of illustrations iii

1 Origins and legacies 1
2 The enforcement of medical law 9
3 Before birth 18
4 Confidentiality and privacy 32
5 Consent 46
6 Clinical negligence 61
7 Research on human subjects 80
8 Resource allocation 90
9 The end of life 96
10 Organ donation and the ownership of body parts 114
11 The future of medical law 124

Cases discussed 129

Further reading 133

Acknowledgements

Every book is a piece of plagiarism—a mosaic of the ideas of others. This is probably particularly true of law books. All an author can do is to rearrange the ideas into a new-ish form, and do some processing. Often the sources are impossible to trace. A source might be a raised eyebrow in a seminar, or the tone of a sentence. So every list of acknowledgements is both incomplete and invidious. Here, however, are some of the people to whom I know I owe a great debt:

Jonathan Herring, Tony Hope, Mike Parker, Julian Savulescu, Richard Ashcroft, Roger Brownsword, Aharon Barak, Mikey Dunn, Mark Sheehan, Dom Wilkinson, John Keown, John Tingle, Jane Kaye, a host of barristers who've pointed out my misconceptions both gently and aggressively, OUP's anonymous reviewers, and the Principal, Fellows, and students of Green Templeton College, Oxford.

I don't know why authors always feel the need to say that all remaining errors are their own. I've always been taught not to state the blindingly obvious, and so I won't.

Charles Foster
Green Templeton College
University of Oxford
April 2012

List of illustrations

1 Hippocrates (c.460–c.370 BCE) **3**
  Neveshkin Nikolay/Shutterstock

2 The developing embryo/fetus **29**
  Hans-Ulrich Osterwalder/Science Photo Library

3 Medical confidentiality **43**
  The Independent

4 *A Rake's Progress*, by Willian Hogarth **52**
  The genius of William Hogarth

5 A surgical site marked up to avoid confusion **71**
  Dr P. Marazzi/Science Photo Library

6 Twins at Auschwitz, used for medical experiments by the Nazi doctor Josef Mengele **84**
  AFP/Getty Images

7 Patients in an African clinic wait for treatment **92**
  Mauro Fermariello/Science Photo Library

8 Philip Nitschke's 'Deliverance machine' **106**
  Dr Philip Nitschke

9 Detail from Andrea Orcagna's *The Triumph of Death* **111**
  Web Gallery of Art

10 Rembrandt's *The Anatomy Lesson of Professor Nicolaes Tulp* **119**
  Geheugen van Nederland

Chapter 1
Origins and legacies

As a discrete subject, medical law is young. But regulation of the medical profession is not. Being able to hack into people's bodies for money is a remarkable privilege, and it entails particular responsibility. It has long been recognized (even if it is being quickly forgotten) that medicine isn't like any other business. An orthopaedic surgeon might have the same skills as a carpenter, but bone and muscle were and are regarded as being made of stuff importantly, if mysteriously, different from pine and plywood. Bone and flesh build boxes for souls. Mess with the boxes and you could affect the soul. That gives physicians and surgeons awesome, high-priestly power.

The accountability of medicine's high priests

Priests are a set-apart caste: they are expected to behave better than the hoi polloi. All priests serve in temples. Those in the temples dedicated to divinities are answerable to the divinities; and those (the doctors) who serve in the material temples of the human soul (by rummaging around inside chests or by putting leeches on limb stumps) are answerable to the body owners, or to the society that represents them. But there is a problem about such accountability. If you're an inaccessibly high high priest—if your work is beyond the ken of the people to whom you're accountable—how can accountability be real?

The doctors persuaded the people that they, the doctors, had to regulate themselves on behalf of the people. The Hippocratic Oath, already extant in the 5th century BCE (and therefore probably borrowed by the Hippocratic School from some mystical Pythagorean ancestors), is the classic example. It's a code drawn up by doctors, for doctors, and is policed, more or less, by doctors.

For most of the next two and a half millennia, the Hippocratic Oath, or one of its many variants, has been the law regulating the medical profession. But here's the point: these codes are not laws in the usual sense of the word. They are sets of ethical principles: the rules of a very exclusive club. Only when self-regulation manifestly failed, or the law acquired a self-confidence it has rarely had, or it became politically desirable to question the propriety of self-rule by an esoteric elite, did the law think it either necessary or appropriate to intrude into the holy of holies where the white-coated, bloodstained priests stood with their votive knives.

By and large, continental Europe, was quicker to regulate doctors than were England, the British Commonwealth, or the US, but it is hard to generalize usefully about why this was. Both France and Germany, for instance, imposed legal duties of confidentiality on doctors far earlier than did Britain, but their motives for doing so were not necessarily the same. Catholic France was perhaps influenced by the analogy between the confessional and the consulting room. If so, the French duty of confidence might be an affirmation of the sanctity of the consultation rather than the human rights of the patient. Germany, on the other hand, has always been keener than many nations on regulation for regulation's sake. But everywhere, until the middle of the 20th century, medical practitioners enjoyed extraordinary social status, and a legal status bordering unacceptably on immunity.

1. Hippocrates (c.460–c.370 BCE), the 'Father of Western Medicine', who is (probably wrongly) credited with the formulation of the Hippocratic Oath, a declaration of ethical principles on which subsequent medical regulatory codes have drawn

The Nazis changed this. Their doctors showed that a professional qualification did not imply a decent conscience.

The seeds of this recognition were sown in the French Revolution and the Great War, when the myth of the infallibility of the upper orders was comprehensively and bloodily exploded. But it's one thing to realize that a moustachioed, titled general is an ass. It's another to recognize that a doctor, pledged professionally to heal, and speaking words of fate in hermetic language, might be incompetent or downright evil. It took Mengele to teach the world that doctors couldn't be trusted to regulate themselves. This was an important moment for the rule of law.

The world learned quickly. Immediately after World War II there was a proliferation of international declarations and professional codes, including the Declaration of Geneva, 1947 (revised 1968 and 1983) and the World Medical Association's international code of medical ethics, 1949 (revised 1968 and 1983).

This change in the *zeitgeist*, crystallized in and evidenced by the codes, was fairly effective in regulating unconscionable conduct (although, as we'll see, some abominable things still continued to happen in the world of medical research, particularly in countries and amongst populations who, it was thought, wouldn't invoke the newly promulgated, if rather toothless, declarations). It was less effective in changing judicial attitudes towards well-meaning but technically inadequate clinical conduct. Judges still tended to regard an assertion of clinical negligence as a piece of insubordination: the thin end of the Marxist revolutionary wedge. The judges, after all, had been to the same schools as the doctors, and drank the same ancient claret. If the professional judgement of a doctor could be questioned, where would it end? Lawyers might be next in the firing line. This led, as we see in Chapter 6, to an abuse of one of the commonest tests for establishing a breach of duty—the '*Bolam*' test'. This is the idea that a doctor is not negligent if what he has done would be endorsed by a responsible body of opinion in the relevant specialty. The abuse continues, although it's on the wane. Constitutional lawyers would assume, and everyone else would hope, that it was self-evident that the law, not the doctors, set the standard by which doctors should be judged. It is not yet self-evident to judges everywhere. English judges have been particularly slow learners.

A new set of medico-legal tools

When the law, belatedly, dealt with the health-care professions, it did so using tools that had been made for other things. It used notions of contract that were originally devised to regulate the sale of wool, concepts of trusteeship that worked well enough in suppressing the skulduggery of executors, and ideas of duty that let ginger beer manufacturers know where they stood if they let snails die in their bottles. These ideas do not necessarily export well into operating theatres. The chance of successful export is not increased if the export is handled (as it was) by legal practitioners (barristers, solicitors, and judges) who know a lot about the conveyance of land, the rule against perpetuities, the construction of bills of lading, and the Oxford and Cambridge Boat Race, but nothing whatever about the circulation of the blood or the anatomy of the bile ducts.

It's surprising that things worked out as well as they did. Long before it was possible to talk about a corpus of medical law, let alone a profession of medical lawyers, the courts, proceeding by more or less bad analogy with commercial and personal injury litigation, and by an instinct for fair play honed or ablated on the cricket field, did approximate justice in the relatively few medical cases that came before them.

No accurate figures exist for the number of medical cases brought in the various jurisdictions. One problem is simply that of definition. What's a 'medical case'? But whatever a medical case is, the number of them increased steadily after World War II, and then, after the 1970s, increased very rapidly indeed. The rise in the number of cases was paralleled by an increasing acknowledgement of medical law as a subject in its own right. The two acted synergistically. The more medical cases, the more law: the more law, the more public and professional recognition of the possibilities of medical litigation, and hence the more cases.

Lawyers, particularly in the US, went into a feeding frenzy. The profit motive isn't always a friend of nuance, but even greedy lawyers are sometimes clever and imaginative, and the desire to win cases and boost reputations gave the judges a chance to mould a distinctive corpus of medical law. And they did.

England typically catches American colds and ideas about ten years after the Americans are immune to them, and it is certainly true that English (and Commonwealth) medical law has borrowed some central medico-legal ideas from the US. But the medico-legal community is more genuinely international and egalitarian than many other legal communities. Everyone wants to learn from everyone else. Authorities from other jurisdictions are cited with less apology and embarrassment in medical cases than in many others. Perhaps this is because medical law deals with the most fundamental questions about humans. Americans might convey land in a different way from the Vietnamese, but they're born and they die similarly. Perhaps, too, it's because the questions are terribly difficult, being laced bracingly with biology and metaphysics. This means that judges are grateful for all the help they can get. At any rate there has been promiscuous cross-fertilization (the cynics would say cross-infection), which has produced some exciting, vigorous hybrids.

The industry of academic medical law

Another important chicken-and-egg-type question relates to the role of academic lawyers. Medical law courses have been taught now for many years, but have mushroomed over the last decade.

They have produced graduates who have gone on to swell both the numbers of medical cases litigated and the sophistication of the arguments ventilated in that litigation. This has given their old tutors more to write about, so generating a demand for more medical law textbooks and courses, and so on, if not ad infinitum, at least to the point of medical law having a recognized status both as an academic subject and a professional sub-discipline. In some ways this is a shame: respectability leads to petrifaction. There was a swashbuckling, rather rag-tag feel about medical law twenty years ago. Now medical law has a paunch, a suit, and a mortgage. You used to be able to say anything. Now there's a growing orthodoxy. When you get orthodoxy you get heresies and burnings.

Medical law and medical ethics: a tense but fecund marriage

Medical law, both in academic courses and textbook titles, often has a partner: medical ethics. The nature of the partnership is obscure and complex. Medical ethics purport to say what doctors should do: medical law purports to say what doctors should do, *or else*. But it's not so simple. There are ethical courts—the disciplinary bodies—which have fearsome teeth.

Lord Justice Hoffmann, in *Airedale NHS Trust v Bland* (1993), said: 'I would expect medical ethics to be formed by the law rather than the reverse.' At first blush it seems that he got it wrong. The influence of the *Bolam* test is profound. In many jurisdictions the liability of professionals is determined by professional peers. A clinician will not be negligent if he's done something in a way that would be endorsed by a responsible body of clinicians in the relevant specialty. Often (for instance in the law of consent and confidentiality) discussions about what amounts to legally responsible conduct have a distinctly ethical flavour. The ethical guidelines from the relevant regulatory bodies will be cited, and experts will opine about whether a rightly oriented professional conscience could reach the same conclusion as the defendant. Ethics seem to lead the way.

But is it really so? Who drafts the guidelines? Often lawyers will have sat on the relevant committees, infusing the drafts with their wisdom and folly. Lawyers are often listened to with entirely unjustified deference. Through guidelines and through dinner party conversations, lawyers may wittingly or unwittingly influence the consciences of surgeons, nurses, and occupational therapists. Hoffmann LJ didn't imagine that the law would exercise its influence like this, but he might have got it right after all.

Practising lawyers, though, tend not to be very philosophically literate or interested. And even if they are, they don't usually have time for anything other than rule-of-thumb, case-by-case-basis pragmatism. This is frustrating in the law of contract: it can be quite literally deadly in the law of medicine, where every question, properly examined, is a version of the Psalmist's: 'What is man, that thou art mindful of him?' If medical law is ruled entirely by the lawyers, it'll be a clunking, mechanistic thing. To deal properly with its astonishing subjects (humans), it needs to be more reflective, polymathic, and multilingual than it is or than it ever realistically can be. It will always fail, but it badly needs the help of the philosophers to help it fail less abjectly and more coherently.

Chapter 2
The enforcement of medical law

When health-care professionals are accused of doing something wrong, they might find themselves in jail, poverty, disgrace, or all three. This chapter maps their journeys.

The journey to jail: criminal jurisdiction

Health-care professionals can find the collars of their white coats fingered by the police for many things. They can and do sexually abuse their patients. This seems to be a particular pursuit of general practitioners/family doctors and psychiatrists, no doubt because of the opportunities that those specialities give, rather than because the specialities attract a disproportionate number of sexual predators. They invent clinically implausible excuses for breast and vaginal examinations, drug or hypnotize their patients into compliance, and misuse clinical photographs.

They can, and do, get involved in various types of medically related fraud, from fiddling their expenses or claiming for work done on non-existent patients, to drilling out and filling healthy teeth.

There's nothing quintessentially medical about the law relating to medical fraud. You can see the principles in any criminal law textbook. We meet the distinctively medical parts of sexual and other assaults in Chapter 5, on consent. But when doctors and nurses kill, the law is particular, particularly interesting, and particularly controversial.

The law of medical murder and manslaughter is dealt with in Chapter 9, on the end of life. There's of course a big and loud debate about whether the state should prosecute doctors who deliberately and compassionately 'ease the passing' of manifestly competent patients who ask for help in dying.

But what about accidental killing? Are the big guns of the criminal law appropriately directed against doctors who simply make a mistake with lethal consequences?

Take two examples:

A patient is undergoing a serious abdominal operation. Unknown and unknowable to the surgeon, the patient starts to bleed badly. The blood pressure plummets. This would be easily correctable if the anaesthetist notices. But he doesn't, since, bored by the long procedure, he's doing the crossword. The patient has a cardiac arrest and dies.

A patient has an epidural catheter placed for pain relief. She screams out for a top-up of her anaesthetic dose. A hard-pressed nurse draws up the anaesthetic and injects it. She has not checked the bottle properly. The drug is a highly toxic cancer chemotherapy agent, and the patient dies.

In both these cases the police are summoned. In both cases the family has an unanswerable claim for compensatory damages, and in both cases the clinicians involved are likely to be hauled before the relevant professional regulatory body. They may never work again. What's to be gained from criminal proceedings?

It might be said that the taking of a life is always a serious business, and must be seen to be taken seriously by the state, rather than only by the individuals most closely involved. The state exists to safeguard the security of individuals: its appearance in the role of prosecutor in criminal proceedings is part of that custodianship responsibility, and the mere fact of the prosecution (perhaps *particularly* where the forensic fuss seems out of proportion to the magnitude of the defendant's default) is shouting something important about the sanctity of human life.

Then there are the arguments which rest on what the state's responsibility entails. It entails a duty to investigate properly the deaths of its subjects (a responsibility embodied, for instance, in Article 2 of the European Convention on Human Rights). This is partly because investigation involves healthy catharsis, and partly so that the lessons of tragedy are not missed. The prevention of future fatalities is important in another way: the drama of criminal proceedings might cause other potential defaulters to be more careful.

Against all this it can be said that there are plenty of other more appropriate ways of saying that lives are important and that the state cares. In most modern states inquests or other fatality investigations discharge the investigatory and, to some extent, the cathartic functions of a criminal trial. Regulatory proceedings ensure that individual doctors learn the lessons their own sense of guilt might not have taught them, and that wider risk management lessons are disseminated to the profession as a whole. Adding yet another set of proceedings simply runs up costs that might better be spent on health care, delays the start of the grieving process, and panders to a prurient press.

And yet patients' families often want criminal proceedings. Revenge is an old and deep instinct.

The journey to poverty: civil claims for damages

Doctors are much more likely to be sued than prosecuted. The claim will typically be in the form: 'You shouldn't have done that. It's caused me damage. I want compensation.' Typical examples are negligence claims (see Chapter 6), claims based on consent (Chapter 5), and claims based on confidentiality and privacy (Chapter 4).

In most jurisdictions these claims are tried by professional judges sitting alone. Those judges may or may not have any particular expertise in medical cases, but the trend worldwide is towards judicial specialization.

There are still jurisdictions (notably the US) where civil claims are commonly tried by lay juries. This scares the life out of defendants and their insurers. If you were an accountant, how would you like your ability to prepare a balance sheet judged by an innumerate panel, none of whom knows what a balance sheet is? It's hard for the presiding judge to keep juries on a tight rein. They're easily led by their noses and heartstrings rather than by the facts.

Where (as is common in the UK) the relevant health care has been given by a public body, the public body rather than the individual doctor concerned is likely to be the defendant. But even in the UK lots of health care is provided by private doctors or by family doctors (general practitioners, or GPs) who, although paid ultimately by the state, are sued in their own name. If the private doctor or GP has paid the necessary insurance premium, and the alleged malpractice falls within the terms of the policy (sexual misconduct, for instance, may well not), the insurer will indemnify the doctor and pay his legal costs and, if he loses, those of the other side. So, generally, if he's kept up his premium payments and has been 'merely' negligent, the doctor's unlikely to lose his house.

Medical litigation is big business. And so, therefore, is professional indemnity insurance. Malpractice insurance premiums form a significant part of the total professional expenses of any doctor—and particularly those in specialties more likely to be sued (such as surgeons of various types) or in specialties likely to be sued for huge amounts of compensation (such as obstetricians, since brain-damaged babies are expensive).

A 2011 study of US doctors showed that 75 per cent of physicians in 'low-risk' specialties, and practically all in 'high-risk' specialties, would face a malpractice suit at some time in their careers. But that doesn't mean they will be successfully sued. The pattern is the same in the US as elsewhere: most claims don't result in a payment to the claimant. More detailed statistics would be meaningless: they depend crucially on the mechanics of the compensation systems in the relevant jurisdiction.

There have been strident calls for reform in many US states. Sometimes reforms have been enacted—typically along the lines of setting up special courts for malpractice litigation (on the assumption that they will deal with cases more speedily, so reducing costs, and will be less likely to be bamboozled by eloquent lawyers), reducing the length of time that a claimant has to bring a claim, and setting limits on compensation for pain, suffering, and loss of amenity (that part of the claim which is not capable of scientific-ish quantification, and which juries sometimes assess in an over-sympathetic and wholly disproportionate way).

The journey to disgrace and unemployment: disciplinary and regulatory proceedings

An appearance before the profession's disciplinary tribunal is what many health-care professionals fear most. They are unlikely, unless they are depraved, monstrously careless, or very unlucky, to find themselves before a criminal court. A civil claim for damages, although troublesome and embarrassing, is dealt with by the insurers. But a complaint that is explored before the regulatory body, almost certainly in public, can have much of the stigma of criminal proceedings, and, since it may lead to removal of the right to practise, can be financially devastating.

Most jurisdictions have some sort of self-regulation of the professions. It's often done using a quasi-criminal procedure, with investigation according to standard protocols, obligations on the part of the 'prosecution' to disclose everything material to the 'defendant', detailed charges, examination and cross-examination conducted as they would be in a criminal court, and a 'sentencing' stage, with provision for testimonials and other mitigation.

Regulatory tribunals are necessarily concerned with the confidence that the public has in the profession. A sanction such as suspension from practice or erasure from the register can be imposed simply because the public is outraged. This can make regulatory tribunals a sophisticated form of lynch mob—more responsive to the media's call for a pound of flesh than they are to the rules of procedure or basic fairness. This is one reason why many of their decisions are reviewed by the courts exercising public law jurisdiction.

Public law jurisdiction

Many important decisions in medical law turn on whether a public authority (typically a local or national health-care provider) has acted lawfully. Examples might include a decision not to fund a particular type of treatment, to permit research on embryos, or to produce national guidelines setting out the criteria that should be used in deciding whether or not to withdraw life-sustaining treatment.

The way in which such questions are litigated depends very much on the quirks of the jurisdiction concerned. In the US, Germany, and South Africa, for instance, the constitution is likely to be invoked; in Israel, the basic laws. In the UK there is a broad provision for judicial review of administrative action. In the UK and other countries which are signatories of the European Convention on Human Rights, national laws or the means of their implementation can be challenged in national courts for alleged non-compliance with the Convention, with eventual recourse to the European Court of Human Rights in Strasbourg. Many cases with a medical taste have found themselves there. Many other jurisdictions have similar arrangements.

Human rights language is particularly common in medical law. It's not surprising. Medical cases often invoke the most fundamental questions we can ask about human beings, their relationship to their bodies, and their relationship to the other bodies that comprise the societal soup in which they swim.

Jurisdiction over patients lacking capacity

Some of the most legally difficult, emotionally agonizing, and politically explosive decisions in medical law involve the court making decisions on behalf of those who cannot make decisions for themselves—for instance children and permanently or temporarily incapacitous adults. Judges regularly order the compulsory sterilization of the mentally incompetent, permit doctors to tie a struggling Jehovah's Witness child to a table and give her the life-saving blood transfusion that her parents think will cause her to be hurled into the lake of fire for eternity, and tell doctors to withdraw artificial nutrition and hydration from unconscious patients (often over the protestations of the patients' families), so killing them.

Treatment decision cases are extreme, dramatic examples of a benevolently paternalistic jurisdiction with which everyone's familiar. Every day, all over the world, thousands of judges in family courts decide whether it will be best for a child to live with his mother or father. The same or similar judges, applying the same or similar criteria, decide whether it is better for the child to live or die. Judges regularly decide whether an incompetent adult's carer should be allowed to take money from the patient's account. To decide whether a doctor should be allowed to take her ovaries out of her pelvis is a very similar process.

A one-stop shop for resolving medical law disputes?

There is much wasteful duplication in medical litigation. If a doctor kills a patient by negligently clamping the wrong vessel during surgery, he might find himself, in respect of that single mistake, prosecuted for gross negligence manslaughter, pursued for damages by the patient's relatives and estate, watching his back at an inquest, and fighting for his registration before a regulatory tribunal. And that's not to mention other internal enquiries at the hospital, which might involve review of his employment contract. If he contends, as part of his defence, that the hospital was dangerously understaffed, it's perfectly possible that the issue of resource allocation might be discussed in one of the public law reviewing courts.

This multiplicity of proceedings makes no one but the lawyers happy. The doctor might have to give identical evidence five or six times, the relatives will have to hear the same distressing story over and over again (putting their grieving on hold until the lawyers have picked the case clean), and many expensive independent experts might be commissioned to comment on the same set of facts. It's possible that different tribunals might come to wholly different conclusions. The judge in the civil proceedings might decide that there was no negligence at all and that the doctor is an exemplary surgeon, but the disciplinary panel that the doctor was grossly negligent and should never practise again.

Can't it all be done in one set of proceedings, depriving the lawyers of their brief fees, the doctor of his stress, and the relatives of their distress?

The answer is no. Although they start with the same set of clinical facts, each of these types of proceedings has its own distinct objectives and corresponding procedures. They are not always compatible with the objectives and procedures of the others. The criminal proceedings, for instance, use a different definition of negligence from the civil proceedings, and have a higher standard of proof. The assessment of damages in the civil claim is a sophisticated process involving evidence about matters that are wholly irrelevant to any of the other jurisdictions. The inquest, concerned to learn lessons that will prevent the repetition of the tragedy, will inquire much more broadly into the background of the case than will the other tribunals.

That's not to say that something can't be done. Some European jurisdictions run criminal and compensatory inquiries to some extent along the same channel. We can learn from them. But, sadly, so long as we acknowledge that all the various objectives are legitimate, most of the lawyers will continue to be paid.

Chapter 3
Before birth

Despite its invasion by ultrasound and, sometimes, more dangerous tools, the uterus is a secret place. What happens there is biologically mysterious. The effects of gestation can be described in a fairly crude anatomical way. So too can a few of their more superficial causes. But the nature of the process and the detailed blueprint of the engine that drives it remain baffling.

The law has been content to leave metaphysics out of its own intrauterine fumblings. It has refused to be drawn into philosophical debate about the status of the early embryo, preferring to navigate the shadowlands of the unborn using its familiar instruments of rights and duties. It uses them with a fitting, deferential caution.

Rights and obligations to reproduce

The position in most places is this: if you want to be a parent, then generally, if nature's left you the option, you can be. You can fuse your gametes with almost anybody's. And if you don't want to be a parent, then you needn't be.

It's not surprising that the law defends the right to reproduce—or, at least, doesn't put many obstacles in the way of people wanting to do so. The urge to parenthood is one of the most fundamental urges there is, and the shadow of eugenics remains rightly scary.

Limitations on the right to reproduce are few and far between. Many cultures have, for obvious genetic reasons, prohibitions on incestuous unions, and, for the same genetic reasons, prohibit the creation of embryos by artificial reproductive procedures from the gametes of (for instance) parents and children, or siblings. Nor may you, in most places, create (or create and bring to term) a chimaeric embryo resulting from the fusion of human and non-human gametes. The state regulates reproduction by the young, too, by insisting that one cannot lawfully have sexual intercourse or marry below a certain age. But, incest, age, and technological bestiality aside, you can go forth and multiply.

Article 12 of the European Convention on Human Rights summarizes the international *zeitgeist*: 'Men and women of marriageable age have the right to marry and to found a family, according to the national laws governing the exercise of this right.' The second clause could drain the first of its significance, but in fact in no jurisdiction does it do so.

It doesn't follow, though, that you've got a right to state funding for in-vitro fertilization (IVF), or, if you've been locked up, that you can force the authorities to let your wife into jail for a conjugal visit at the time of your choice (see *ELH and PBH v United Kingdom* (1998-))- although if she's teetering on the edge of infertility it might be different: see *R (Mellor) v Secretary of State for the Home Department* (2002).

While it might be unsurprising to hear that there's a right to reproduce, it's so utterly unsurprising that there's no *obligation* to reproduce that it might seem odd to mention it at all. In fact there's a perfectly sensible reason for mentioning it—a reason that has been much discussed in the courts.

Before Diane Blood's husband died, some of his semen was harvested. Diane Blood wanted to use it to conceive a child. No, said the court. The rules prohibiting this were entirely reasonable: they were made to avoid the spectre of a man being confronted, emotionally or financially, by a child of whom he had no knowledge. The rule had a brutal consequence in that case, but that was no reason to overturn it: see *R v Human Fertilisation and Embryology Authority ex p Blood* (1997).

One might have thought that the situation would be different if it involved the implantation of already existing embryos, rather than the mere use of sperm. Perhaps the weight of the embryo's interest, joined to that of the mother's desire, would prevail over a man's reluctance to propagate. But no, the autonomistic right not to be a father trumps all the countervailing considerations: see *Evans v United Kingdom* (2006).

We see the same thinking at work where the father of an embryo asks the court to prevent his wife or girlfriend from having an abortion. Where abortion is lawful these applications have failed. The right not to be a parent outweighs the right to be one: see *Planned Parenthood of Central Missouri v Danforth* (1976); *C v S* (1988) and *Paton v United Kingdom* (1981).

From all this one might conclude that the rights of embryos and fetuses don't amount to much—at least where they conflict with almost any other rights. As a general proposition that's not inaccurate.

The rights and non-rights of the embryo and fetus

The law can't be accused of inflexible consistency. And still less of philosophical sophistication. At the time of writing, abortion was permitted in some circumstances in all countries in the world except for a very few, very Catholic Latin American countries. But those circumstances vary very widely. Some permit abortion only where it is necessary to save the woman's life; others permit it under any circumstances. Generally, and unsurprisingly, the more religiously committed the country, the harder it will be to have a lawful abortion. But that doesn't necessarily mean that countries with liberal abortion laws are blithe about the status of the embryo. On the contrary, their jurisprudential rhetoric often indicates a thoughtfulness sometimes lacking in the more stridently anti-abortion states. It's just (they'd say) that, having considered the matter carefully and painfully, they've decided that the plainly identifiable rights of a solid, adult mother should prevail over the misty, conditional rights (if any) of the mysterious embryo.

This is nonsense, say the anti-abortion activists. Yes, you've got two sets of rights in competition here: those of the mother, and those of the embryo. Only very rarely will the mother's right to live be at stake. When it is, even the most conservative Catholic agrees that it's a different matter.

What's usually at stake is the mother's right to avoid an uncomfortable few months of inhabitation by a growing parasite, and then some truncation of her ability to live her life in exactly the way that she chooses. These, say the pro-lifers, are essentially convenience rights—the sort of rights protected, for instance, by Article 8 of the European Convention on Human Rights. And, goes the argument, they must always be trumped by the hugely more weighty right to life (expressed, for instance, in Article 2 of the Convention) possessed by the fetus. Isn't this obvious? Convenience rights must, logically, be conditional on and subservient to the right to live: if you don't live, you can't experience convenience.

Much has been said about this argument. We return to it in a moment. But for now it's enough to say that it has been thought to have enough force for legal writers and judges (many of whom want to keep open the option of legal abortion) to be wary of according any rights at all to the embryo—at least in its early stages. That's often taken the form of denying to the embryo/fetus/unborn child (and what a storm erupts whenever one uses the term 'unborn child' incautiously) any legal personality at all. In such a scheme a child magically becomes a fully human being, invested with all the protection of the law, when (and essentially because) it moves the few inches from inside the uterus to outside the vagina. That has the advantage of neatness, but the disadvantage of discordance both with biological facts (the facts, for instance, of incremental fetal sophistication and the possibility of viability from about 23 weeks gestation) and with intuition.

In some areas of the law, though, it's legally convenient for the fetus to exist. And so, for those purposes, it does. In English law, for instance, a fetus can inherit an estate. But for other purposes it is not so convenient. And so, by legal sleight of hand, it vanishes. Now you see it, now you don't.

Here's how it's put:

'It is established beyond doubt for the criminal law, as for the civil law... that the child *en ventre sa mere* does not have a distinct human personality, whose extinguishment gives rise to any penalties or liabilities at common law.' *Attorney General's Reference (No. 3 of 1994)* (1998): UK House of Lords

'To permit an unborn child to sue its pregnant mother-to-be would introduce a radically new conception into the law; the unborn child and its mother as separate juristic persons in a mutually separable and antagonistic relation...' *Winnipeg Child and Family Services (Northwest Area) v G* (1997): Canada, Supreme Court

'There can be no doubt that in England and Wales the foetus has no right of action, no right at all, until birth.' *Paton v Trustees of the British Pregnancy Advisory Services* (1979): UK, Court of Appeal

The device of the inconsistently existing fetus has been used for various purposes. In Canada and in many other places, for instance, a fetus cannot sue its mother for causing it damage during pregnancy. And yet if a doctor, or anyone else, causes the fetus harm (for example by negligently administering drugs to a pregnant mother), the fetus, once born, can sue the doctor for damages. The doctor couldn't say: 'At the time of my negligence you didn't exist: how can I possibly have injured a non-existent person?' or 'Your identity was inextricable from that of your mother, and so she should be suing, not you.'

There's a glaring anomaly here. What the law is really doing is saying to the fetus: 'If you survive gestation and become a person, we will retrospectively credit you with sufficient personality to be legally injured.' That's intellectually uncomfortable. So too is the mother's immunity—particularly if retrospective credit is really what's going on. Why should the person who is most obviously connected to the child, who has the greatest ability to harm and protect it, who should (surely) be regarded as having some sort of trusteeship responsibility to the unborn child, be the only person incapable of being fixed with meaningful legal responsibility?

At other times it's useful for the embryo/fetus/unborn child to exist *in some sense*. And so, it's now unsurprising to hear, it does. It is given sufficient existence and the necessary qualities for the purpose in hand.

Some examples. In IVF procedures, many 'spare' embryos are produced. How should they be treated? Intuition suggests that they should be treated with respect, and so they are given sufficient status to justify that respect. Most jurisdictions have legislation or case law that says more or less that. The UK Polkinghorne Committee on the use of embryos/fetuses in research (1989) expressed the international consensus. It spoke of the fetus having 'a special status ... at every stage of its development which we wish to characterize as a profound respect based on its potential to develop into a fully formed human being'.

In the context of forced treatment of a pregnant mother, in order to save the child, the English Court of Appeal observed that 'Whatever else it may be, a 36-week foetus is not nothing; if viable, it is not lifeless, and it is certainly human': *St George's NHS Trust v S* (1998).

This convenient but slightly disreputable agnosticism about the legal status of the embryo/fetus is the current position of the European Court of Human Rights. That position emerged out of the tragic events in Lyons General Hospital.

Two women, both called Mrs Vo, were there on the same day. One was six months pregnant. The other was there to have a contraceptive coil removed. There was a mix-up. The doctors tried to remove the non-existent coil from the pregnant Mrs Vo, puncturing her amniotic sac. The pregnancy was doomed. A termination was performed.

The case found its way to Strasbourg. The question was whether the unborn child had a right to life under Article 2 of the European Convention on Human Rights. The relevant part of the Article states: 'Everyone's right to life shall be protected by law.' But did 'everyone' include an unborn child? The consequences of an unqualified 'yes' were of course profound. Abortion laws would be in jeopardy.

So the majority opted for equivocation. It decided not to decide, observing that 'at European level...there is no consensus on the nature and status of the embryo and/or fetus...At best, it may be regarded as common ground between States that the embryo/fetus belongs to the human race. The potentiality of that being and its capacity to become a person—enjoying protection under the civil law...require protection in the name of human dignity, without making it a "person" with the "right to life" for the purposes of Article 2...Having regard to the foregoing, the Court is convinced that it is neither desirable, nor even possible as matters stand, to answer in the abstract the question whether the unborn child is a person for the purposes of Article 2' (*Vo v France* (2004)). So: it has some status, but we're not going to tell you what that status is, or its corollaries.

The position in the US is very similar. The fetus isn't a 'person' within the meaning of the 14th Amendment of the Federal Constitution (see, for instance, Blackmun J in *Roe v Wade* (1973)) and yet in some circumstances (and particularly once it reaches the crucial watershed of about three months' gestation) may nonetheless, by analogy, or by legal wriggle, or by political expediency, be entitled to 14th Amendment protection.

So it is that the law has been able to limp by with piecemeal solutions. Without a clearly identifiable status, it's going to be hard for embryos to resist harm. They will be outgunned by just about any real person. And even unreal people. One of the objections to granting embryos rights in the same currency as the rights of real people is that embryos are only potential people. And yet research on embryos is often permitted (for instance in the UK) on the grounds that the research may be of value to people as yet unborn. I'm not saying that's wrong; but it is untidy.

The state rarely insists that a mother must not carry a child to term, although it insists that children of a particular genetic complexion should not be conceived in the first place (the laws against incest). But it may happen. An incapacitous patient who becomes pregnant may be forced, against her will, to have an abortion. The judgment will typically be expressed in the language of the best interests both of the mother and of the welfare (were it to be born) of the child. What's happening here?

The maternal best interests part of the analysis is fairly straightforward. This isn't really an abortion against the mother's will. She's got no (rightly directed) will. But what about the interests of the putative child? A couple of points. First: it is given a voice in the debate (although for other purposes it has no legal existence) because it is convenient for it to have it. It will obligingly deliver a speech saying that it doesn't want to exist, and will then shut up. It's allowed no other speech. Second: in the law of the UK and in many other jurisdictions a child cannot bring a claim based on the assertion 'It were better that my mother had not borne me.' It's regarded as offensive to public policy: see, for instance, *McKay v Essex AHA* (1982). If public policy forbids such a claim by a child, why should it permit it-still less invite it and rely on it-from an unborn child?

There's widespread public unease, and some judicial unease, about claims by parents in relation to the financial costs of unwanted children. These typically occur where a sterilization has been performed negligently, or there's been a failure to warn about the risk of a sterilization operation reversing. The parents then claim the costs of upkeep.

These are uncomfortable claims. They involve the parents unwishing the child. In the UK, the discomfort spread to the House of Lords, which said that the birth of a child should conclusively be presumed to be a blessing which more than cancelled out the associated financial detriment: see *McFarlane v Tayside Health Board* (2000). That's policy speaking. But it's a policy that doesn't seem to extend to regarding the unborn child as a blessing. Fair enough: who said that the law had to be internally consistent? Which brings us back to abortion itself.

There are two legal ways of looking at abortion. The first is expressed in terms of rights. One jurisdiction might say—perhaps at a particular time of gestation—that 'Abortion is a mother's right' or 'The fetus has a right not to be killed.' The second is that abortion is a prima facie wrong, but that there are defences to it. The first of these approaches is exemplified by the US, and the famous Supreme Court decision of *Roe v Wade* (1973). The second is exemplified by the UK.

The majority in *Roe* discovered, in the 14th Amendment's concept of personal liberty and restriction on state action, a constitutional protection of 'a woman's decision whether or not to terminate her pregnancy'. But the woman's right, said the court, was not absolute: a state, according to the majority, 'may properly assert important interests in safeguarding health, in maintaining medical standards, and in protecting potential life. At some point in pregnancy, these respective interests become sufficiently compelling to sustain regulation of the factors that govern the abortion decision.'

The state, then, legitimately acts as a referee in a struggle between two competing rights—those of the mother and those of the fetus. The fetus's rights grow incrementally. During the first trimester the state's primary interest is in protecting maternal rights. During this period 'the attending physician, in consultation with his patient, is free to determine, without regulation by the State, that in his medical judgement, the patient's pregnancy should be terminated'. But the state also has an interest in protecting fetal life. When might that justify interference with the woman's continuing right to determine what happens to her own body? The tipping point, held the court, was fetal viability. Then the fetus could have a 'meaningful life', independent of its mother.

Accordingly: in the first trimester, the state must leave the woman to choose. Thereafter, until fetal viability, the state may regulate abortion in ways that are reasonably related to the mother's health (which was clarified in *Doe v Bolton* (1973) to be determined as a medical judgement in the light of all the factors pertinent to maternal well-being). After the time of fetal viability the state may, if it chooses, regulate abortion, even to the point of banning it (except where abortion is necessary to preserve the mother's life or health).

There's an odd asymmetry here. The state is required to leave the mother alone in the first trimester. Put another way, it is required not to protect the fetus then. But it is not required (although it is permitted) to protect the fetus during the time of viability. Its two obligations (to protect maternal health and fetal life) are not equally onerous.

Many jurisdictions analyse abortion problems in a similar rights-based way. Often, in such analyses, the fetus is better protected than it is in the US. Many of the countries which assert that the right of the fetus to live should trump that of the mother to be uninhabited rest that assertion on theological presumptions about the status of the embryo (many Catholic and Islamic countries) or on some dignity-based beliefs about its status (for instance Germany).

The UK, in common with many of the Australian states, does not speak of abortion as a 'right' (although no doubt a contention along those lines could be advanced in the language of Article 8 of the European Convention on Human Rights which, very broadly, gives a right to live our lives as we please—which might include a right not to be encumbered with an unwanted child). It chooses instead to say that abortion is unlawful, except where it isn't. The fact is, though, that until 24 weeks of gestation (when the rules change) there is abortion on demand in the UK. That's not to say that there's a right to it: it's just to say that you won't have any difficulty finding a clinic to do your abortion for you in a way that will leave it entirely immune to prosecution.

This, ironically, makes life more dangerous for the fetus than in rights-based jurisdictions. Where the notion of rights is taken sufficiently seriously to be the basis of the mother's security, there's at least the possibility (theoretical though it often is) of the fetus putting up its developing arm and demanding, by the same token, a right to be heard.

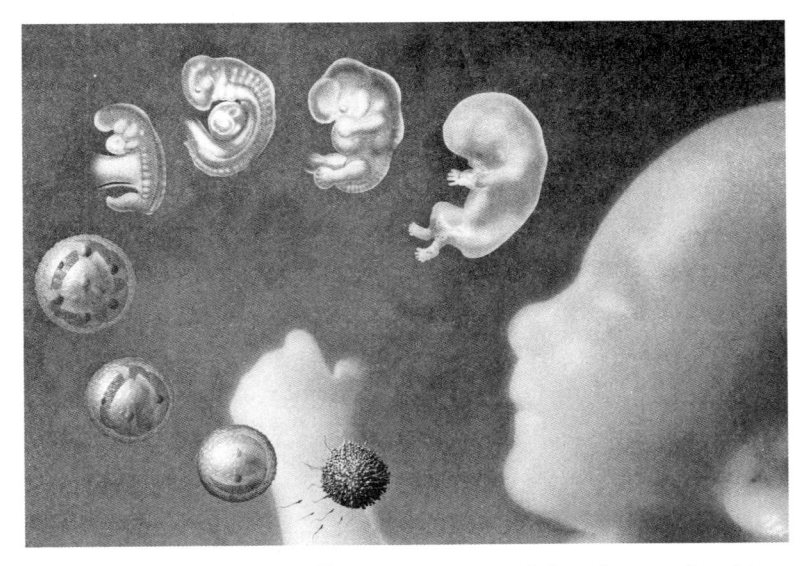

2. The developing embryo/fetus. Some contend that the moral and/or legal status of the embryo or fetus changes as it develops

The cloning debate

Identical twins are clones. They're not especially frightening or necessarily dysfunctional. And yet the spectre of creating clones is scary to almost everyone.

In relation to reproductive cloning (the cloning of an embryo with the intention of bringing it to term) the fears don't seem to be located consistently in respect for the status of the human embryo. Instead they are fears about overstepping the limits of legitimate interference with nature ('playing God'), or distaste at the thought of a woman giving birth to herself or her partner, with all the psychological fallout that would entail for everyone involved.

The ethics are complicated. The law, by and large, is not. Human reproductive cloning is unlawful almost everywhere. The regulation of therapeutic cloning (the creation of cloned embryos with the intention of using them for research) is more politically controversial. It is permitted in the UK, for instance, with decisions about the permissibility of a particular application being delegated to an independent scrutineer (the Human Fertilisation and Embryology Authority). In the US, regulation is a patchwork of state and federal legislation. When a Republican government is in, embryo research will tend to be out.

Where embryo research is unlawful, the legislature has made some sort of judgment about the status of the embryo, and decided that the respect the embryo deserves warrants the disadvantage to potential beneficiaries of research that prohibition of research will entail—some sort of calculus along the lines of: 'The moral bad involved in the creation of embryos and their destruction outweighs the moral good of a chance of curing motor neurone disease.' That sort of calculus is easy enough if the potential good is to unidentified people. It's easy to dismiss a faceless abstraction. It's much harder to look a real person in the eye and say: 'For my belief in the inviolability of the eight-cell embryo you must die.' That's often what the 'saviour sibling' cases boil down to.

Saviour siblings

Zain Hashmi, aged three, had beta-thallasaemia. His best chance of survival was by receiving stem cells from the umbilical cord of a sufficiently well tissue-matched sibling.

The chances of conceiving such a sibling naturally were not good. So his parents sought permission to create embryos by IVF. Then, at about the eight-cell stage, a cell would be taken from each embryo and tested to see if the embryo would do the job. The application was approved by the UK regulatory body, but a pro-life group, opposed both to the destruction of the unused embryos and to what they saw as the instrumentalizing of human life, challenged the approval. It lost: see *Quintavalle (on behalf of*

Comment on Reproductive Ethics) v Human Fertilisation and Embryology Authority (2005). The case turned on some technical niceties, but the point of principle remained painfully clear. It divided even the pro-life lobby. Are you really pro-life if you're content for a three-year-old to die?

Similar cases have made judges in several jurisdictions pace the floorboards in the early hours. Lawyers tend to like absolute positions: to say that something has a definite, inalienable status. They tend to think that such positions make life easier. But if everything with a human genome has inalienable human status, the most religious, conservative judges are forced into a moral and legal relativism that is visibly uncomfortable for them. Life's not straightforward if you abandon your stereotypes and see it as it really is. And since life isn't straightforward, nor can the law be.

Chapter 4
Confidentiality and privacy

Patients tell doctors intimate things. At least since about 500 BC, when the Hippocratic Oath required doctors to declare that 'Whatsover I shall see or hear in the course of my profession... if it be what should not be published abroad, I will never divulge, holding such things to be holy secrets,' everyone has agreed that there are some times when doctors shouldn't disclose them. Most agree that only rarely should doctors disclose any of their patients' confidences. But should there be an absolute rule of non-disclosure? If not, why not? When is disclosure justified? Is disclosure ever mandatory? These questions have made lots of normally prosaic judges express themselves in unusually philosophical language.

National and international codes of medical ethics acknowledge, in their equivocation, the undesirability of an absolute rule. That equivocation is there in Hippocrates. He seems to recognize that there may be some things that can ethically be 'published abroad'. One of the American Medical Association's 'Principles of Medical Ethics' is: 'A physician shall... safeguard patient confidences within the constraints of the law'—so handing the really difficult questions to the lawyers. The World Medical Association's International Code of Medical Ethics, revised in 2006, is more helpful. It anticipates some of the caveats the law has found necessary. 'A physician shall respect a patient's right to confidentiality. It is ethical to disclose confidential information when the patient consents to it or when there is a real and imminent threat of harm to the patient or to others and this threat can be only removed by a breach of confidentiality.' The UK General Medical Council tells doctors that '[p]atients have a right to expect that information about them will be held in confidence by their doctors. You must treat information about patients as confidential, including after a patient has died,' but peppers that principle liberally with caveats in a mass of detailed supplementary advice. Other health-care professionals have similar guidelines.

Why should confidences be respected?

Many reasons have been identified by the courts. Some are utilitarian. It's typically said, for instance, that a law of medical confidentiality facilitates the flow of information from patients to doctors. If patients think that their secrets will be the stuff of gossip in the hospital canteen, they will be less likely to tell the doctor the full story. That's not good either for the patient or for the doctor: it reduces the chance of the patient getting the treatment he needs. The point doesn't apply just to that particular doctor and that particular patient: it applies more broadly to the medical profession. If doctors as a whole aren't bound by a duty of confidentiality, patients *generally* will be less forthcoming, and the general confidence that the public reposes in the medical profession will be reduced.

Some reasons for keeping tight-lipped are more fundamental. Patients, it is commonly said, have a *right* to secrecy.

Confidential to whom?

Of course it's important for treating clinicians to talk intelligently to one another about patient care. Both law and ethics are pragmatic about this. The pragmatism is based on an assumption about what patients expect. If a confidence is divulged to doctor X, X will be entitled to tell it to doctor Y, as long as the disclosure is necessary for the proper care of the patient. Why? Because the patient will be taken to expect this disclosure, and therefore impliedly to have consented to it.

But there are limits to this implied consent, and those limits are often exceeded. Patients at a teaching hospital no doubt expect their medical secrets to be discussed with medical students, but does a woman going to her family doctor for an abortion referral really know that the referral letter will be typed by the receptionist, who probably lives round the corner and will bump into her at the supermarket?

From ethics to law

Several different types of language have been used to translate these ethical positions into legal principles.

Some analyses see the patient's secrets as a sort of intellectual property which is handed to the doctor on the strict understanding that the property will only be used for the purposes for which it is being given. The doctor is a sort of bailor or trustee. To deal with the secrets other than in the authorized way is a breach of the trust: it's like using a borrowed car for joyriding. Or it's a breach of an express or implied contract with the doctor, by which the doctor agrees that his lips will be sealed. Which brings us to another way of looking at the issue: the doctor's conscience. Decent doctors, with properly oriented consciences, don't go metaphorically joyriding, or break their promises. A British Court of Appeal judge, Simon Brown LJ, having reviewed a number of authorities, concluded that:

> To my mind the one clear and consistent theme emerging... is this: the confidant is placed under a duty of good faith to the confider and the touchstone by which to judge the scope of his duty and

whether or not it has been fulfilled or breached is his own conscience, no more and no less… (*R v Department of Health, ex p Source Informatics Ltd* (2000))

Trustee- and conscience-based analyses feed happily into the notion of duty. Indeed much of the law of confidentiality has been forged in the crucible of tort litigation for damages for breach of confidence, where, of course, the notion of duty is so at home.

Some of these models clunk. Today, in many jurisdictions, they are being eclipsed by human rights analyses. The European Convention on Human Rights is one good example. Article 8(1) of the Convention provides that '[e]veryone has the right to respect for his private and family life, his home and his correspondence'. This is the most elastic of all the Convention articles. It has been found to stretch to areas of the law undreamt of by the draftsman, and it certainly extends to the medical consultation room. It makes patient autonomy the starting point. And often the end point. 'The protection of personal data,' said the European Court of Human Rights in *Z v Finland* (1998), 'not least medical data, is of fundamental importance to a person's enjoyment of his or her right to respect for private and family life as guaranteed by Article 8 of the Convention.' Quite right.

Although the language of human rights is rather different from that of contract, trusteeship, and duty, there's hardly a difference in substance. Just as dutiful doctors don't normally breach contracts, dutiful doctors don't normally breach their patients' human rights. The UK House of Lords, in *Campbell v MGN* (2004), suggested that the test to apply in deciding whether or not a claim for breach of confidence gets off the ground is whether the claimant had a 'reasonable expectation of privacy'. That neatly conflates the demands of the common law and the Convention. The European Convention has changed the way that lawyers frame their medical confidentiality claims: it hasn't, by and large, changed the outcome of those claims.

Privacy and confidentiality are closely related and, in most countries, creeping gradually closer. The UK judges, for instance, nervous about being over-creative, insist that there is no tort of the invasion of privacy per se, but that there is a tort of misuse of private information. There's nothing wrong, then, with a press photographer taking a salacious photo of a celebrity, but if he does anything at all with it the law gets stern. In most real medical contexts confidentiality and the embryonic law of privacy can be safely regarded as identical.

Take, for instance, the whiteboards that appear in many hospitals above the nurses' station. They often identify the patient and her date of birth, and may go on to indicate the condition for which she's in the hospital. The boards are visible to everyone when they come onto the ward. Is this a breach of privacy? Yes, although English lawyers would look troubled when they admit it. It's also a breach of confidentiality. At least in England, both the law of confidentiality and the tort of misuse of private information have the muscle to do something about it.

Balancing competing interests: the basic position

So far, easy enough. Confidences matter. There's no controversy about that. Their importance, and the corresponding obligations on doctors, can be described in many ways. But from now on the plot thickens. For patients are not islands: they are relational entities. They cannot coherently be considered except as part of the nexus of relationships in which they exist and of which, to a large extent, they consist.

Mr W was a very dangerous man. He was locked up in a secure hospital. He optimistically applied to be released. He asked a psychiatrist, Dr Egdell, to write a report saying how outrageous his continued incarceration was. Dr Egdell wasn't fooled, and instead wrote that W had a long-standing and morbid fascination with explosives, and would pose a serious risk if released.

W's solicitors' optimism faded, but their determination did not. They did not disclose the report to the tribunal. This worried Dr Egdell. Without W's permission, he disclosed his report. W was outraged. He sued Dr Egdell for damages for breach of confidence.

The case illustrates well the way that medical lawyers in most jurisdictions look at the law of confidentiality. There's a widely accepted checklist of core questions.

Was the information disclosed in circumstances of confidentiality? Of course. Almost all information disclosed in most normal medical circumstances will be. You can say, if you like, that a duty of confidentiality arose. It doesn't much matter how you describe that duty, but if you choose to use duty language you need to recognize that the duty to the patient is not an absolute one. It is hedged round with phrases like '...except where...' Does this mean that the physician has a competing duty to someone else? Well, possibly. We'll come to that.

Was there disclosure? Plainly, yes. It might have been different if the information was already in the public domain. A well-recognized defence to the allegation of letting cats out of bags is that the cat is already out of the bag and on the front page of a newspaper.

Was that the end of the matter? Did W therefore succeed? No. He failed. The crucial question, the court decided, was whether the public interest in disclosure outweighed the *public* interest in non-disclosure. The italics are important. The relevant interest in maintaining the confidence was not W's: it wasn't like a property right. The court implicitly endorsed the utilitarian reasons for keeping confidences. Here, there was a public interest in major buildings staying upright and shoppers staying alive. That interest outweighed the utilitarian considerations that apply to this and all other medical confidence cases: see *W v Egdell* (1990).

Nowadays, if Dr Egdell were acting on behalf of a public authority, the arguments would be framed additionally in terms of Article 8. A similar balancing exercise would be done. Was there a prima facie breach of W's Article 8(1) right? Certainly. But Article 8 has two parts. 8(2) provides that: 'There shall be no interference by a public authority with the exercise of [the right in 8(1)] except such as is in accordance with the law and is necessary in a democratic society in the interests of national security, public safety or the economic well-being of the country, for the prevention of disorder or crime, for the protection of health or morals, or for the protection of the rights and freedoms of others.' An interference with W's right could plainly be justified on all or any of the grounds identified in 8(2).

Where the duty of confidentiality *must* be breached

Very broadly, courts across the world have approached problems of confidentiality like this. And legislatures and courts worldwide have indicated that there are some cases in which the doctor must disclose information given to him in confidence. These cases are best seen as determinations that the public interest in disclosure is so overwhelming that no other considerations could possibly prevail against it.

Doctors must disclose information when a court says they must. If they don't, they will be in contempt of court, and can be locked up. It is obviously in the public interest that the truth emerges in legal proceedings. But what if the truth can only emerge by breaching patient confidentiality?

In England, there is no blanket rule of doctor–patient privilege, entitling or requiring a doctor to keep quiet. But in both civil and criminal proceedings the fact that patient confidentiality will be breached by an answer to a question or the production of a document is a factor that the court can consider in deciding whether or not to require that answer or that document. The court conducts the now familiar exercise, balancing the public interest in disclosure against that in non-disclosure. It often expresses itself in terms of proportionality.

In the US, most states have rules of evidence that give patients some patchy, conditional protection against disclosure by their doctors. These rules tend to be particularly keen on sealing the lips of psychotherapists. The Federal Rules of Evidence contain no such privilege, although the Supreme Court's respect for the sanctity of the modern confessional—the shrink's couch—has created an arguable but fragile privilege in relation to disclosure by psychotherapists: see *Jaffee v Redmond* 518 US 1 (1996).

As one would expect, jurisdictions come to illuminatingly different conclusions about what type of disclosure is perceived to be in the public interest. But there are some common elements. It is generally thought to be good for societies to know more or less who lives among them (hence rules for the mandatory disclosure of the medical facts of births and deaths), for their members not to be struck down by contagious diseases (hence public health laws requiring doctors to expose the otherwise private fact that a patient is suffering from a notifiable disease), and to be protected from terrorism (hence, in many places, such as the UK, a requirement to hand over information about terrorists, even if that information is contained in medical records or disclosed in the course of an otherwise confidential consultation).

Outside these fairly clear (and usually statutory) cases, the position is much more ethically fuzzy and legally difficult.

Suppose that a patient tells his psychiatrist that he is going to kill his wife. The psychiatrist believes him, but tells no one what he has been told, thinking that it would be an unpardonable breach of medical confidentiality to do so. The patient bludgeons his wife to death. Can the wife's family successfully sue the doctor? What they would be saying is: 'You had a duty to breach the patient's medical confidentiality. That duty to breach was a duty owed to his wife.'

Several jurisdictions have smiled on that contention—for instance California (*Tarasoff v The Regents of the University of California* (1976)) and England (*Palmer v South Tees Health Authority* (1999)). Those were claims in tort. Tort is concerned with the question of whether the defendant, X, owes a duty to the claimant, Y. It is understandably reluctant to impose on X a duty to the whole world, and restricts the ambit of duties using the devices of proximity, foreseeability, and reasonableness.

What would the law of tort say, then, about the liability of a psychiatrist who failed to disclose not a specific threat to the wife, but a conclusion that the patient was generally dangerous to unspecified people? If one of the unspecified people got very specifically stabbed in the throat, would he be able to sue the psychiatrist, saying, as the dead wife did in the first example: 'You had a duty to me to breach the patient's confidentiality'?

The law of tort would be more queasy about this submission, but should that queasiness determine what, as a matter of public policy, the law should say about the psychiatrist's obligation to disclose? The questions of public good that govern the general law of confidentiality don't fit neatly in the private law world of tort claims, but it would be little comfort to the stabbing victim to say: 'It's important that public and private law are concordant and, I'm afraid, private law trumps public. You've no claim.' Shouldn't ethics, rather than artificial legal theory, cut the Gordian knot? Shouldn't one ask simply: 'Is it so obviously right to blow the whistle on the patient that the psychiatrist cannot be excused for not blowing it?'

In most jurisdictions the law sees the force of this question but, in almost all cases, has refused to agree that it is so obviously right to disclose that the doctor *must*, and has contented itself with saying, in most conscience-troubling instances, that the doctor *can* disclose without sanction. It will very often be, therefore, that a doctor will not be condemned by the law either for disclosing or for not disclosing.

The law has often, and rightly, taken its cue from the professional regulatory organizations that are deemed to be the conscience of the profession. If, for instance, the UK General Medical Council says that disclosure in particular circumstances is mandatory, then the law will agree, and conscientious obligation becomes crystallized into law. That there are so few examples of mandatory disclosure is a mark of the professions' own reluctance to legislate for every conceivable set of facts.

Where the duty of confidentiality *may* be breached

There are two points here. The first is that there's an ethos of judicial liberality—of sympathy with the awful dilemmas that face the doctor at the clinical coalface. The second is rather more black-letter.

First: judicial sympathy. The medico-legal landscape is composed mostly of no-man's-land, stretched messily between bordering principles, and pockmarked by the craters made by litigious shells. The law of confidentiality is the classic example. In most real cases, lawyers and health-care professionals have to navigate their own way through this mess, guided by more or less bad analogies with decided cases, by the guidelines given by their professional organizations, and by the compass of their own conscience.

The law says that a breach of confidence is not actionable if the public interest in the disclosure outweighs the public interest in non-disclosure. That's often a very difficult balancing exercise. In practice it is delegated to individual clinicians: you can't litigate every problem that involves a question of confidentiality. Clinicians have to undertake the exercise without the (theoretical) benefit of detailed arguments from counsel, or the (actual) benefit of ample time for reflection. And so it is not surprising that the courts judge clinicians' judgements kindly. The doctor disclosed? Fine: we can understand why. The doctor didn't disclose? Fine: we can understand why.

Second: the black-letter law of lawful but not mandatory disclosure.

The starting point for the lawyers is set by the professional organizations. The law is rarely stricter on the profession than is the profession itself, and is often more lenient. The bigger the professional organization, though, the more unhelpfully general the guideline. The World Medical Association, for example, suggests that a doctor may disclose secrets if 'a real and imminent threat of harm to the patient or to others' may be averted only by a breach of confidentiality. That puts the test too liberally for most jurisdictions. Does a remote risk of an infinitesimal harm to a third party justify disclosure? The WMA would seem to say that it did. Many other regulatory organizations have been more cautious. The UK General Medical Council indicates that disclosure without the patient's consent may be appropriate where failure to disclose 'may expose others to a risk of death or serious harm... You should still seek the patient's consent to disclosure if practicable and consider any reasons given for refusal... Such a situation might arise, for example, when a disclosure would be likely to assist in the prevention, detection or prosecution of serious crime, especially crimes against the person.' The American Medical Association advises that 'When a patient threatens to inflict serious physical harm to another person or to him or herself and there is a reasonable probability that the patient may carry out the threat, the physician should take reasonable precautions for the protection of the intended victim, which may include notification of law enforcement authorities.'

How might these issues arise in practice? Well, a doctor might feel obliged to turn in a predatory would-be axe murderer. But even today, this is not part of most doctors' daily diet. Much more common is the risk posed by infectious disease.

A businessman comes into a doctor's surgery and confesses that on a recent trip to Thailand he had unprotected sexual intercourse with a prostitute. He is concerned that he might have contracted HIV. He's right to be worried. He has. The doctor questions him about his wife. She doesn't know, says the patient, and she's not going to know. And, what's more, he's not going to stop having sex with her, and he's not going to use a condom.

What should the doctor do?

In most jurisdictions the doctor can, entirely safely, tell the wife that she's at risk. Indeed the law is tending increasingly in the direction of insisting that he should. Tort will be more likely to

The Independent

Doctor who died was HIV positive, confirms Trust

WEDNESDAY 19 FEBRUARY 1997

A junior doctor who died suddenly at a Devon hospital last week was HIV positive, the local health trust confirmed last night. The doctor died after falling ill but the actual cause of death has yet to be established, said the Royal Devon and Exeter Healthcare NHS Trust. A Trust statement said the Exeter coroner had confirmed the doctor was HIV positive. The doctor worked at the hospital between 15 and 19 July, 1996, and between 5 and 7 February this year. On both occasions he worked in gynaecology and obstetrics departments.

3. Sometimes clear breaches of medical confidentiality are justified because the public interest in disclosure outweighs the public (or private) interest in keeping the secret

condemn him for non-disclosure if the wife is his patient, but neither ethics nor the general law of confidentiality should mind whose life he endangers: it's a *public* interest in disclosure that's being considered. The wife is just the part of the public that's most directly in the viral firing line.

Children, incapacitous patients, and the secrets of the dead

The law of consent and the law of confidentiality are close relatives. Confidentiality is happy about disclosure when the patient consents, and uneasy about it when the patient does not. But there are some classes of patient who cannot give consent. Young children do not have the neurological software necessary to understand what's at stake in the disclosure or non-disclosure of their secrets. Capacity can be truncated by illness or injury. And the dead, so far as we know, have no opinions.

It's therefore no surprise that, in relation to children and incapacitous patients, the law of confidentiality trundles in the wake of the law of consent. That is so in all jurisdictions. The starting point in England, therefore, is accordingly the best interests of the patient. If disclosure is, prima facie, against the patient's best interests, there is a presumption against disclosure. But, as in the rest of the law of confidentiality, that's not the end of the story. The interests of others fall into the balance too, and are weighed in precisely the same way as for any other confidentiality case.

An area that gives particular trouble is the provision of contraceptive services to children. Suppose a 14-year-old girl comes to see a doctor. She wants to go on the contraceptive pill because she is having sex with her 14-year-old boyfriend. (It might be different if the boyfriend were 45: then the girl might have been giving the doctor information about a dangerous sexual predator, and other considerations might come into play.) Should the parents know what's going on? In England the court has said that it should be assumed that parental involvement will be helpful (which means that it is in the girl's best interests) (*R (Axon) v Secretary of State for Health* (2006)), but that this assumption can be displaced. The American Medical Association has given more or less identical advice: see Opinion 5.055: Confidential Care for Minors: 1996. It's easy to understand why the assumption of disclosure is readily displaced: girls would often be discouraged from seeking medical help if they thought that their parents would be told.

The dead, in many countries, can't be libelled, but, anomalously, their secrets may be protected. Professional organizations (for instance the GMC and the AMA) presume that medical secrets should be kept confidential after the patient's death, subject to the usual balancing exercise. It seems, though, that the interests of family members or friends in knowing the circumstances of a death will weigh heavily. While one might see this as acknowledging a public interest in the truth emerging and angst being dissipated, it seems rather artificial.

The law, while smiling broadly on these well-meaning expressions, has generally been content to sit on the fence. The English case of *Lewis v Secretary of State for Health* (2008) is typical. It held that it was *arguable* that the duty of confidentiality survived the grave.

Consent and confidentiality are close cousins. Let's visit the cousin.

Chapter 5
Consent

People tend to assume that they have an absolute right to control what is done with their bodies. But it's not so simple.

A group of homosexual sadomasochists met in private. Their idea of a good night out was to nail one another's genitalia to pieces of wood. They were all adults, and it was all consensual. No one complained, but the police got to hear of it. The participants were prosecuted for various assault offences. They simply said: 'Everyone consented. Consent is a defence to assault.' They were convicted by the English courts, and the convictions survived a trip to the European Court of Human Rights: see *R v Brown* (1994); *Laskey, Jaggard and Brown v UK* (1997).

The judges who upheld the convictions and those who would have quashed them all based their decisions on an appeal to public policy. No one thought that sadomasochism should be encouraged. Lord Templeman's attitude was typical: 'The evidence discloses that the practices of the appellants were unpredictably dangerous and degrading to body and mind...Society is entitled and bound to protect itself against a cult of violence...'

The judgments turned on the extent to which the state should be allowed to reach into the private lives of citizens. Some judges were more liberal than others, but it's as trite a proposition as one can get that the law restricts what individuals can do. Indeed one might even *define* the law as that which restricts individual freedom. Normally a curtailing of X's freedom is justified on the grounds that if X is not restricted, Y will be adversely affected in an unacceptable way. That adverse effect might be direct and physical (which is why, for instance, X's freedom to rape Y is curtailed by the criminal law), psychologically corrupting (which is why some forms of censorship of violent video games might be justified), or by an insidious transformation of ethos or atmosphere (which is one reason why legislation prohibiting assisted suicide, and so asserting the value of human life, might be justified, although it interferes with an individual's ability to end their life in the circumstances they wish).

Brown is sometimes cited as establishing that one cannot validly consent to serious bodily injury. The state, on this analysis, has a paternalistic duty to protect us from ourselves. But if that's right, it discharges its duty in a very inconsistent way. Boxers can injure themselves grievously for money, and crowds can roar enthusiastically as noses break and blood spurts. Skiing and bungee jumping are lawful, and when you get injured doing either you will get free medical treatment from the state in many countries. The state has a duty to prevent the suicide of an entirely mentally competent prisoner. And no one suggests that a surgeon acts unlawfully if he does wholly unnecessary breast augmentation or female genital cosmetic surgery—in the course of which he will inflict what amounts to (at least until the wounds heal) significant bodily injury.

The law of consent is so suffused with policy that it is sometimes difficult to map the outlines of the law. The policy itself is a creature of the tension between autonomy on the one hand and community interest and state ideology on the other.

That said, there are some generally recognized principles.

Competent adults

What's a competent adult?

Competency or capacity in relation to a particular decision is the ability to receive, weigh, process, and retain the relevant information. It also implies an ability to communicate the decision made once the information is processed. The words 'in relation to a particular decision' are crucial. Capacity is not an all-or-nothing thing. One might well have capacity for one decision but not for another. You don't need much neurological processing power to understand sufficiently what's involved in the dressing of your bedsore. You need much more to ponder the pros and cons of a cancer chemotherapy regime.

Capacity can fluctuate. If I drink 20 pints of beer, my ability to make decisions about my own medical treatment, or indeed about anything, will be seriously reduced. But in the morning it will be restored. Therapeutic drugs can have a similar effect. So can some diseases. Depression might impair my capacity: nature, TLC or Prozac might restore it.

Legal systems across the world rightly value autonomy, and fear terribly the thought of forcing unwanted treatment on a patient. They accordingly tend to require clinicians and others to presume that a patient is capacitous unless the contrary is proved, and to seek to ensure that, if at all possible, decisions are made by the patient herself, rather than by someone else on her behalf. It might follow, for instance, that if a decision about treatment can safely be delayed until a temporarily incapacitous patient regains capacity, there should be a delay.

Suppose a surgeon, while operating to break down pelvic adhesions, finds an ovarian tumour. It's not *immediately* life threatening, but the surgeon feels that it should be dealt with. Unless the woman wants to die, the tumour will have to come out some time. He removes the tumour. The patient, of course, has not given express consent. The surgeon justifies his action by saying that, since the patient is anaesthetized and thus incapacitous, he can and should do what is objectively in her best interests, or (depending on the jurisdiction) what she would want were she in a position to say.

The court would not be impressed. The patient's incapacity is temporary. She could have been woken up and her real wishes ascertained.

Competent adults: the general rule

At least within the walls of a hospital, a competent adult can generally consent to anything, and her refusal to consent to anything must be respected.

The classic statement of this principle comes from the US. Cardozo J in *Schloendorff v Society of New York Hospital* (1914):

> Every human being of adult years and sound mind has a right to determine what shall be done with his own body; and a surgeon who performs an operation without his patient's consent commits an assault, for which he is liable in damages.

And in Canada:

> The state's interest in preserving the life or health of a competent patient must generally give way to the patient's stronger interest in directing the course of her own life... The right to determine what shall be done with one's body is a fundamental right in our society. The concepts inherent in this right are the bedrock upon which the principles of self-determination and individual autonomy are based. Free individual choice in matters affecting this right should... be accorded very high priority. (*Malette v Shulman* (1990))

It doesn't matter that a choice might be deadly. Competent adult Jehovah's Witnesses can refuse life-saving blood transfusions. As long as you understand the consequences of what you're asking for, you can insist that the doctors switch off the ventilator which is breathing for you. The basic rule is: autonomy's respected to death.

This doesn't mean, of course, that you can require someone actively to do anything to you. Generally you can't demand that an individual doctor provides a particular treatment, or, in a publicly funded health system, that the state provides a particular treatment that no clinician believes is in your best interests. You can require someone to stop your life-sustaining ventilator because the continued ventilation is, without your consent, an inappropriate act—indeed an assault. So one can demand omissions (refuse treatment), but not demand acts (insist on specific treatment).

Incompetent adults

If a decision has to be made about (for instance) medical treatment, and someone can't make it for themselves, someone will have to make it for them. Making someone submit to medical treatment that they haven't themselves endorsed is philosophically draconian, and may be physically draconian. It might do more harm than good. One might have to get burly nurses to hold the patient down on a table until they are anaesthetized. That shouldn't be done lightly, and by and large isn't.

How does one decide how to make a decision on someone else's behalf, and who does it?

The 'who does it?' is more difficult to summarize than one might think. The real answer is either the patient themselves (where the patient has made a binding advance decision saying what they would like to happen should they become incapacitous), a proxy decision-maker appointed by the patient while they have the capacity to do so, or the court.

Part of the law's respect for autonomy is expressed in its respect for the wishes of a patient, recorded at a time when they were capacitous, regarding what they would like to happen if they lose their capacity. (Some of the difficulties with advance decisions are discussed in Chapter 9, on the end of life). If an advance decision has complied with any relevant formalities, was appropriately informed at the time it was made, applies to the relevant clinical circumstances, and if there is no indication that the patient might have decided differently were she to be able to make the decision himself as of now, the advance decision will be honoured, and quite right too. But there are many 'buts' here.

In many jurisdictions a person can appoint a proxy decision-maker. When they do, and the proxy is acting within the scope of the authority delegated to them, the proxy's decision is as valid as if it were uttered capacitously by the patient.

If there is no relevant advance decision and no validly exercised proxy, the court decides.

It might not always seem like that. Indeed it is actually very rare indeed for the court to be troubled with medical decision-making. Almost all decisions on behalf of patients are taken by the clinicians concerned or, in the case of non-medical decisions (such as where to live, where to bank, what to eat), by carers or family. What's really going on here?

What the doctors or carers are doing, if they're acting lawfully, is to act as the agents of the relevant national court, which itself is the custodian of the law. The court retains ultimate jurisdiction. A decision made on behalf of an incompetent patient by anyone can always be overruled by the court.

How, then, can the doctor or carer act lawfully? It depends on the particular jurisdiction concerned. If the patient is in the UK, for instance, the decision will be a lawful one if it is in the best interests of the patient. In many states in the US the test is, instead, that of substituted judgement: the decision-maker must divine what the

4. Tom, the subject of Hogarth's series *A Rake's Progress*, is finally incarcerated in 'Bedlam', a London psychiatric hospital. The law has long recognized that some mental states justify treatment to which the patient will not or cannot consent

patient would have done in the relevant circumstances had she capacity to make the decision. These tests are discussed in Chapter 9, in the context of end-of-life decision-making, where the questions present in the most dramatic form.

Children

Every jurisdiction has a formal definition of a 'child' for legal purposes. In the UK a 'child', for the purpose of medical decision-making, is anyone under the age of 18. The definitions sometimes create curious anomalies. A court might find a boy of 12 guilty of murder, but he's not entitled to refuse treatment for his own acne.

Very broadly, children do not have (or it is assumed that they do not have) the ability of competent adults to understand the consequences of their decisions. But this statement is too broad to be the sole basis of responsible law-making. It's plainly foolish to assume that as midnight strikes to usher in her 18th birthday, a child is suddenly given a completely new set of cognitive faculties. And many 17-year-olds (and 16-year-olds, and no doubt some eight-year-olds) will have a maturity and sophistication denied to many legally competent 50-year-olds. Nonetheless, lines have to be drawn somewhere.

The lines can work injustice. In most jurisdictions treatment can be given to non-consenting children which is deemed to be in their best interests. But compulsorily treating a perfectly comprehending, sophisticated 17-year-old is a terrible thing. And so, generally, the law has allowed the lines to bend. Thus in the UK, which is fairly typical, there's the notion of '*Gillick* competency' (see *Gillick v West Norfolk and Wisbech AHA* (1986)). A child has the capacity to consent to medical treatment when she 'achieves a sufficient understanding and intelligence to enable... her to understand fully what is proposed'. That includes, of course, the ability to understand the consequences of not being treated. Whether a particular child has that understanding and intelligence is a question of fact.

In many legal systems there's an asymmetry between the law relating to a child's ability to consent to treatment and to refuse treatment. In the UK, for instance, statute provides that a 16- or 17-year-old's consent to treatment is as valid as that of an adult. But the same does not apply to refusals of treatment. There the common law, *Gillick* rule applies.

At first blush this looks illogical. But in fact it makes sense. It reflects the law's presumption that clinicians are likely to suggest to a child only treatment that is in the child's best interests. Accordingly the court can say, in response to a 16- or 17-year-old's refusal: 'We've looked at the case carefully, and it's clear that doctor knows best. You'll have the treatment.'

The question of parental consent or refusal of consent is vexed. It's often said, even by lawyers, that parents (or, more accurately, those with parental responsibility) have a right to make treatment decisions on behalf of their children. Consent forms are printed and hospital protocols devised with that in mind. But it's not the full legal truth.

What's really happening is that the law presumes that parents (being, usually, uniquely concerned and knowledgeable about their children) will be the best arbiter of what is in the child's best interests. But that presumption can be displaced. The final decision in relation to a child's treatment always rests with the court.

Take a seven-year-old child in a family of Jehovah's Witnesses. The child is knocked down by a car. If the child does not have a blood transfusion he will die. The devout parents refuse to give their consent. In their view, the eternal consequences of receiving the blood will be more serious than the child's physical death.

This is the sort of consent case that often reaches the court. In almost all such circumstances the court overrules the parents—deciding that it is in the child's best interests to live. In the US, for instance, the court said:

> Parents may be free to become martyrs themselves, but it does not follow that they are free in identical circumstances to make martyrs of their children... (*Prince v Massachusetts* (1944))

But the court does not overrule the parents blithely. It considers carefully the sad fact that a child who receives blood may be rejected by her parents and cold-shouldered by the community. That fact is factored into the best-interests equation. One can imagine extreme circumstances where a child, if she survives, would in any event have a seriously diminished quality of life. If one adds to this the burden of ostracism, one may be forced to the conclusion that it is not in the child's best interests to have the life-saving transfusion.

The best-interests test has a long chronological perspective. It looks far into the future.

Imagine, for instance, that child X has leukaemia. His only realistic chance of survival lies in receiving a bone-marrow donation from his eight-year old sister, Y. This will involve sticking a large needle into Y and aspirating marrow. Y refuses to agree to the procedure. She hates her brother because he has just stolen her teddy bear. In fact, of course, her refusal is legally irrelevant: she cannot validly either give or refuse consent. The teddy bear incident will just make the business of getting the marrow that much more traumatic than it would be with a compliant child.

The test of whether Y should be forced to donate the marrow is simply whether it is in Y's best interests.

Courts in such circumstances have typically found that donation is in Y's best interests, although the aspiration itself is clearly a medical detriment. It is in Y's interests that her brother lives. Not only will Y have the benefit of growing up with X (dubious though she might see that benefit to be, just at the moment), but she will be spared the stigma of being her brother's de facto executioner. One could hardly expect her parents' attitude to her to be unaffected by the fact that she could have saved her brother but failed to do so.

When is consent not consent?

In Victoria, Australia, a perverted doctor inserted an instrument into a woman's vagina. His motivation was purely sexual: there was no clinical indication. The woman consented because she thought it was diagnostically necessary.

The doctor was tried for sexual assault. He was acquitted, the Supreme Court of Victoria finding that there was no assault. The woman's consent was real. There was no fraud as to the nature and quality of the doctor's act (*R v Mobilio* (1991)).

This decision, which seems bizarre to many, was the legacy of an old English case, *R v Clarence* (1988). Clarence was infected with gonorrhoea. He knew it, although his wife did not. He had sexual intercourse with her. She contracted the infection. He was prosecuted.

It was said that he had assaulted his wife. Nonsense, he said: consent is a defence to assault. She's a grown woman, and she knew exactly what she was consenting to—namely sexual intercourse. The prosecution responded that her consent was not real, and that had she known that he was infected she would not have agreed to sex. The appeal court was no doubt worried about the dire social consequences of suggesting that a wife (who shared, per the Bible, one body with her husband) might have any excuse not to have sex at the husband's whim. It agreed with Clarence. Mrs Clarence had consented to an act of the 'nature and quality' of that which had occurred.

Clarence continued to wreak injustice in England until 2004, when, in the context of transmission of HIV, it was finally held that where one does not know but a sexual partner has a sexually transmissible infection, consent to sex (*R v Dica* (2004)). Another way of putting it is that the court looks more to the mind of the defendant than to the state of knowledge of the victim in deciding on liability in sexual assault cases. That's no surprise.

That's the criminal law. Medical gropers are less safe from prison than they were. If you're going to touch someone, whether in the course of a medical consultation or otherwise, you will do so criminally unless you do it with their express or implied consent, and that consent will not be real (at least in a sexual context) unless the real reason for the touching is what the patient thinks it is.

But the criminal law, slanted towards acquittal as it must be, is necessarily more forgiving to defendants than the civil law. If you're convicted of a criminal offence your liberty is in jeopardy. If you're found liable for a civil wrong, at most your wallet, and perhaps your reputation, will be. A lower quality of consent is required to exculpate in the criminal law than in the civil law.

The whole notion of 'informed consent' permeates, and sometimes paralyses, medical practice. 'Informed consent' itself is a US idea, but, like so many ideas, it has crossed the Atlantic and metastasized throughout Europe and the common-law world. It's got a good pedigree. We can argue about the age of that pedigree, but a sensible point to start is 1957, when the California Court of Appeals stated that 'a physician violates his duty to the plaintiff and subjects himself to liability if he withholds any facts which are necessary to form the basis of an intelligent consent by the patient to the proposed treatment' (*Salgo v Leland Stanford Jr University Board of Trustees* (1957)).

The US courts built on this and other observations a massive edifice that supposedly protects patients, and certainly terrifies doctors. In the enormously influential case of *Canterbury v Spence* (1972), a US District Court observed that the doctor's duty was not merely a duty to answer questions, but a duty to volunteer information. Rejecting conclusively the operation of the English *Bolam* test in the law of consent, the court held that the right to self-determination was so crucial that the law, rather than doctors themselves, should set the required standard. The doctor must disclose all 'material risks'. A risk is material when 'a reasonable person, in what the physician knows or should know to be the patient's position, would be likely to attach significance to the risk or cluster of risks in deciding whether or not to forgo the proposed therapy'. Only where disclosure of the risks would pose 'a serious threat of psychological detriment to the patient' could non-disclosure be justified.

The Canadians agree (*Reibl v Hughes* (1980)). So do the Australians (*Rogers v Whittaker* (1992)).

The English law in the area is harder to describe. The leading case is *Sidaway v Board of Governors of the Bethlem Royal Hospital and the Maudsley Hospital* (1985), but it's terribly difficult to work out what it says.

There were five judges, and four very different judgments. There has been a tendency to read only those judgments supporting the notion that the *Bolam* test applies (and accordingly that the doctor will have discharged his obligation if he counsels the patient in a way that would be endorsed by a responsible body of medical opinion). But English lawyers are beginning to read and apply the other judgments—and in particular those which hint at the US way of looking at things: see *Pearce v United Bristol Healthcare NHS Trust* (1999). In any event, professional regulatory codes are increasingly using the US language of informed consent, and if that's the case, it's hard to say that *Bolam*-responsible UK doctors shouldn't feel obliged to treat their patients as if they practised in New York.

There's another reason, too, why Europe is becoming more and more wedded to the notion of 'informed consent' as understood in the US. That's the European Convention on Human Rights. Article 8 of the Convention robustly protects patient autonomy. Even if *Bolam* doesn't insist on full disclosure, Article 8 may do so—unless it can be contended under Article 8(2) that such insistence is likely to gum up the health-care system to the overall detriment of society.

In fact such a contention isn't fanciful. Full disclosure of risks sounds fine, but is it possible? And if it is possible, is it practicable?

Every drug ever produced, and every procedure ever devised, has actual or potential complications, some of them vanishingly rare and recorded only in highly obscure journals. It's simply not possible to run through them all. And if it were, it's neither practicable (it would leave no time for any treatment at all) nor desirable (because many people would be scared stiff by the mention of a horrifying but almost unknown possibility, and would irrationally decline treatment, or be inappropriately worried while undergoing it). Some sort of balance needs to be struck between full disclosure and sensible disclosure. It may be that the balancing exercise demanded by Article 8 is the sensible way to strike that balance.

But perhaps there is another, even more fundamental, reason to be less dumbstruck than we often are by our awe of informed consent. And that is that it's not possible to identify the *person* who's really giving consent. By all means respect autonomy: a system that doesn't do so is malignant. But ask: 'Whose autonomy?' Consider a person who is faced with a decision about whether to have life-prolonging treatment for cancer. The biological man may want to cling onto life with the help of any available technology. The sentimental family man might want to see his children for those extra few months. The considerate family man might want to die early so as 'not to be a burden' to his family. The man who has read John Stuart Mill and drafted a 'life-plan' might want to die as he has lived, with a proud independence unfettered by morphine and incontinence. The religious man might think that sophisticated therapy frustrates the will of God. And so on. Few of us are, at least when it comes to ontological challenge, well-integrated people. We'll be one person one minute, and another the next.

The consequences of failing to obtain the patient's consent

One example makes the point. You go to your dentist. He tells you that a lot of work needs to be done, and that if it's not, the consequences for your dental health will be dire. You sign a form agreeing to the treatment. He drills and fills. You pay him.

Criminal consequences

If the treatment was unnecessary, and the dentist knew it, he has procured your consent by fraud. He might try to run a *Clarence*-type argument (saying that you knew the nature and quality of what you consented to), but he's likely to fail. Quite apart from committing an offence of dishonesty, which could have its own criminal consequences, he has assaulted you, and can be prosecuted in the criminal courts. If there was a sexual motive, of course (if he'd gassed and groped you), he can be prosecuted too.

Civil consequences

Assault is a civil wrong too. Touching someone without their (sufficient) consent is an assault/battery. If the treatment was, to the dentist's knowledge, unnecessary, he can be sued for damages for assault.

But perhaps your dentist was not dishonest. Perhaps he should just have given you a better explanation than he did of the risks and benefits of the treatment. In the US and many other places you're entitled to know the material risks. It's negligent not to explain them. Your autonomy rights have been outraged. The way the law looks at such negligence in consent cases is complex: it's discussed in Chapter 6. It's enough to say here that it may be possible to get damages representing the consequences of that negligence.

Disciplinary consequences

The dentist is accountable to his regulatory body. He is obliged to comply with a set of professional standards. Depending on the facts, he may have breached those obligations. This may have put his registration at risk, or attracted some other disciplinary sanction.

Chapter 6
Clinical negligence

Doctors, being human, make mistakes. Since doctors' business is with human bodies, and human bodies are really rather important for much of the business of living, loving, and earning, those mistakes can be far-reaching and expensive.

But does that mean that an honest mistake by a well-meaning doctor should give an injured patient a right to sue? If so, what yardstick should be used in deciding that a doctor has fallen short of the mark? If a doctor has made a mistake, should all consequent damage, however remote, and however amorphous, be placed at the doctor's door?

This is the world of clinical negligence—a term that makes the eyes of many (and in particular Americans) roll. To many it speaks of shiny-suited, ambulance-chasing, claim-inflating lawyers, whose greed makes clinicians and insurers tremble, and causes patients to be hysterically over-investigated in an effort to see off the litigators. Clinical negligence claims are agonizing for everyone but the lawyers. The lawyers should be impoverished if they can be. But it's hard to get rid of them completely.

'No fault' or tort?

In theory the clinical negligence industry isn't inevitable. The state, or a consortium of insurers, could simply decide that they will pay out compensation on a no-fault basis to the victims of medical mistakes without the need for the elaborate and expensive ballet of the courts. But in practice this rarely happens. There are two main reasons. The first is the sheer expense that would be involved in such a scheme. In the UK, today, a baby whose cerebral palsy has been caused by obstetric negligence could get an award of £10 million—reflecting a lifetime's loss of earnings, the need for a lifetime's care, therapy, equipment, and so on.

Suppose there's a modest (25 per cent) chance of avoiding a £10 million liability. To get that chance you've got to go into the casino (it's called a court). Most casinos have an entrance fee, and this one certainly does. It's made up of lawyers' fees, expert witness costs, and many other elements. But even with the sleekest lawyers, the most eminent experts, and the 75 per cent probability of having to pay all of the claimant's costs too, it will often be financially sensible to pay the entrance fee, spin the wheel, and see if that one in four chance comes up.

The second reason why no-fault schemes are unattractive in the clinical negligence context is the frequent difficulty of establishing causation. A no-fault scheme in relation to road traffic accidents is one thing. If car A hits car B, and the occupants of car B get hurt, it's often not hard to attribute that hurt to car A. But in clinical negligence claims causation is often much murkier. Many cases end with the defendant having been found to be in breach of duty, but with the claimant failing to prove that that breach of duty has caused any loss. No-fault schemes have to presume that causation is straightforward. You can't do that in medicine. Cells and enzymes are less predictable than trucks.

The New Zealand experience illustrates this well. New Zealand has a no-fault scheme of compensation for medical injuries, but it requires a claimant to prove that her injury was caused by 'medical or surgical misadventure'. Many clinical negligence claims in tort jurisdictions are concerned solely and agonizingly with precisely that.

Other supposedly no-fault schemes in fact find themselves edging back towards fault. Sweden is a good example. Fault, it insists, is irrelevant: claimants are compensated for injuries that result from inaction on the part of a clinician that is 'medically unjustified'. But to argue about whether something is medically unjustified is, very often, to argue about whether the doctor is at fault.

Tort is surprisingly hard to escape.

The elements of a clinical negligence claim in tort

Just as in any negligence claim in a tort-based system, to be successful in a clinical negligence claim in tort a claimant must prove that:

- the defendant owed him a duty of care
- there has been a breach of that duty
- the breach has caused damage
- of a type recognized by the law of tort.

Claims in contract

Private medicine is performed according to contracts. The relevant contract will often be between the patient and the doctor who provides the care. The position is sometimes complicated by the involvement of medical insurers and private hospitals: it may therefore be that a contract exists between the insurer and a hospital, rather than the patient and the doctor.

In the simple situation of a contract for treatment between the patient and a doctor, the contract, in practice, adds little or nothing to the law of tort. Many countries (for instance France, Belgium, Germany, Austria, Switzerland, and Greece) use contractual models for establishing the liability of a doctor, but the courts in all jurisdictions have been very reluctant to read the governing contract as anything other than an agreement by the doctor to use the skill and care reasonably to be expected of a doctor holding himself out as having the expertise of the defendant. The law of tort makes an identical demand. In particular the courts are unhappy about construing an agreement as an agreement for a particular medical or surgical result—for instance a cure of the patient's cancer, or a pair of breasts that look like the ones in the surgeon's brochure. This is because they recognize the vagaries of biology. The clinician never has complete control, and so it is unfair for a contract to assume that he does.

This is not to say that analogies with contract aren't sometimes enlightening. Sometimes they are—and particularly in relation to the question of damages for loss of a chance. As we shall see.

Duty of care

The existence of a duty of care is seldom an issue in medical cases. By and large there is no obligation to be a Good Samaritan. When the tannoy pleads 'Is there a doctor in the house?' the doctor can sit quietly and ignore it. In most (but not all) jurisdictions he will be safe from the law, if not from his conscience, if he watches an entirely salvageable patient die. Doctors, in short, usually owe duties only to their patients, and can decide who is their patient and who isn't.

Usually it's obvious when someone is a patient of a particular clinician, and of course clinicians have a duty to take reasonable care of 'their' patients. Often several clinicians will owe a duty to a single patient. In a state health-care system the appropriate defendant will usually be the statutory provider (for instance the National Health Service Trust or the hospital) which employs the clinicians directly responsible for the patient's care.

Very occasionally, though, there are arguments about the existence of a duty.

Imagine, for instance, that a doctor is employed by an insurance company. His job is to look through the medical notes of potential clients to see if they are a good insurance risk. He is looking through X's notes when he discovers a clear indication that X is suffering from an entirely curable cancer. It is plain that X's own clinicians have missed the cancer. What should the doctor do? Does he have to tell X what he has found, so that X can get the necessary treatment?

Or suppose that a surgeon performs a vasectomy on Boy, and then, negligently, assures him that he is sterile and need take no more contraceptive precautions. Boy later meets Girl. Over wine and dinner in a candlelit restaurant, Boy romantically assures Girl that he is sterile. Accordingly Girl has unprotected sex with Boy. The assurance was wrong, and Girl becomes pregnant. Can Girl sue the surgeon?

There is wide variation between jurisdictions as to how these issues are resolved. But most countries use a formula akin to the English one, asking whether the relationship between the claimant and the defendant is sufficiently close, whether the damage suffered by the claimant is a foreseeable result of the defendant's negligence (a test more obviously at home in the law of causation, but which has had a home in the law relating to duties at least since the canonical case of *Donoghue v Stevenson* (1932)—the one about the snail in the ginger beer bottle), and whether it is just and reasonable to impose such a duty on the defendant: see *Caparo Industries plc v Dickman* (1990). Policy considerations play a big part in the determination—particularly in relation to this third element.

The insurance company case would be difficult to call, but many judges would find that the doctor's duty was restricted to the duty he owed by contract to the employing insurer (compare *Kapfunde v Abbey National plc* (1999)). The vasectomy case is a real example: the English Court of Appeal held that one could not owe a duty to all the potential sexual partners of a patient, and accordingly that Girl had no claim: *Goodwill v British Pregnancy Advisory Services* (1996).

This doesn't mean that a doctor cannot owe a duty to unknown third parties.

A psychotic patient tells his psychiatrist that, if released from his secure hospital, he will kill the first person he sees. The psychiatrist negligently discharges the patient and, true to his promise, the patient strangles, on the hospital steps, the first passer-by he sees.

Could the victim's family sue the psychiatrist? Almost certainly: see *Tarasoff v The Regents of the University of California* (1976); *Palmer v South Tees Health Authority* (1999). What if the victim were the second person the patient saw? Very likely. Or the twentieth? Very probably.

Can it not be said that there's a duty to *any* victim? That goes directly against authorities like the vasectomy case (*Goodwill*). But to say otherwise is to give a negligent doctor an immunity simply because the patient has been incautious enough to blurt out his plans. Why should that blurt have the effect of restricting the doctor's duty? Shouldn't it rather have made the release *more* negligent? The doctor has loosed into society a deadly weapon which might go off at any moment with obviously foreseeable loss of life. Shouldn't the law have something to say about that?

The answer is that the law should and does, but what it says is stuttering and inconsistent. This is a fast-evolving area. The next big steps in that evolution are likely to occur in relation to the liability for damage done by psychiatric patients, liability for transmission of HIV or other sexually transmitted diseases by sexual partners of a doctor's patient, and liability for psychiatric injury to people other than patients.

This sort of psychiatric injury is common. A father might watch the delivery of his dead child—dead through the negligence of the obstetrician—and be traumatized as a result. A mother might be depressed by the burdens of bringing up a negligently brain-damaged child. The worry about compensating these apparently deserving claimants is that it will open the floodgates to a tsunami of claims. Many people far removed from the scene of the tort can be mentally affected in various ways by clinical negligence.

Various devices are used to keep the floodgates shut, including a requirement that a claimant is in a close relationship to the patient, or has witnessed the 'immediate aftermath' of the negligence.

Breach of duty

In England and many other jurisdictions the test for breach of duty is the *Bolam* test (see *Bolam v Friern Hospital Management Committee* (1957)). This says that a professional will be in breach of duty if what they have done would not be endorsed by any responsible body of opinion in the relevant specialty. It is a test both of substantive law and of evidence, and has become ubiquitous in professional negligence law, being used to determine the liability of everyone from heart surgeons to plumbers (who, after all, have a lot in common).

It has sometimes been abused by defendants and defendant-friendly judges, some of whom, seeing any attack on fellow professionals as a general attack on the middle classes, have been happy to acquit a doctor of negligence on the basis of the evidence of another doctor who, having miraculously remained on the register for an undistinguished professional lifetime, is prepared to say (at £200 an hour) not that *he* would have done an operation in the way that the defendant did, but that he once met someone in the golf club who'd also astonishingly escaped erasure who did it that way.

Claimants rightly railed against this. Their complaints led, in England, to a revisiting of the test in *Bolitho v City and Hackney Health Authority* (1998), in which the court pointed out something that had tended to be forgotten—namely that the old test referred to *responsible* opinion. There may be cases, it said, where, notwithstanding evidence that the defendant adopted a common practice, the defendant might still be negligent—if the practice did not stand up to logical scrutiny.

This provoked howls of worry from doctors, concerned that their professional practices would be second-guessed by medically unqualified judges. To many, those howls sounded petulant. The doctors were really insisting that they and only they should set the standards by which they should be judged. And if you are the law, aren't you above the law?

It was precisely those concerns that had made other jurisdictions reject the *Bolam* approach and leave the setting of legal standards in the hands of the courts. The best examples relate to the law of consent: see below.

Bolam is on the retreat. *Bolitho* chased it into its proper place, but medicine itself has eroded *Bolam*'s authority significantly. Medicine is increasingly evidence-based. Proper medical practice is increasingly based on large, statistically significant studies of efficacy which are embodied in clinical guidelines. There's a diminishing amount of room for opinion. If the literature conclusively shows that practice X is better than practice Y, then (economic considerations aside) how can anyone *responsibly* adopt practice Y?

Consent cases occupy a curious corner of the clinical negligence world. They are very common. A patient might, for instance, say that she was not appropriately warned about the risks of surgery, that had she been warned she would not have consented to it, and accordingly that she would have been spared the damage wrought by the surgery.

Even in jurisdictions where *Bolam* rules, it is not self-evident, according to a number of eminent authorities, that the test for liability in relation to allegedly negligent consenting of a patient should be the *Bolam* test. In the leading English authority, *Sidaway v Board of Governors of the Bethlem Royal Hospital* (1984), a case whose effect is famously obscure, the House of Lords, while upholding the broad proposition that the *Bolam* test applied, did so cautiously, suggesting that judges might be more ready than in other classes of case to make up their own minds about whether the doctor in question had done what was necessary.

Lord Scarman, dissenting, approved the position in the US case of *Canterbury v Spence* (1972), in which the US court, while not saying that evidence about medical practice was irrelevant to the question of what amounted to appropriate care, insisted that the court, and not the medical profession, was the arbiter. Lord Scarman was embraced in several Commonwealth countries. Even in conservative England he's slowly being rehabilitated. Ever since *Canterbury v Spence, Bolam,* cold-shouldered elsewhere, has been shown emphatically to the door in consent cases in Canada (see *Reibl v Hughes* (1980)), Australia (*F v R* (1983)), and South Africa (*Castell v De Greef* (1994)).

Canterbury v Spence articulated the 'reasonable patient' test, which we met in Chapter 5. Material risks must be disclosed. A risk is material if it would be regarded as significant by a reasonable person in the patient's position. There's an exception, inconsistently recognized by judges across the world, and apparently frowned on by some professional regulatory bodies:

this is the 'therapeutic privilege'—the notion that information can be withheld if to disclose it might be psychologically harmful.

Once a revolution starts, it's difficult to stop. If the unthinkable could be thought in relation to consent cases, why stop there? Why not abolish all reference and all deference to expert medical evidence in all clinical negligence cases, and let the law do the job (which many presume is its only, or at least main, job) of setting standards?

That was indeed the view of Gaudron J in the High Court of Australia case, *Rogers v Whittaker* (1992):

> ...even in the area of diagnosis and treatment, there is, in my view, no legal basis for limiting liability in terms of the rule known as 'the *Bolam* test'...[I]t may be a convenient statement of the approach dictated by the state of the evidence in some cases. As such, it may have some utility as a rule of thumb in some jury cases, but it can serve no other useful function...

This was fighting talk. It was not adopted by the majority of the court in *Rogers v Whittaker*, who restricted their restriction of *Bolam* to counselling cases, observing that 'There is a fundamental difference between, on the one hand, diagnosis and treatment and, on the other hand, the provision of advice and information to the patient... Because the choice to be made calls for a decision by the patient on information known to the medical practitioner but not to the patient, it would be illogical to hold that the amount of information to be provided by the medical practitioner can be determined from the perspective of the practitioner alone or, for that matter, of the medical profession.'

There are many who would like to see *Bolam* excised wholly from the law books—and not just those sections that relate to counselling. For them, *Bolam* stinks of medical paternalism; of the closing of the white-coated professional ranks against the desperate patient.

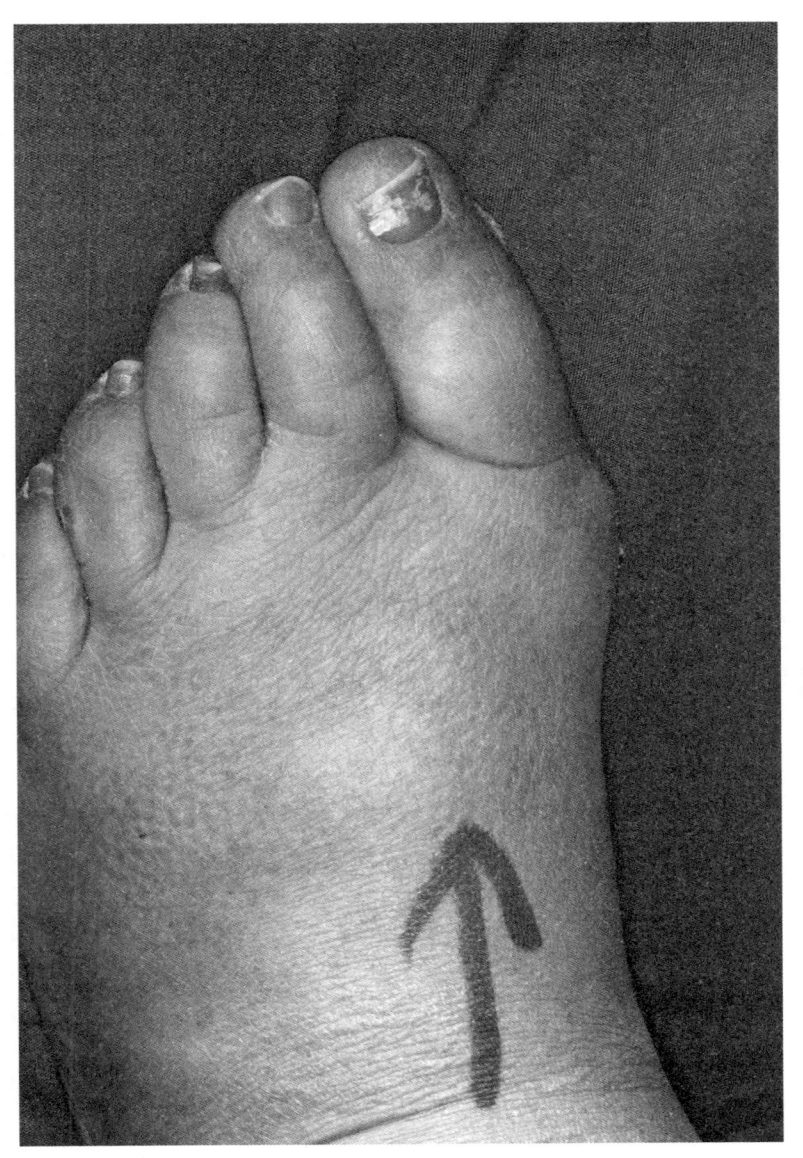

5. A surgical site marked up to avoid confusion. However forgiving *Bolam* might be, there is no responsible body of medical opinion which operates on the wrong finger, arm, or leg

But despite the political, sociological, and jurisprudential objections to *Bolam*, and despite *Bolam* being ousted from its throne by the evidence-based medicine revolution, it is hard to imagine that it will vanish altogether. It can't. The judges need it—especially in cases of diagnosis and treatment.

Consent cases are rather different. They are really about patients' human rights, and judges, being, by and large, human, are qualified to opine about whether or not human rights have been breached. But questions of diagnosis and treatment are technically complicated. Something akin to the *Bolam* approach will inevitably persist, simply because judges aren't equipped to make judgements about the appropriateness of a particular medical approach without the help of expert evidence. The nature of that inevitable help will inevitably boil down to something like *Bolam*. Just as judges aren't equipped to decide, without the benefit of expert evidence, which medical approach is correct, so they're not equipped, in most cases, to decide which of two competing medical approaches (the claimant's and the defendant's) is the right one in the relevant clinical circumstances. Should they decide on the basis of the cut of the expert's suit, or the number of peer-reviewed publications that each has to his name? Of course not. And hence there will have to be an appeal to a standard along the lines of 'a responsible body of medical opinion'. *Bolam* has lost some status, but it's far from dead.

Causation

The basic rule: 'but-for' causation

However rankly negligent a defendant has been, the claim will fail unless some loss has been caused. The basic test sounds common-sensical: it is for the claimant to show that, but for the defendant's negligence, she would have been spared the injury that she has in fact suffered.

So: a patient attends her family doctor, worried about a lump in her breast. The doctor examines the lump and wrongly reassures her that it is benign. In fact she should have been referred for further investigation. Had she been, breast cancer would have been diagnosed, and treatment would have been started. Her chances of complete cure at that point would have been 49 per cent. By the time her breast cancer is diagnosed, the chance of cure has dropped to 5 per cent.

The doctor admits breach of duty, but the claim, insofar as it is a claim for loss of cure, fails. Statistically the patient was doomed at the time of the first consultation. The doctor's negligence is causally irrelevant.

Loss of a chance

This conclusion troubles many. Hasn't the doctor deprived the patient of something that is capable of grounding a claim in tort? The law commonly compensates claimants who, because of breach of contract, lose a chance of gaining a benefit or avoiding a detriment. In an old English case, a girl paid money to a newspaper in order to enter a beauty contest. Due to the paper's administrative incompetence (in breach of its contract with her), she was not entered into the contest, and was therefore deprived of her chance (which would not have been better than evens) of winning it. She was entitled to damages: *Chaplin v Hicks* (1911). If a solicitor's incompetence robs a client of a (say) 30 per cent chance of succeeding in litigation, it is no answer for the solicitor to say: 'You'd probably have lost anyway, so there's no claim against me.' And yet that is precisely the assertion that lets the negligent doctor escape.

Why the discrepancy? Some would say that there is no discrepancy, pointing to the fact that the newspaper and the solicitor are acting under a contract, and that one might construe those contracts as contracts to take reasonable care to give the client the very chance of which she has been deprived. But many medical services are provided under contract. Can those contracts not be read in an identical way? And if so, is it acceptable to deprive a National Health Service patient of a remedy when a private patient, in identical circumstances, would get compensation? Some would contend that there's a difference between the chance of obtaining a benefit (as in the newspaper and litigation case) and the chance of avoiding a detriment (as in the breast cancer case). But that doesn't work either, for many reasons, one of which is that it is legal child's play to transform a benefit into a detriment, and vice versa. Who would like to tell the cancer victim that she hadn't really been deprived of the benefit of living and seeing her children grow up, but had instead merely failed to avoid the detriment of death? Nothing of any moral substance (and surely the breast cancer case has moral substance in spadefuls) should turn on such distinctions. It brings the law into disrepute.

What is operating here is not logic, but policy, and it would be better for the law's reputation if that were frankly admitted. The policy, in fact, is a sound, pragmatic one. We've seen it already in other contexts: the courts would be hopelessly clogged if damages for a lost chance were routinely allowed in clinical negligence cases. Many (arguably most) medical mistakes cause a patient to lose a chance of *something*. If loss of a chance were sufficient to allow a claimant to recover damages, one might effectively be doing away with the requirement to prove causation at all in clinical negligence cases: a breach of duty would be followed by judgment for damages to be assessed. Perhaps that sounds just. But the vagaries of biology being what they are, quantifying loss is often nightmarishly difficult and expensive. Whether the difficulties of some cases should defeat justice in all is a literally moot point.

Material contribution to injury and risk of injury

The law doesn't always run scared from biological uncertainty. Sometimes it recognizes that defendants shouldn't always be able to shelter behind the statement 'This situation is terribly complex'—effectively getting a windfall from the sometimes banal simplicity of the 'but-for' test.

Take an industrial disease case. Over a working lifetime, during the course of his work for several employers, the claimant has inhaled noxious dust. Some employers were negligent in letting him inhale it; some were not. He gets a disabling lung disease, and seeks compensation. He sues the negligent employers. They respond: 'The but-for test applies. You cannot prove that but for our "guilty" dust you would not have the disease. Who knows exactly what the trigger was, or when the threshold was reached? The innocent dust might have triggered the disease.'

The law, generally, doesn't like this response. Most jurisdictions have developed a way of compensating a claimant in this position—often by saying that it is sufficient for a claimant to prove that the defendant's negligence has materially contributed to his injury (*Bailey v Ministry of Defence* (2009)). Sometimes it goes further, holding that, in some circumstances, a material increase in the risk of a condition will be enough (if the claimant has in fact developed that condition): *McGhee v National Coal Board* (1973).

Many situations in medical law are analogous to these industrial disease cases. A vulnerable brain might have been exposed to negligent and non-negligent periods of hypoxia, for instance. Or the state of medical knowledge might be such that the experts cannot say that a negligent act probably caused the injury, but are happy to say that it increased the risk of it. While the policy considerations that dictate caution in loss-of-chance cases make the courts wary of accepting analogies with industrial disease, the law in many places is evolving towards acceptance.

Consent cases

From the point of view of causation, consent cases might look easy. Suppose that a surgeon negligently fails to warn about the risks of a proposed operation. Had the patient been appropriately warned, she would not have consented to the operation. The operation goes ahead, and in the course of it, or afterwards, as a result of it, the patient suffers injury.

The but-for test has no problem with such a case. Whether or not the injuries were those about which the surgeon should have warned the patient, they wouldn't have occurred but for the negligence, and (subject to the rules about remoteness—see below) causation is usually established.

But wait a moment. Take the following case. Its facts are not unusual.

A patient goes to see a consultant spinal surgeon. She needs a laminectomy to decompress her spinal cord. The surgeon fails to warn her about a 1 per cent risk of urinary incontinence. She agrees to the operation. The operation is done entirely competently, but the 1 per cent risk eventuates, and the patient is left incontinent. She sues the surgeon. The court finds that had she been properly warned, she would have consented to the operation, but would have pondered for a bit before consenting, and accordingly would not have had the procedure on the day that she had it. Since the 1 per cent risk hovers over every patient undergoing the procedure (and just happened to alight on her when she in fact had the operation), a short delay would probably have meant that she avoided it. So: same surgeon, same counselling, same operation, same operating table, different day. Does she succeed? And if so, should she?

The but-for test, narrowly applied, says that she does and should. And indeed she did in a controversial English case: *Chester v Afshar* (2005) (although not simply on a 'but-for' basis). But many are outraged by this result. The connection between the surgeon's negligence and the damage suffered by the patient is mistily metaphysical.

There's a better way to see such cases. The patient did indeed suffer harm, but it was harm not to the nerves supplying her bladder, but to her right to be properly informed—her autonomy right. Violations of human rights, even when they don't involve physical harm, are routinely compensated.

Hypothetical causation

Very often clinical negligence claims involve omissions rather than acts. A clinician negligently fails to attend a patient, or fails to arrange a particular investigation. The court then has to determine what would have happened had the clinician attended or the investigation been performed. Usually these questions turn on the but-for test, or a gloss on that test along the lines of material contribution. But commonly things are more complicated.

An example. A paediatrician negligently fails to answer her bleep. As a result a baby suffers an episode of hypoxic brain damage which leaves it irreversibly disabled. The expert evidence is that the only intervention that would have prevented the damage would have been the immediate insertion of a tube into the baby's trachea. But the paediatrician says (and the court accepts) that, had she attended, she would not have intubated the baby. The court finds that a responsible body of paediatricians would not have intubated—in other words that it would not have been negligent for the paediatrician, had she come, to have failed to give the only treatment that would have prevented the injury.

Does the claimant succeed? In England, and many other places which hallow *Bolam*, she does not: see *Bolitho v City and Hackney Health Authority* (1998). The question is whether, but for the negligence, injury would have been avoided, and negligence is defined according to the *Bolam* test. The negligence here is causally irrelevant: nothing different would have happened had the doctor rushed diligently to the ward.

This is not the only way of looking at it. The pressure on the non-attending doctor to convince herself (and therefore the court) that she would not have given the only effective treatment must be intense. One might argue that the law should compensate for that pressure by assuming that the doctor would give effective treatment. That argument is easier in a jurisdiction that is not in thrall to *Bolam*. If *Bolam* rules absolutely in the law of breach of duty, it is hard to stop it holding sway over causation too.

Damage of a sort recognized by the law

There is a lot of negligence by doctors, but there are few clinical negligence cases. One of many important reasons for this is that most of the negligence doesn't cause loss of a type that the law thinks should be compensated: it is usually hurt feelings, upset, or inconvenience.

A patient goes into hospital for a corneal graft. After the operation the surgeon comes to see him on the ward. The good news, says the surgeon, is that the operation went very well, and the patient's sight will be restored. The bad news, however, is that the hospital's tissue bank has just told him that the cornea came from a patient who, many years before, had had syphilis. It's unfortunate that this wasn't picked up by the tissue bank: it should have been. But, the surgeon goes on, there's no need to worry. There is no case reported in the literature of anyone contracting syphilis this way, but just to be absolutely safe, the patient will be given a course of prophylactic antibiotics.

The patient walks out of hospital (for the first time in years not bumping into things as he does so), and sues the hospital.

But what's the loss? The patient doesn't have syphilis, and will never get it. He's just been rather shaken up by the whole experience of being told about the origin of the cornea. No psychiatrist will give that 'shaking up' the label of a recognized psychiatric illness.

In most jurisdictions this claim would fail. There's negligence, the negligence has caused *something*, but the something is not in one of the categories of compensable damage.

This isn't because upset, worry, and so on are too nebulous to be quantified. Pain, loss of amenity, and loss of reputation are no easier to value, but are routinely valued in the courts. Rather it is, again, policy. A minimum threshold of severity is arbitrarily imposed to stop the courts from being swamped by claims.

Assessing quantum

Compensation in negligence cases aims to put the claimant in the position in which she would have been had the defendant not been negligent. In a typical clinical negligence claim there are several elements.

'Pain, suffering, and loss of amenity' are valued by reference to published guidelines and reported cases. In England, for instance, quadriplegia was typically valued in 2013 between £255,000 and £317,500, and the loss of a leg below the knee at £177,000–£104,500.

Then there are the heads of claim that are, in theory, capable of more scientific quantification: loss of earnings, travel expenses, the cost of aids and appliances, and the cost of care. Life expectancy (assessed either in relation to the individual patient or, if the patient is likely to die at the time predicted by the actuaries, by reference to population mortality data) is used to calculate the number of years over which future loss will run—a number discounted to take account of presumptions about the amount of money that the sum of damages, invested, will yield. It's a laborious process.

Perhaps clinical negligence lawyers deserve their fees after all.

Chapter 7
Research on human subjects

The world looked at what Mengele and the other Nazi doctors had done, and said 'Never again.' In fact the Nazis were (as some of them pointed out in their subsequent trials) in a long, dishonourable, and well-established tradition of abusive medical research. J. Marion Sims, in the 1840s, repeatedly operated on unanesthetized slave women; Leo Stanley, in the first half of the 20th century, implanted pig, goat, and sheep testicles into prisoners; and countless patients in many countries were deliberately infected with deadly and disabling diseases in the name of science.

From Auschwitz, to Helsinki, to the African bush

The immediate response to the revelations from Auschwitz, Buchenwald, and elsewhere was the Nuremberg Code (1947), which declared that the consent of all participants to all research on them was essential, and the Declaration of Geneva (1948), which set out doctors' ethical duties towards their patients.

The Nuremberg Code gave way to the World Medical Association's Declaration of Helsinki (1964). This has gone through six revisions. The latest was in 2008. It has no legal force in itself, but has had profound influence on national and international research ethics and law. As we've seen, authoritative ethical guidance has a way of becoming actual or de facto medical law. Most countries have given at least a nod to the Declaration—or at least to some version of it—and so the best way of identifying the international legal consensus is to look at it.

It has done a lot to change the thoughtlessly utilitarian or downright callous ethos of pre-war medical research. But not enough. Mengele-esque abuses continued. In Tuskegee, Alabama (1932–72), syphilis patients were told that they were being treated for syphilis. They weren't, although they could have been. Many died; many fathered children with congenital syphilis. In Staten Island, until 1966, mentally disabled children were secretly infected with viral hepatitis. Until 1971, women attending a contraception clinic in San Antonio were given placebos instead of effective drugs, without their consent. There were several pregnancies. Between 1960 and 1971 the US Department of Defense and the Defense Atomic Support Agency funded whole-body irradiation experiments on non-consenting patients. A 1994 study showed that a drug called zidovudine was extremely effective in reducing mother–infant HIV transmission. Some subsequent trials withheld the drug from patients in Third World countries, while ensuring that US patients had it. And so it went on.

The Declaration, in its present form, emphasizes the importance of autonomy and informed consent, and insists that the subject's welfare outweighs the welfare of society or the march of science.

The Declaration is a well-meaning document. It's an honest attempt to protect the rights of individuals while at the same time acknowledging that scientific progress is crucial, and that a communitarian perspective sometimes makes sense. But it's hard to be philosophically consistent if you're that ambitious, and the Declaration isn't consistent. It's a patchwork quilt, not seamlessly woven from the yarn of one principle. That in itself isn't a criticism. Some of the best law is made from several philosophical materials. But since the Declaration does pay explicit lip service to autonomy, it's worth observing that it outlaws research on humans unless the importance of the objective outweighs the inherent risks and burdens to the subject (Article 21). That's a highly paternalistic restriction. If a pharmaceutical company wants to pay me a huge amount of money to participate in potentially dangerous research that might lead to the development of a new brand of shampoo, why shouldn't it be able to do so? Isn't my body my own (unless I choose to engage in rado-maroditic bondage: see Chapter 5)?

The Declaration has evolved very significantly through its many revisions. Many of the revisions have generated hot and anxious debate. Here's why.

Imagine that you're the head of a multinational pharmaceutical company. You have the patent for a very promising drug for the treatment of malaria. Malaria is very important. It kills millions each year, almost all of them in the poorer countries of the world. If the drug works, your share price and your bonus will rocket.

The efficacy of the drug needs to be established. That means clinical trials in hot, poor places.

The most scientifically satisfactory results (which would lead to the fastest acceptance of the drug by the market) would be obtained by trials in which a large cohort of infected patients in a remote part of Africa, all of whom need treatment, is divided into two. Half would receive the drug; half would receive a pharmacologically inert placebo. It would be a 'double blind' trial, in which neither the patients nor the administrators of the drug/placebo knew who was getting the drug and who the placebo.

But there's a problem. Patients receiving the placebo are likely to die. That's a shame. It's also avoidable. There are already drugs available which would stop them dying.

What should be done?

The answer's not obvious. If this trial is vetoed on the grounds that it's unethical, no one at all will get treatment. Many of them will die. Certainly (if the drug is as good as it is thought to be), more will die than would die if the trial happened. Wouldn't the potential participants prefer a 50 per cent chance of salvation to a 0 per cent chance? And, since the alternative trial methods, not involving the ethically dubious placebo group, won't produce such a clear result, there will be a longer delay before the drug is commercially available—so leading to the loss of more lives.

If those essentially utilitarian arguments hold water, is there anything to be said against entirely non-consensual research on the same cohorts? Every participant might think that they're receiving, say, a free drink of lemonade, but in fact they're getting either the drug or the placebo. The science would be good, lives would be saved. What's the problem?

I don't seek to adjudicate. The Declaration is unhappy about either version of the malaria trial. It disapproves of placebo-controlled trials except where there is no intervention that is known to work, or where, for 'compelling and scientifically good methodological reasons', a placebo control is necessary and patients who receive a placebo or no treatment will not be subject to any risk of serious or irreversible harm (Article 32). The Declaration cautions that '[e]xtreme care must be taken to avoid abuse of this option'. The US Food and Drug Administration has refused to be bound by these limitations—essentially on the grounds that they hamstring science, which isn't in the world's ultimate interest.

Subsequent revisions sought to meet these concerns by providing that research is only justified if there is a reasonable likelihood that the 'population or community' in which the research is carried out stands to benefit from the results of the research (Article 17), and that when a study is completed participants should be provided with whatever the study has shown to be the best thing for their situation (Article 33).

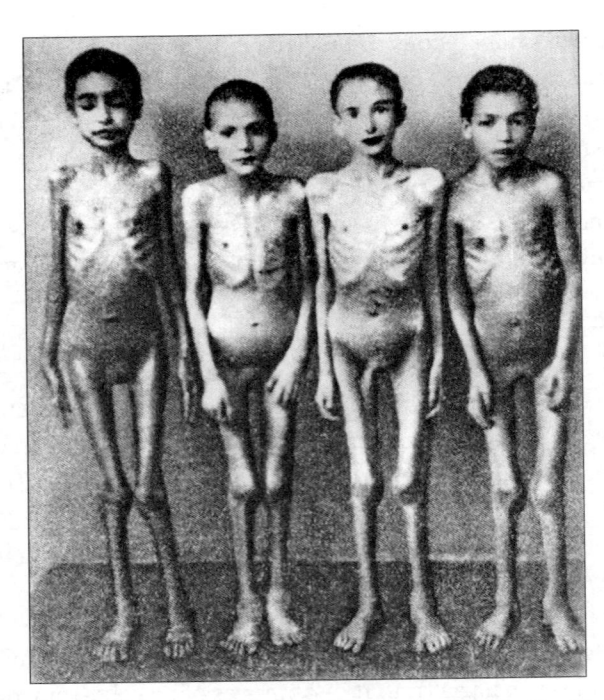

6. Twins at Auschwitz, used for medical experiments by the Nazi doctor Josef Mengele. The horrors of the Nazi regime have had a profound influence on modern attitudes towards experiments on humans

When the only hope is in the Unknown

The Declaration is rightly conservative. It talks a lot about the proper communication of risks to research subjects. Usually, when a trial of a novel product begins, there will be *some* evidence to suggest that it will work. But that's not always so: there's still some genuine pharmacological mystery in the world.

A drug company has been working for years on a new drug for colon cancer. The drug has done exciting things in mice. It shrinks their metastases to nothing, bringing them back from the grave. But then we're not mice, or not necessarily so. The next step is to test it in humans. But the pharmacologists are worried: it might cure, but it might kill or maim. Can it be tested? Or must the clinical trial go on hold unless and until the researchers can show that the risk of death or serious injury is as low as you'd expect it to be in a trial of healthy volunteers?

The Declaration is pragmatic. We'd want it to be. If the options are certain death from cancer or a 50 per cent chance of cure associated with a 50 per cent chance of death, many would unhesitatingly opt for the potential magic bullet. The Declaration deals specifically with this situation (Article 35), although it hardly needs to do so. It says that the trial can be done. The other Articles, taken together, produce the same result. Mix informed consent with the principle that the inherent risks should be outweighed by the importance of the research, add the centrality of the individual research subject, and you've got Article 35. If the subject will die anyway if you don't give the magic bullet, the Declaration isn't offended if the magic bullet ends up going through the roof of the subject's mouth.

When should you stop?

You start your malaria study. The wonder drug works wonderfully—so wonderfully that it is very quickly clear that it's better than the competition. You're going to earn a lot of money from it, and so you're anxious to rush it onto the market. But too much rush is a bad idea. To annihilate the competition you want to continue the study for a little longer. Then the statistics buttressing your product will be unassailable.

But again, there's a problem. To continue the study in these circumstances might mean even more robust science (you'll prove your case to an extreme level of probability), but it also means more deaths. People in the control group will die in order to refine your scientific (and hence commercial) case. Is it worth it?

The Declaration (Article 20) demands that a study is stopped immediately when 'the risks are found to outweigh the potential benefits or when there is conclusive proof of positive and beneficial results'. This, of course, begs many questions. When, statistically, can one say that the risks outweigh the potential benefits? When does proof of a positive result become 'conclusive'? The Declaration gives no guidance. Presumably if this issue were to be litigated by people who had been harmed by or failed to benefit from a trial, it would turn on the relevant domestic law. Was it, for instance, *Bolam*-negligent to fail to stop the trial at a particular time? In theory such issues will have been decided in advance and built into the diligently vetted trial design. But it's not always so.

Children and incompetent adults

The spectre of experimentation on people who cannot validly give or refuse consent is terrifying. The Declaration seeks to exorcise it by tight controls. Such potential subjects cannot be used (my word, designed to raise Kantian hackles) in a research study that has no likelihood of benefiting them personally, unless it's intended to promote the health of the population from which the subject comes (say children, or adult patients with Down syndrome), the research can't be done with competent subjects, the study entails only minimal risk and burden, and informed consent has been obtained from the relevant proxy decision-maker, where one exists (Article 27).

What happens, though, where the test for lawful proxy consent is the 'best interests' of the individual patient, and there's no conceivable benefit to the individual subject? This is very common indeed. Take studies of normal child physiology, for instance. Typically blood samples will be taken. That poses only minimal risk, but it's uncomfortable, and confers no benefit whatever to the screaming child. To say that participation is in the child's best interests is to take an unfashionably wide, communitarian view of 'best interests'. The result has been massive under-testing of products for use in children. Many of the drugs used routinely in paediatric medicine are, for this reason, not specifically licensed for use in children. The studies that would be necessary to get the regulator's rubber stamp haven't been thought to be ethically or legally appropriate.

Payment

Everyone has seen adverts for medical research participants. Depending on the country, they might say 'Remuneration of expenses', or, more brazenly, 'Generous compensation for your time and trouble'. But everyone knows what's being offered. Money is given as an inducement to allow bodies to be experimented on. And people are induced.

The Declaration itself is silent about the payment of money to research subjects. It contents itself with saying that researchers must ensure that consent is real. There are many things that might taint the reality of consent. Money is one of them, says the orthodoxy. That orthodoxy is embodied in many local protocols, which typically insist that payment is restricted to the reimbursement of expenses and compensation for the time taken. Those protocols are ignored. The law, whose main concern is coercion of a darker kind, turns a Nelsonian blind eye. Across the world there's payment for participation. Research on healthy volunteers would stop if there weren't. There aren't enough genuine altruists out there, happy, just for the love of science and their fellow men, to give up their afternoons and their blood.

There's nothing offensive about this pragmatism. The relationship between money and voluntariness is too complex to be summarized in one or even many paragraphs of a code. Most people wouldn't go to work if they weren't paid, and yet rarely is it suggested that there should be laws to stop them working. Workers in dangerous occupations tend to get paid more: again it is rarely suggested that compensation for risks is contrary to public policy.

Project review and the outlawing of mavericks

The amateurish, ad hoc 'let's-start-it-and-see-how-it-goes' maverick is dead. Or dead-ish. The Declaration has certainly done its best to see him off. It seeks to entrench its own principles by demanding that research is done systematically and thoughtfully, with due regard to the ethical issues at stake. Its main entrenching tool is the research ethics committee, to which a research protocol must be submitted, by which the protocol must be approved, and which has the right to monitor the progress of the research.

Each country has a slightly different way of arranging this regulatory oversight. All too often the policemen of the ad hoc and amateurish are ad hoc and amateurish themselves—sometimes failing to understand the science they are supposed to be regulating, sometimes too cavalier about the ethics. Perhaps the real problem is a crisis of identity: they don't know what they are meant to be. Are they meant to be the eyes and conscience of the public? Or the guardian of the rights of the research subjects? Is there a difference between these functions? How should the interests of researchers and potential beneficiaries be represented? Does a committee discharge its function if it goes through a thorough, transparent, and consistent procedure, or is there a notional 'right answer' to each problem it faces? There is no consistency within nations, let alone worldwide, about these central questions. It's not surprising that academic and political observers of the committees haven't been deafening in their applause.

Perhaps the most embattled committees are the Institutional Review Boards (IRBs) in the US, and the most damaging criticisms levelled against them are of conflicts of interest. Many have spent a lot of time in bed with big pharmaceutical and medical device manufacturers, and have come away with some nasty ethical diseases. A 2006 study of IRB members at university medical centres showed that over a third rarely or never disclosed their conflicts of interests to other members of the IRB, and over a third had financial ties to relevant industries. The US government has promised to clean up the IRBs. It remains to be seen how successful it is.

Chapter 8
Resource allocation

There is an infinite amount of suffering in the world. There is a distinctly finite amount of resources to deal with it. How do we decide who gets what? The dilemmas are agonizing. One man's treatment is another man's denial of treatment. To save X is to condemn Y.

Medical creativity has made the problem worse. If the options available to doctors were now what they were 100 years ago, we would stand a reasonable chance of being able to give everyone the treatment available. But so much more can now be done. Each new advance generates a new moral dilemma.

Each dilemma is politically explosive. Should life-saving and life-enhancing innovation be available only to the rich who can afford to pay for it themselves? If there's a state health service, should the government say frankly: 'We'll provide the basics. If you want anything exotic, you'd better go private'? Or should it say instead: 'We can't give everyone everything for free, but to show that we're true democrats, we'll give some patients the world-class, cutting-edge treatment'? But if so, which patients? And if the obligation is to provide the basics, what are those basics?

We tend to look at these problems through exclusively western, or at least narrowly national, eyes. About 40,000 children died today of hunger. Tens of thousands more died of malaria, and tens of thousands more of waterborne infectious diseases. Almost all of these were preventable. The money spent on a few heart transplants in elderly westerners would have saved almost all those lives.

Who'd get involved in all this if they could possibly help it? Well, not the judges. They've made that very clear. Wherever in the world an advocate stands up to suggest that health-care resources have been deployed unlawfully, there's a sharp intake of judicial breath, followed by the noise of Pilatian hand-washing. When the courts are pressed to give reasons for their non-intervention they come over all democratic, insisting that interfering with health-care resource allocation policy would be to usurp unacceptably the function of the legislature, or, where the question is whether a particular treatment should be provided to A rather than B, that this turns on clinical judgement, and accordingly it would be inappropriate to interfere.

They are not consistently deferential, of course. Legislative decisions are often pre-empted or struck down in the course of judicial review—usually by reference to a constitution or a set of human rights principles. And in many jurisdictions that bulwark of judicial deference to clinical opinion, the *Bolam* test, has been demolished or eroded. Judicial reluctance to say 'Yes' or 'No' to life-sustaining treatment has more to do with human reluctance to make hard decisions than with legal principle. Judges want to be able to sleep at night. And who can blame them?

The people who do blame them are the desperate litigants.

There are few more desperate than the parents of 10-year-old 'Child B'. She suffered from leukaemia. The prognosis didn't look good, but there was one possible treatment, which had a 20 per cent chance of success. The health authority refused to fund it, and the parents challenged that refusal in the English Court of Appeal. They failed. Unless the authority could be shown to have acted irrationally in its decisions about resource allocation, the court could not interfere (*R v Cambridge Health Authority ex p B* (1995)).

That's how it works in most places in the world.

It's hard to be irrational. Most claims of irrationality in the arena of health-care funding are framed not as an outright assault on the outcome (such assaults are generally hopeless), but as attacks on the decision-making process. Suppose that an authority decides not to fund gender reassignment surgery for transsexuals. If its reason is simply that it thinks it is more important to buy kidney dialysis machines for the money that it would otherwise spend on the surgery, the decision is likely to be unimpeachable. But if the same decision is reached because the authority thinks

7. Patients in an African clinic wait for treatment. In every country medical needs outstrip medical resources, creating agonizing dilemmas about which the law has to take a view

that, as a matter of public policy, sex change ought to be discouraged, the outcome might be very different.

Discrimination itself isn't unlawful. It's essential. The law simply requires discrimination to be transparent and reasonable. In most jurisdictions, for instance, it wouldn't be unlawful to deny cardiac bypass surgery to smokers as long as the decision was justified carefully. The justification wouldn't be hard. The success rate for the surgery is significantly lower for smokers. Put another way (the utilitarian way beloved of hospital accountants), you get fewer Quality Adjusted Life Years per dollar when you spend your dollars on smokers. The surgery is not good value for money.

Human rights legislation has had surprisingly little impact on the law of health-care resource allocation. One might have thought that, in countries that apply the European Convention on Human Rights, Article 2 (which imposes a liability on states to institute measures to protect life), Article 3 (which prohibits inhuman and degrading treatment), and Article 8 (which, broadly, protects autonomy and gives people a qualified right to live their lives as they wish) might have made decisions about health-care funding rather more justiciable. But it hasn't happened.

Article 14 prohibits discrimination in the way that the other Convention rights are recognized or effected, but it's hard to point to a case where Article 14 would give a claimant a remedy but the domestic law would not. The transsexuals whose surgery had been denied on the basis of public policy would be able to frame their claim in terms of Article 14, but why bother? In most western countries discrimination of that sort is irrational and unlawful without Article 14's help. Some countries, of course, aren't so enlightened, and would endorse a public policy of discrimination. But although the Article 14 challenge might succeed against them in the European Court of Human Rights, the victory would be a pyrrhic one. The errant country would just be less candid in future about its reasons for denying the surgery.

So much for policymaking. What about decisions about individual patient care?

A patient in permanent vegetative state (PVS) lies on the ward, being fed through a nasogastric tube. If the diagnosis is right, by definition she does not get, and cannot ever get, anything at all out of life (although her family may get some comfort from visiting her). It's very expensive to keep her there. She might lie there for years. Her existence is killing and disabling lots of perfectly salvageable patients. She is, in particular, a lethal parasite on the patient in the bed next to her. That patient, a 35-year-old mother of four, has an entirely curable type of cancer. But the hospital doesn't have the money to pay for the necessary drugs.

Should one kill the PVS parasite (who many would say was really dead already) so that the mother can live? Well, perhaps. But the law in most jurisdictions—with a wary eye on the consequences of saying that one human life is worth more than another—will not say so. Indeed the UK House of Lords, in *Airedale NHS Trust v Bland* (1993), said that in deciding whether to withdraw life-sustaining treatment from the PVS patient, it was illegitimate to take into account the funds that would be released to treat others. Most other countries agree.

Let's examine that. It's lawful to have in place a policy that says that one will treat a class of patient with condition X, but not one with condition Y. It's lawful for the clinicians on the ward with the PVS and the cancer patient to decide on clinical grounds to maintain the PVS patient but not the cancer patient, or even to say to the cancer patient: 'Sorry. We've run out of money in this year's budget. You'll have to die.' If the cancer patient says to a court: 'It's irrational to condemn me and save the PVS patient,' she'll get short shrift. The court won't interfere.

Some judges are unhappy with this abdication of responsibility. Judges are, after all, paid to judge. They already make awesome decisions about the withdrawal of life-sustaining treatment; they sometimes (for instance in cases involving the separation of conjoined twins, where the separation will kill one but save the other) weigh one life against another (although they typically protest, unconvincingly, that that's not what they're doing). Hospital funding committees have to take decisions about whom to treat and whom to deny. They don't do that with the benefit of much more information or skill than a judge could, with the help of expert evidence, bring to bear on the same questions. Individual clinicians no doubt take financial considerations into account when deciding whether to treat X rather than Y—it's just that the law as it presently stands requires them to deny they're doing it. If clinicians can do it, why can't judges? And wouldn't it be healthier if clinicians were encouraged to be honest about the basis of their decisions?

The problem, of course, is not just a lack of judicial will or expertise. It's not, either, that it would be hard to devise a system of substantive law that did the job. The real problem is the old one of the floodgates. Make it too easy to challenge funding decisions, and the courts would be swamped by patients and their relatives scrabbling for the money. Very often the substantive law is shaped by practical considerations: health-care resource allocation is a classic example.

Chapter 9
The end of life

A terminally ill patient lies in a hospital bed. A doctor comes in and stands beside her bed. He draws the curtain around, so that no one can see what he's doing. He takes an instrument out of the bag he's holding. He does something to the patient using the instrument. Whatever he does causes the patient to die.

What should the law do?

The answer, of course, is that it depends on many, many things. Lots of crucial information is missing.

We'd need to know where the hospital was. If this is a case of euthanasia or assisted suicide, there are some juridictions where it would not be unlawful. If it was euthanasia, and took place somewhere where euthanasia was lawful, we'd need to know whether the procedures prescribed by the euthanasia law had been followed. Those procedures might include certification by independent practitioners that the patient was terminally ill within the meaning of the relevant law; that the patient had voluntarily requested euthanasia, having been fully informed of the prognostic and palliative facts; that there was no undue influence on the patient from relatives or carers; that there had been a 'cooling-off' period since the request for euthanasia; that the request was signed and duly witnessed; and so on.

We'd want to know what instrument the doctor used. If it was a syringe, and he'd given an injection that caused death, we'd want to know what was in the syringe. If it was potassium chloride, we'd probably want to call the police. A bolus of potassium chloride stops the heart immediately. It has no therapeutic use at all, unless you think that death is a type of healing. But even if the agent were potassium chloride, we couldn't immediately conclude that the doctor was guilty of murder (which is killing someone, intending to kill them or to cause them serious bodily harm). The doctor might have injected the drug thinking that it was something benign. In that case we'd be thinking about gross negligence manslaughter, and we'd have to ask questions such as: Did the doctor draw up the drug himself? And if so did he check the ampoule sufficiently carefully? (It sounds as if we'd have trouble establishing that.) Was he handed the syringe, ready filled, by a nurse? If so, does the law say that it's fine for him to assume that the nurse will have done her job properly, or is it grossly negligent (or merely negligent) to have delegated that duty? If the nurse handed him a syringe full of potassium chloride knowing that he would inject it into the patient with fatal consequences, is *she* guilty of murder?

If the syringe was full of morphine, some of the same questions would be asked, but there might, depending on the dose and the patient's condition and clinical history, be some others. The doctor might be able to take refuge in the doctrine of double effect, which distinguishes between intention and foresight, saying that if you do an action with intention A, but knowing that B might happen too, then you may be able to escape criminal liability for B.

Here, if the doctor injected morphine with the intention of relieving the patient's pain, but knowing that the dose required for proper pain relief might tip the patient into the grave, he would not be guilty of murder.

Perhaps, though, the instrument that the doctor took out of his bag was simply a pair of scissors. Perhaps he had used them to cut the tape around a tracheostomy tube that connected the patient to the ventilator that was keeping her alive. Perhaps the doctor had then removed the tube, causing the patient to die.

Those facts would generate a host of other questions. Some we've met already. This might be murder or gross negligence manslaughter. It may be, though, that the doctor might have been guilty of assault if he had *not* removed the tube. The patient might have been entirely mentally capacitous, and might have insisted on the removal. Or the patient might have been incapacitous, but she might have made a binding advance directive (living will), saying that if she got into the state that she was in when the doctor arrived, she wanted to refuse all life-sustaining treatment. It may be that the doctor was withdrawing the feeding tube that was keeping her unlawfully alive, or the catheter through which she was getting the antibiotics that were staving off the deadly bacteria that, were she capacitous, she would see as her merciful friends.

In short, death is a complicated business. Even saying what it is is difficult.

The definition of death

The heart of a hanged person sometimes continues to beat for 20 minutes after the plunge through the trapdoor. Some cells can continue to function for a long time after the body of which they are a part has ceased to ventilate them and pump blood. We all die slowly and incrementally.

Some injuries can wipe out a person's cerebral cortex. The person will never again be capable of pain, pleasure, communication, or any other sensation. Their relatives often talk about them as if they were dead. And yet the patient's heart will be beating and their chest rising and falling as they breathe unaided. Is there anything wrong about burying such a patient?

The law has two broad concerns. It wants to ensure that people are irrevocably dead before they are buried, cremated, or their vital organs are harvested for donation. And it wants to protect the sensibilities of relatives and friends. However biologically certain it is that a person will never recover, the traumatized family is unlikely to be happy about shovelling earth onto a heaving chest.

The brain stem—the evolutionarily ancient, vegetative part of the brain—contains, among other things, the respiratory centres which drive ventilation. If the brain stem is knocked out, not only is it immensely unlikely that there will be any higher cortical function (making many people unwilling to distinguish between brain-stem death and whole-brain death), but unaided respiratory function is also impossible. The heart may, however, continue beating for a while. If the patient is ventilated, it may continue to beat for a long time.

There are undoubted advantages in adopting a definition of death based only on demonstration of brain-stem death. It may mean, for instance, that organs can be taken from a patient when they are still being perfused by the patient's own beating heart, and when the organs are therefore in optimal condition for transplantation. It may mean that resources are not spent ventilating a patient who is certainly doomed and who has no conceivable interest in remaining, in a narrow, biological sense, alive.

These are the sort of considerations that have led the UK, amongst many other jurisdictions, to adopt a definition of death based on brain-stem death. The protocols to be followed in reaching the diagnosis of death are tightly controlled. They always involve demonstration of a patient's inability to breathe spontaneously, and may be supplemented by other investigations such as cerebral angiograms.

The difficulty with legislating in this area is that legislation has to cover all possible cases. We've already noted that the heart of a brain-stem-dead patient on a ventilator may beat happily for a long time. Legislators, therefore, have tended to hedge their bets. The US Uniform Determination of Death Act 1980 provides, for instance, that a dead person is one who has sustained irreversible cessation of either 'circulatory and respiratory function' or 'all functions of the entire brain, including the brain stem'.

Deadly acts and deadly omissions

At the heart of much legal thinking about death and dying is the distinction between acts and omissions.

Tony Bland was crushed in a football stadium. Much of his cerebral cortex was wiped out. He went into a persistent vegetative state (PVS). He was insensate, and always would be. He knew nothing of the devoted relatives who, for years, came to sit beside him in hospital. His heart worked, he could breathe, and he had a functioning gut. But that was about the limit of his life. He was kept alive by being fed and hydrated through a tube.

Eventually his family decided that enough was enough. It was time to acknowledge that the Tony they loved had gone. His doctors agreed. The best way to deal with this, they all decided, was to withdraw his feeding tube. Deprived of food and fluids he would soon be dead. By definition, if the diagnosis of PVS was right, he would have no idea what was happening to him.

But there was a problem. If the withdrawal of food and fluids amounted to an act, it would be an act done with the intention of causing death. If it in fact caused death, his doctors would be guilty of murder. If, instead of pulling out a feeding tube, they, with identical intent, pressed the plunger of a syringe containing a lethal drug, they would certainly be guilty of murder. What was the difference?

The difference, said the UK House of Lords (*Airedale NHS Trust v Bland* (1993)), was that the withdrawal of food and fluids was an omission.

This has caused lots of brow-furrowing. It doesn't take much legal sleight of hand to transform an act into an omission and vice versa. If I starve a child to death by refusing to feed it, I should expect a frosty reception to my submission at my murder trial that I was only omitting to do something. And there are various thought experiments devised by philosophers that seek to indicate that there is no distinction of substance between acts and omissions. Perhaps the most famous is the 'Trolley problem': perhaps the most accessible is the story of the two wicked uncles.

Uncle A stands to gain a huge inheritance if baby C dies. He offers to bath the baby. He pushes its head under the water. It drowns. He is guilty of murder.

Uncle B, too, will be massively enriched by baby C's death. He too gives the baby its bath. Just as he is reaching out his hand to push C's head beneath the water, C accidentally knocks her own head on the side of the bath and sinks beneath the water. It would require no effort at all for B to raise C's head and save her. But of course he's delighted by this windfall. He stands and watches, rubbing his avaricious hands, as C drowns.

In most jurisdictions B will have committed no criminal offence at all. A few jurisdictions impose a duty of rescue in these circumstances, but they don't regard failure to rescue as murder. And yet the action of Uncle A is ethically identical to the omission of Uncle B. Isn't the law being absurd in failing to acknowledge it?

Well, possibly. But many feel that, however many anomalies can be pointed out by imaginative philosophers, there is a distinction of great emotional weight and intellectual utility between acts and omissions. One of the uses was demonstrated in *Bland*:

well-meaning doctors don't get locked up for refusing to continue pointless treatment.

Murder, euthanasia, and assisted suicide

If you went into a bar and injected a fatal dose of a drug into someone, intending to kill them or to do them really serious harm, you'd be guilty, wherever you were in the world, of murder. Note, importantly, that motive and intention are different. Many people commit murders with compassionate motives. The classic example is the 'mercy killer' who, wishing to spare his wife more agony, puts a pillow over her face and suffocates her. His motives are love and mercy: his intention is to kill.

Lilian Boyes suffered for many years from rheumatoid arthritis. It became increasingly agonizing. She howled like a dog when she was touched. Palliative options were exhausted. She repeatedly begged her physician, Dr Cox, to put her out of her misery. He repeatedly refused. There were no doubts about her mental capacity. She continued to beg and to howl. At last Dr Cox gave her a lethal injection. He wrote up in her medical notes what he had done. A nurse contacted the police, and Dr Cox was tried for attempted murder (an attempt rather than the completed offence, notionally because the prosecution could not prove definitively that the injection was the cause of the death—it was theoretically possible that she had died of an entirely unrelated arrhythmia just as the plunger was pressed—but more likely because the prosecution realized that a jury would be more likely to convict of attempted murder since a murder conviction carries a mandatory life sentence in the UK). The case was indefensible. The law was clear. He was legally indistinguishable from the husband with the pillow, and was duly convicted. His benign motive was reflected in his sentence—a short and wholly suspended sentence of imprisonment: see *R v Cox* (1992).

All of us surely have sympathy both for Lilian Boyes and for Dr Cox. The question is whether that sympathy is a good reason for a change in the law of murder.

Proponents of the legalization of euthanasia tend to use two strands of argument. First, they contend that compassion makes euthanasia morally mandatory. We wouldn't let our dog continue to scream for years with uncontrolled pain: we'd take it to the vet to be put down. Why should we deny to humans what basic decency makes us do to our dogs? And second, they emphasize autonomy. Our lives are our own, they say. We can decide what to do with them. If we choose to end them, that's our business.

The opponents of a change in the law are often, but by no means always, motivated by a belief in the sanctity of life which is often rooted in the notion of the Imago Dei—the idea that God's image is stamped on all humans, and that to take life is to efface that image. They are typically suspicious about the primacy of autonomy, suggesting that it is not the only principle in play. They note that the exercise of X's autonomy necessarily affects the life (and the exercise of the autonomy) of Y. A special and important example of this is the asserted slippery slope from voluntary euthanasia to involuntary euthanasia (the killing of a patient who has not consented to it, or not consented to it when in possession of all the relevant facts, or who has consented to it under some sort of duress from relatives or carers, or who simply feels that their continued existence is a burden to others).

Whether this slippery slope exists in jurisdictions where euthanasia is lawful, and if so whether any block can be placed on it to stop practice sliding disastrously all the way down to the bottom, are matters of intense debate. It is probably true that capacity-truncating depression is a common and under-diagnosed condition in patients who ask for euthanasia. This means that there is reason to wonder about the validity of the consent they give, and reason to wonder whether, if their depression were treated, the desire for death would recede. But it does not necessarily mean that no sufficient safeguards can be put in place to relegate these concerns to the status of mere slogan.

If autonomy is the sole arbiter of action, say the opponents of euthanasia, why restrict the right to die to terminally ill patients (as is usually the case in those jurisdictions where euthanasia is permissible)? Why not allow a tired, bored person to drop in at a euthanasia booth on the way home? They assume, in this argument, that this will be unthinkable.

The proponents of euthanasia have three responses. First, and most radically: 'Why not indeed? But sadly society's not yet mature enough for such a dramatically enlightened step.' Second, and often bolted on to the first: 'That's not the law we're asking for at the moment, so don't introduce irrelevancies.' And third, and more disarmingly: 'There may be real concerns about whether a request from a physically well person is made with full capacity. Autonomy would therefore be suspicious of the booth.'

Another argument from the opponents is based on the role of doctors, who would be doing the killing. If we say for the sake of argument that X has a right to be killed when, where, and in the circumstances that they wish, should that imply that X can say to Y: 'You must kill me, whether you want to or not?' If Y is society, perhaps this demand is not so offensive. If Y is a person, or perhaps even a profession, it becomes more tricky. And ultimately it is a profession, and a person within a profession, who has to do the killing.

Individual doctors, whatever their broader views on euthanasia, have tended to express distaste for doing the killing themselves. The medical profession in many countries, concerned about what euthanasia laws would do for the doctor–patient relationship, has been slow to endorse those laws. But this is not always the case: it is hard to make useful generalizations, particularly since so few countries have experience of euthanasia.

Significantly absent from the ranks of pro-euthanasia doctors are palliative-care physicians—those who deal with the reduction of pain and distress at the end of life. Their stance has tended to be that euthanasia is never necessary: that modern palliative care enables a good death for all. Even in the very rare cases where satisfactory analgesia is impossible, one can always sedate to unconsciousness—effectively anaesthetizing the patient until she dies.

The pro-euthanasists respond that good palliative care isn't available to everyone, and that it is absurd and intellectually dishonest to say that there's an ethical difference between ablating someone's consciousness permanently by anaesthesia and ablating it permanently by causing their death.

And so it rumbles on.

Assisted suicide is a close ally of euthanasia. But there are some important differences.

Most jurisdictions do not now make it an offence for a person to attempt to commit suicide. There are compelling reasons for this. Pressure for change came from doctors who noted that being the principal prosecution witness against a patient they had successfully pumped out was unlikely to help the therapeutic relationship with that patient. Often, however (for instance in the UK and many US states), it is an offence for someone to help someone commit suicide.

Assisting suicide of course covers a multitude of legal sins. Some are downright evil. Take, for instance, a recent UK case where the defendant persuaded his girlfriend that she was worthless, demon-possessed, and better off dead. She eventually believed him, drank the bottle of vodka he'd handed her to give her Dutch

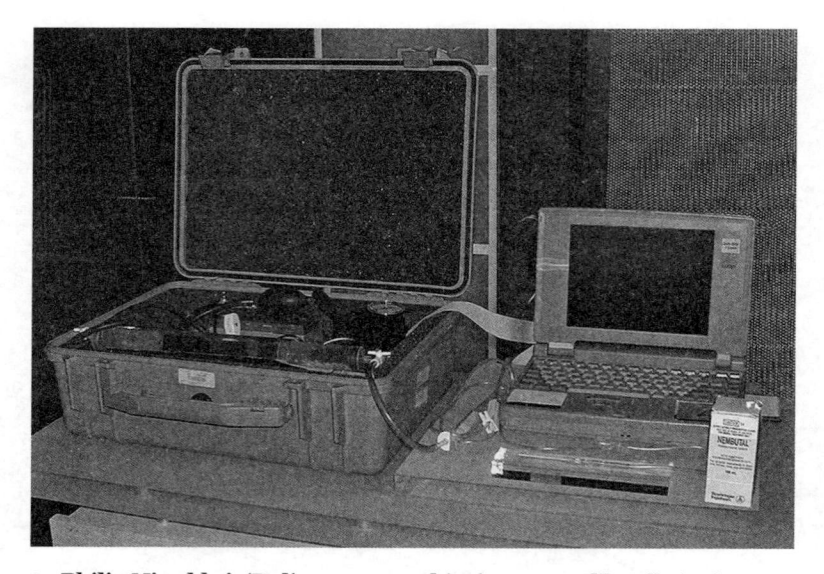

8. Philip Nitschke's 'Deliverance machine', once used legally in the Northern Territories of Australia. If the patient answered correctly a series of questions posed by a computer, a lethal dose of barbiturates was automatically injected

courage, and, at his encouragement, jumped off a bridge. Some are motivated simply by compassion. Some sort of legal control of assisted suicide seems appropriate, but so does a good deal of prosecutorial discretion.

Any sensible law permitting assisted suicide will, as all jurisdictions that have such laws recognize, need robust safeguards to ensure that requests for suicide are made voluntarily, without coercion, and in full knowledge and understanding of the relevant facts.

Withholding and withdrawing life-sustaining treatment

Ms B had a bleed into her cervical spinal cord. It paralysed her from the neck down. She couldn't breathe for herself: a ventilator had to do it for her.

She found her life unbearable. She asked her clinicians to turn off the ventilator and let her die. They refused. They were very fond of her, and they thought her life was worth living.

She took them to court, asking the court for an order that her continued ventilation was unlawful.

The only issue for the court was whether she was mentally competent to make the decision—whether she had the cognitive apparatus to understand what she was asking for—and whether she was properly informed. She was competent, and so the ventilation constituted an assault. The UK NHS body in charge of her care (as opposed to the doctors who had expressed their reluctance) was ordered to stop the ventilator and let her die: *B v An NHS Trust* (2002).

This was not a suicide or an act of euthanasia. It was a natural death. What killed Ms B was not the flick of the ventilator switch, but the bleed and the consequential respiratory paralysis. The case illustrates a principle respected in all jurisdictions: competent adults can decline even life-sustaining treatment. The alternative would be a frightening paternalism. For US examples, see *Satz v Perlmutter* (1978), *McKay v Bergstedt* (1990), and *Georgia v McAfee* (1989).

It is much more difficult with incapacitous patients.

A 45-year-old man is involved in a catastrophic accident. Like Tony Bland, he is in PVS. He has no sensation, nor will he ever have again, but he normally needs no active medical care other than tube feeding. He gets a chest infection. A five-day course of oral antibiotics would cure it. If it is not treated it will kill him. What should be done?

There are four common legal strategies.

Substituted judgement

Here, the decision-maker seeks to make the same judgement that have been made by the incapacitous patient were that patient not incapacitous. This will involve an inquiry into the patient's wishes and values.

This is a common approach in the US, but many states have recourse to the best interests strategy if the views of the patient cannot be determined with sufficient certainty.

The substituted judgement approach sounds good: its rhetoric is straightforward patient autonomy. But patients' supposed views are often inaccessible, or can be determined only by looking through the possibly jaundiced eyes of those, such as relatives or carers, who may have a stake in the patient's death. Few of us are articulately philosophical when it comes to considering how we'd like to die, and even fewer of us have the medical knowledge necessary to tailor our utterances closely to the clinical circumstances in which we are likely to approach death. There are, too, plenty of studies showing that, when we find ourselves in the medical situation that, when healthy, we feared most terribly, we find our lives much more valuable and bearable than we thought we would. I doubt that most of us factor that literature into those depressing end-of-life conversations we have in the early hours—precisely the sort of conversations that are likely to take centre stage in a determination of substituted judgement.

Substituted judgement, of course, can have no place in making decisions on behalf of people who have never been able to make or express decisions on their own behalf (for instance children or people who have never had capacity). Since most of us are more or less incompetent and inarticulate, and do not record our views reliably, it seems strange to say that there's such a rigid division between the technically incompetent and others that a wholly different test should be applied to each.

Best interests

The test used, for example, in the UK, is the best interests test, whereby an action or inaction will be lawful if it is in the best interests of the patient. 'Best interests' are considered holistically: they are not a mere audit of the 'medical best interests'.

In theory this is an objective test: something either is or is not, as a matter of fact, in someone's best interests.

In PVS cases judges have struggled (notoriously in *Bland*) with the question of whether a permanently, irretrievably unconscious patient has any interests at all, but surely such a patient does: he would want, for instance, to be remembered well. A PVS patient is not a mere piece of meat on a slab. Suppose it were proposed that medical students practised rectal examinations on a PVS patient. Would that be right? It would not, and that is because the patient has residual interests (perhaps best described as dignity interests, protected in Europe under, I suggest, Articles 8 and/or 3 of the European Convention on Human Rights) which can still be violated. You don't have to be cognate to be human or to be abused.

In practice, best interests determinations are often infused with substituted judgement. The English Mental Capacity Act 2005, for instance, requires a decision-maker to consider, when deciding where someone's best interests lie, any previous expressions of opinion by the patient. It's assumed, therefore, that it may not be in the best interests of a patient to be dealt with in a way with which they've previously indicated they'd be unhappy.

The courts often encourage a 'balance sheet' approach. They conduct an audit of the patient's life, listing in one column the factors in favour of continued existence, and in the other the factors in favour of death. Obviously not all factors have the same weight: judgement has to be applied. But once the factors are appropriately weighted, one theoretically adds up each column. The column with the highest score wins, and the judicial thumb is turned up or down accordingly.

This sounds easier and more scientific than it is. 'Best interests' are notoriously elusive. Sometimes (and particularly where the patient is very young and very disabled—perhaps even unable to manifest, by vocalization or facial expression, signs of pain or pleasure), it may be necessary for the law to make certain presumptions. One important presumption is the presumption in favour of continued existence. If you choose, you can call it a foundational respect for the sanctity of life. It has a long and distinguished lineage. It is crucially important in deciding how the various factors in the best interests audit are weighted. It is often decisive. But it can be (and often is) displaced.

Proxy decision-making

Sometimes people appoint someone to make decisions for them. This is typically done by a durable or lasting power of attorney. Often (for instance in many US states and in the UK), a power of attorney entitling the attorney to decline even life-saving or life-sustaining treatment on behalf of a patient has to comply with particular formalities that may not apply to more general powers of attorney.

Parents typically make proxy decisions for their children, of course. And that includes treatment decisions. But parental views are best regarded as an aid to determining where the child's best interests lie. They're a very helpful aid: so helpful, indeed, that they are presumed to be definitive of those best interests in most jurisdictions. But the presumption can be rebutted. The court has the last word.

It's broadly the same for proxy decision-making on behalf of adults. All the legislation that permits lasting powers of attorney reserves to the court the ability to review an attorney's decision. So the fate

9. **The blind and the crippled call out for death: detail from Andrea Orcagna's *The Triumph of Death*. Death is not always seen as an unwelcome predator**

of a person who has executed a power of attorney may nonetheless be decided according to (depending on the jurisdiction) the best interests or the substituted judgement test.

Advance directives

Otherwise known as 'living wills', these are expressions by a person made, when they are still competent, about how they would like to be treated when they are no longer competent. They may apply to the withdrawal or withholding of life-sustaining treatment, but particular formalities are often required when they do. They may take the form either of a statement of principles that the person would like to have applied in relation to their end-of-life decision-making, or of a medically specific direction such as: 'If I become mentally incapacitous and doubly incontinent I do not want any life-sustaining treatment.'

Their legal effect varies between jurisdictions. In some places they are merely evidence which can be taken into account in deciding what to do. In others they have the same effect, if valid and applicable, as a refusal by a competent patient.

Importantly they are almost always *refusals*. That's because it is very unusual to be able to compel a doctor actively to do something she's unhappy about. But stopping her doing something that she might consider worthwhile is very different.

They can be useful, but they need to be approached cautiously. They need to be kept updated. Medical science moves on, and patients' views change. By the time an advance directive becomes relevant, the therapeutic or palliative options, or the patient's personal circumstances or philosophical convictions might be very different from those that pertained when the directive was made.

Sometimes, too, disease can transform personality. Suppose X is terrified of Alzheimer's disease. He makes a directive saying that if he gets the disease he refuses life-sustaining treatment. His fears are realized. He is diagnosed with Alzheimer's dementia. It strips away a lot of his cortex, but it also strips from him much of the angst that, when he was capacitous, made his life hell. He seems to have been transported into a child-like Eden. He laughs with the nurses, giggles happily with his fellow patients, and watches, with apparent enjoyment, the very worst daytime TV. So far as anyone can tell he's happier than he's ever been.

But then he contracts a chest infection. Just as in the case of our 45-year-old road traffic victim, it will kill him in five days if it's not treated with oral antibiotics. The daughter, who is the sole beneficiary under his will, produces the advance directive, saying that if he is given the antibiotics she will sue for assault.

What should the doctors do? Doesn't it seem as if X has died, and that a different person, Y, has risen from his ashes? There's only a superficial biological continuity between X and Y. They share some cells. Why should a document signed by X, who is dead, be the warrant of execution of another person, Y, whom X never met and whose condition X never anticipated?

There is no straightforward answer to this question from any jurisdiction, although textbooks often suggest that there's nothing here to discuss—and that the death of Y is legally inevitable.

Withdrawing and withholding: no distinction

A final point: it's usual for lawyers and ethicists to assert that there's no material distinction between withdrawing and withholding treatment. The reason for that is clear enough. If there were a distinction, it might prove legally or ethically hard to stop treatment that had been started. That might make doctors reluctant to start potentially valuable treatment. And that would be in no one's interests.

Chapter 10
Organ donation and the ownership of body parts

At least if I'm in England, I don't own my own body. Indeed it is incapable of being owned. I don't even possess it: *R v Bentham* (2005).

This might seem odd. I feel and talk as if I own it. But when I feel and talk that way I'm being legally very sloppy. What I'm really saying is that I have a right (or at least more of a right than anyone else) to control what happens to my body. And if the proposition is put like that, the law agrees with me. Indeed, as we've seen when we looked at the law of consent, the law agrees very robustly indeed—as long as you're a legally competent adult who's in a hospital rather than in a sadomasochistic salon.

But the law has a problem with the notion of the living body as property. Yes, there's a problem with the dead body too, of ancient origins, but this is really a corollary of the problem with the living body. Why should my descendants have a claim to my corpse when I have no claim, when alive, to the same mass of cells?

The law's distaste has two roots. The first is theological. The law was framed by believers who thought that to assert ownership over oneself was blasphemous. We didn't create ourselves, and so we don't possess title over ourselves. This attitude (perhaps buttressed by a deeply entrenched instinct) persists, although the beliefs, by and large, do not. The second is related to it, but is a creature of Kant and the Enlightenment. It's a hatred of commodification.

'Distaste'; 'instinct'; 'hatred': these words sound anomalous in a book about the law. But in this area, perhaps more than any other (which is saying a lot), judges shoot from the intuitive hip. It's hard to trace consistent strands of reasoning: policy is dressed up, often very implausibly, as logic.

Now it's property, now it's not

But it's hard to get away completely from the notion of property. Property thinking and property language are sometimes very useful. And, by and large, the courts haven't bothered to get away. They have been messily pragmatic. To the extent to which it's convenient to see body parts as property, they have done so (peppering their judgments with caveats). The overall result has been that body parts are sometimes, sort of, property, and sometimes, most emphatically, they're not.

Here's an example of that pragmatism. The English Court of Appeal in *R v Kelly* (1999) reaffirmed the old, basic rule that there was no property in unmodified body parts. It went on: 'It may be that...on some future occasion...the courts will hold that human body parts are capable of being property for the purposes of [theft], even without the acquisition of different attributes, if they have a use or significance beyond their mere existence. This may be so if, for example, they are intended for use in an organ transplant operation, for the extraction of DNA, or...as an exhibit in a trial.' This is remarkable judicial frankness. It's saying, in effect: we'll invest something with whatever attributes it needs to have in order for us to do the Right Thing. That's no bad thing. Getting the right result is rather important. Its importance tends to be underrated by legal scholars.

The Germans are unusual in being forthright and consistent about the status of severed body parts. For the Germans, these are property. Most other jurisdictions try to find ways to avoid the simple, unequivocal label 'property' and its consequences.

The High Court of Australia is typical. Clinging, in *Doodeward v Spence* (1908), to the historical insistence that there was no property in a corpse (grave robbers were charged with theft of the shroud, or with obscure ecclesiastical offences concerning grave desecration), it said that someone who puts work or skill into the treatment of a dead body or a body part so that it acquires 'some attributes differentiating it from a mere corpse awaiting burial' acquires a right to retain possession.

Doodeward was the nemesis of the thieves who stole body parts from the Royal College of Surgeons. They argued that they could not be convicted of theft, since no property had been taken. Not so, said the English Court of Appeal. The parts had been preserved: labour had been expended on them. Accordingly they were sufficiently 'property' to be stolen: *R v Kelly* (1999).

Cases about the ownership of parts or products of a living human body have tested the judges' ability to get by without the notion of property.

In *Moore v Regents of the University of California* (1990) (Supreme Court of California), the claimant had leukaemia. His spleen and other body parts were removed and, without his consent, cells were used to establish a very economically and medically valuable cell line. The cell line was patented. It earned a lot of money, but not for the claimant.

He sued, contending, amongst other things, that his cells were property which had been 'converted' to the use of another. The court disagreed with this, concerned about the stifling effect on research that might result if entirely innocent researchers might be liable in conversion for working in good faith on a cell line of whose provenance they knew nothing. There were other remedies available to the claimant: the doctor who had removed the tissue without consent was liable for breach of fiduciary duty and for operating without consent. But those claims weren't worth anything like the billions of dollars represented by the cell line.

In *Hecht v Superior Court for Los Angeles County* (1993) (California Court of Appeals), semen could be property for the purposes of being disposed of under a will because the man who had ejaculated it had had sufficient decision-making authority in relation to that semen. It was that authority that rendered it property. The effect of this was that his girlfriend could recover the semen and use it for the purpose for which it had been ejaculated—namely to inseminate her. (Similar cases in England, such as *R v Human Fertilisation and Embryology Authority ex p Blood* (1999) and *Evans v Amicus Healthcare* (2004), are best seen as cases about reproductive autonomy and specific questions of statutory construction: they are considered in Chapter 3).

Policy, rather than legal logic, is behind both these decisions. In *Moore* it was thought that a property analysis would do, on balance, more harm than good, and so it was rejected. In *Hecht* it would do more good than harm, and so it was adopted.

In the English Court of Appeal case of *Yearworth v North Bristol NHS Trust* (2010), semen ejaculated for the purposes of conceiving children after chemotherapy for cancer was negligently destroyed. A wrong had clearly been done, but how should it be described? It was held that, although a statute restricted the use that the men could make of the semen, that restriction did not mean that they could not 'have ownership' of it for the purposes of a claim in negligence, and that accordingly 'it follows a fortiori that the men had sufficient rights in relation to it as to render them capable of having been bailors of it'. Both ownership and bailment (looking after a chattel) imply the recognition in that semen of some sort of property.

So, in the US, England, and elsewhere, body parts and the products of bodies are regarded as property if that gives the right answer.

What about trading in body parts, or things that my body produces? There's a market for human blood, for instance. Can I turn myself into a blood farm, milking myself of blood for profit? Selling one kidney could go a long way towards paying off my mortgage, and could well save someone's life.

If my blood and my kidney are my property, why not? Indeed, why should the lawfulness of the sales turn on the arcane and, as we've seen, rather arbitrary question of whether the label 'property' should be applied to each? Even if my kidney isn't property, and I have no right to possess it in the sense understood by land lawyers, I've still got much more right than anyone else to decide what happens to it. If I choose to wreck my kidneys by marinating them each night in gin, the law won't stop me. Why should it stop me doing something financially sensible and socially useful? A prostitute in many jurisdictions can lawfully sell her body for sex. Why should she not sell her blood for the manufacture of life-saving blood products?

The knee-jerk ethical answer, of course, is 'commodification'—an answer that begs endless questions. Yes, this is commodification, but so what? A proper answer perhaps has to deploy the language of human dignity.

Many jurisdictions have prohibited commercial dealings in human organs and body products. The general international tone is heard in Article 21 of the Council of Europe's Convention on Human Rights and Biomedicine (1997), which provides that: 'The human body and its parts shall not, as such, give rise to financial gain.'

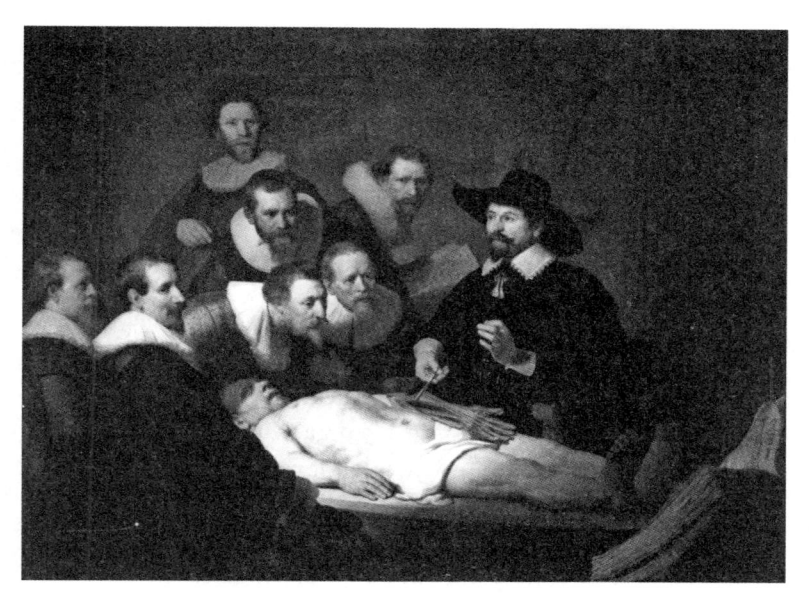

10. Rembrandt's *The Anatomy Lesson of Professor Nicolaes Tulp*.
Should you have an absolute right to determine what happens to your body after your death?

Organ donation

The demand for organs massively exceeds supply.

One solution, in relation to some organs, such as kidneys, is to encourage donation by living people. That is discussed briefly above. Altruistic donation of, for instance, bone marrow or even a kidney by live donors is lawful in many jurisdictions, often, and particularly in the case of a significant sacrifice such as a kidney, after an extensive investigation by a regulatory body to check that the would-be donor is making the offer freely, and understands fully what is involved. But this obviously won't work for hearts, lungs, and so on. If they are to be used at all, they have to be retrieved from dead bodies.

There are two main legal worries about this. The first concerns consent: have the deceased or, where appropriate, the relatives, given the appropriate permission? And the second concerns death: is the deceased really, irretrievably dead?

The ability of people to decide what happens to their bodies after their deaths is, in most countries, largely governed by statute. Those statutes generally tend to assume that autonomy extends into the grave, and that we should each be able to decide whether we rot, burn, or are recycled.

Several mechanisms are used to honour autonomy. Some jurisdictions say that if you haven't indicated what you want done with your body, it is wrong to use any organs. One therefore has to 'opt in' to donation. Others assume that if you had any objection to donation, you'd have said so, and accordingly that silence indicates consent: ('opt out'). Others require you to make a choice, for instance as a requirement of obtaining a driving licence ('mandated choice'). There is a great deal of discussion among ethicists about the acceptability of these options, and among politicians and doctors about their efficacy in increasing donation rates, but they are legally not very interesting.

More legally interesting are the questions that concern the definition of death (discussed in Chapter 9) (on which turns the propriety of harvesting organs from 'beating-heart donors') and the suggestions that are sometimes made about taking organs from patients in permanent vegetative state (universally unlawful at the moment, on precisely the same grounds as it would be unlawful to remove organs from a healthy person who happens to be undergoing an anaesthetic for an appendectomy) and from anencephalic children (which turns in all countries, at the moment, on satisfaction of the standard criteria for determining death, but which one might coherently argue should be more readily done, since the prognosis is so obvious and so dire).

Guidelines from the World Health Organization embody the broad international consensus on the safeguards to be applied when it is proposed to remove organs from a beating-heart donor, including—for ghoulishly obvious reasons—a requirement that death is certified by someone other than the clinicians who want to effect the transplant.

Intellectual property rights

The idea that a biotechnology company should point to a piece of the genome and say 'That's mine: I alone have the right to make money from knowledge of the sequence' raises all sorts of political, philosophical, and theological hackles.

As one might expect from the case of *Moore* (above), the Americans are more laissez-faire about this than the Europeans. Their deep-seated free-market tendencies, in this respect at least, get the better of their religious conservatism. The Supreme Court, endorsing a patent for a genetically engineered oil-eating bacterium, observed that the legislature had intended the patent laws to include 'anything under the sun that is made by man', and that 'made by man', in this context, included the manipulation by man of naturally occurring nucleic acid: *Diamond v Chakrabarty* (1980).

The difference between the US and Europe was shown clearly by a mouse. Harvard University produced a mouse (the OncoMouse), which was a sort of biological time bomb. It had a human cancer gene stitched into its DNA, so that it inevitably developed cancer. Harvard patented the mouse without any problem in the US. But the Europeans were more cautious. The mouse eventually got its patent, but not without a struggle against the contentions that it was immoral to patent a living organism and unlawful to patent an animal variety (both objections that arose out of the European Patent Convention).

For fewer patents for human gene sequences have been granted in Europe, than in the US. But for a time it seemed that Europe was easing up. DNA, it has been held in Europe, is not 'life', and accordingly the 'playing God'-type objections fall away. It would be disastrous for research funding, it was said, were it otherwise. But the Europeans remain intrinsically conservative when it comes to the patentability of human material. That conservatism is now embodied in the 1998 EC Directive on the patentability of biotechnological inventions. It indicates clearly where the battle lines for future legal and ethical debate are drawn. Article 5(1) provides that 'The human body, at the various stages of its formation and development, and the simple discovery of one of its elements, including the sequence or partial sequence of a gene, cannot constitute patentable inventions.' And, by Article 6(1), '[I]nventions shall be considered unpatentable where their commercial exploitation would be contrary to *ordre public* or morality...the following, in particular, shall be considered unpatentable:...processes for cloning human beings... [and]...uses of human embryos for industrial or commercial purposes.' The general position of those battle lines is similar in most jurisdictions.

Confidentiality: where the body tells a story

A celebrity stays in a hotel. The chambermaid scrapes the flakes of dandruff off the pillow and sells them to a national newspaper, which proposes to analyse the DNA with a view to saying whether or not the celebrity is the father of a much discussed lovechild. Can the celebrity say that the dandruff is his property and should be returned to him? Is it property at all? If it is, has the celebrity abandoned it, so that anyone who picks it up acquires title in it?

The example isn't so far from the real world of medical law. In the storerooms of many hospitals across the world there are tissues, legitimately removed in the course of operations and autopsies, which have been retained without the explicit consent of their erstwhile 'owners'. They too can disclose valuable information— valuable to medical researchers, but potentially valuable too to insurance companies, who might be able to tell from scanning the genome whether the person from whom the tissue was claimed is a good insurance risk.

The dandruff and the hospital storeroom cases are very similar. The storeroom sample is bigger, which hardly seems like a sound reason for treating it in a different way from the dandruff. And yet, largely because of the sample size, lawyers across the world are much more ready to worry about whether the storeroom sample amounts to property and should be treated as property than they are about the dandruff.

We've seen already some of the problems about viewing body parts, whether of the living or the dead, as property. We've seen that the law is pragmatically happy to dub something property if that helps to give the right answer. But in both these cases, there's really no need to begin to use property language to protect the interests that need protecting. What's important is not the tissue itself, but the information that it bears. The best analysis is in the law of confidentiality or privacy, not of property.

Lawyers and legislators in many jurisdictions are slowly realizing this. In the UK Human Tissue Act 2004, for instance, the unauthorized analysis of DNA is specifically recognized as a mischief in its own right. That's surely the way forward—tailoring the remedy to the harm, rather than squeezing the problem into artificial and archaic boxes (such as the 'property' box), so complicating and distorting the law.

Chapter 11
The future of medical law

Medical law, as a distinct speciality, is young. But young, in the law, doesn't necessarily mean fit. And the medical law needs to be fit to keep up with the dramatically fast-moving professions it seeks to regulate.

How is that fitness best achieved? Should we rip up the rag-tag, piecemeal, ad hoc collection of principles, rules, and speculations that comprise medical law, complaining that they're irredeemably contaminated with Victorian notions of contract, duty, and trust, and draft a brand new, up-to-the-minute code, informed by neuroscientific understandings of human volition and purged of metaphysics?

I suggest that we muddle on: that we evolve rather than revolt. The subject matter of medical law has always been and will always be the same: humans. The law that we've got was devised for humans by clever, reflective humans. The new problems that we'll get will be variations of old problems. You can't safely purge metaphysics from the law because you can't purge the metaphysics from humans.

But the speed of evolution needs to increase. Lawyers need to become more medically and philosophically literate. Good law presupposes a good understanding both of the medical facts and of the philosophical repercussions. That's a big brief. The proliferation of medical law and ethics texts and courses suggests that it can be mastered. In Chapter 1 we looked at the complex relationship between law and ethics. But in the end the nature of the relationship doesn't matter so much, as long as it's close and amicable. The conversation between the two is ever more vital.

Medicine is becoming increasingly technical, evidence-based, and protocol-driven. Despite a desperate rearguard action by the advocates of medical humanities, it's increasingly embarrassing to talk about the Art of medicine. Talk about the death of the Art becomes a self-fulfilling prophecy. The medicine of the future will be run by technically brilliant nerds. They'll look at their screens, or their shoes, but never at the patient, let alone at Sophocles. They haven't got the time, even if they had the inclination or the ability, to wonder about whether a particularly sexy new intervention is dehumanizing. And if they concluded that it was, they might think that that was not a contraindication at all.

It's therefore very important that medical law isn't over-deferential to medicine, as it has tended to be. *Bolam* should be nudged towards extinction, or at least put on the back foot, not because medicine is increasingly the business of accurately following a definitive guideline (which is the threat to *Bolam* at the moment), but because the law, not the doctors, should set the law's standards. Law has the opportunity and the duty to be appropriately holistic. Medicine has the duty, but has just about lost the opportunity.

It needs confident medical lawyers to do law's job properly. Some of *Bolam*'s more extravagant abuses arose simply because the advocates and the judges didn't have the first idea what the doctors were talking about, and so decided that they ought to give the defendant the benefit of the doubt. There would have been no doubt in the minds of better-educated judges. So we should have specialist judges. They will be faster, more medically fluent, and (at least because they're not thumbing, intimidated, through a medical dictionary during the lunchtime adjournment) will have more chance of becoming properly steeped in the wider literature—the literature that will allow them to take the wide, deep, and long view that medicine has denied itself.

There are dangers with having a professional medical judiciary. It might attract the brothers of the medical nerds. It might mean that medical law is denied the cross-fertilization from other legal disciplines that has proved so fecund in the past. It doesn't matter so much if a commercial court judge is simply a bewigged brain on a stick: he's just got to deal with money. Medical judges have to deal with bodies, minds, and souls, and with whatever strange glue sticks them together. An interest in the mechanics of bodies might denote a lack of interest in the mechanics of souls. That would be sad. But, by and large, expert medical judges are a risk worth taking. We've already got, in many jurisdictions, a cadre of expert medical lawyers. They are made of good stuff.

They need to be. There are some intellectually epic challenges ahead.

What's the status of the human embryo? Is it equivalent for all purposes (and if not, why?) to the adult? Is it ever permissible to kill X to save Y? If not, what should you do with the patient in PVS whose continued existence is consuming the funds that would buy life-saving treatment for many? Suppose the money spent on a cosmetic breast enlargement operation in London would save the lives of 10,000 children in the Congo. Should a judge in a London court conclude that it's rational to enlarge the London breasts? Is life legally an all-or-nothing thing? Does a patient who hovers in the no-man's-land between unconsciousness and death have precisely the same rights as a fully alert and healthy child? Does a woman have a right to inseminate herself with the semen left in a condom her boyfriend and she have just used? If so, what are the consequences for the boyfriend? Is it lawful to remove surgically the healthy legs of a patient because she decides she wants them mounted as an exhibit in her bathroom? A deaf couple, wanting to have a child with whom they can share the intimacy of the deaf world, create embryos by way of IVF, screen the embryos for a 'deaf' gene, and implant a 'deaf' embryo into the mother's uterus. The child, when she's born, sues the clinicians involved for her deafness. 'But you wouldn't have existed if you hadn't been deaf,' they retort. A drug is available which, if taken in pregnancy, gives the child a lifelong immunity to all types of cancer. The parents refuse to take it. The child develops cancer and sues the parents. A doctor engages in a project to produce bionic soldiers who can run faster, jump higher, and see in the dark. Should he be stopped? What's the difference in principle between this sort of enhancement and the provision of a hip prosthesis to an elderly, arthritic woman? A doctor prescribes cognitive enhancement drugs to a university student about to sit her exams. They will allow her to revise for much longer. Should that be allowed? What if they're very expensive drugs, so that their prescription will mean that rich students do better in their exams? Is there anything wrong with genetic cognitive enhancement which increases the IQ of the subject by 50 points? If there is, does that mean that it's wrong to buy your child private education which will have the effect of multiplying the number of neuronal connections in his brain so that he has a cognitive advantage? And so on.

That's an exhilarating in-tray.

Cases discussed

Where cases are mentioned in the body of the text, the year given is that of the report cited in this section. That year is sometimes not the year that the case itself was decided. The authoritative law reports sometimes take a significant time to emerge.

Chapter 1: Origins and legacies

Bolam v Friern Hospital Management Committee [1957] 1 WLR 583
Airedale NHS Trust v Bland [1993] AC 789

Chapter 3: Before birth

ELH and PBH v United Kingdom (1998) 25 EHRR CD 158
R (Mellor) v Secretary of State for the Home Department [2002] QB 13
R v Human Fertilisation and Embryology Authority ex p Blood [1997] 2 WLR 806
Evans v United Kingdom (2006) 1 FCR 585
Planned Parenthood of Central Missouri v Danforth (1976) 96 S Ct 2831
C v S [1988] QB 135
Paton v United Kingdom (1981) 3 EHRR 408
Attorney General's Reference (No. 3 of 1994) [1998] AC 245
Winnipeg Child and Family Services (Northwest Area) v G (1997) 3 BHRC 611
Paton v Trustees of the British Pregnancy Advisory Services [1979] QB 276

St George's NHS Trust v S [1998] 3 All ER 673
Vo v France [2004] 2 FCR 526
Roe v Wade (1973) 410 US 113
McKay v Essex Area Health Authority [1982] QB 1166
McFarlane v Tayside Health Board [2000] AC 59
Doe v Bolton (1993) 410 US 179
Quintavalle (on behalf of Comment on Reproductive Ethics) v Human Fertilisation and Embryology Authority [2005] 2 AC 561

Chapter 4: Confidentiality and privacy

R v Department of Health, ex p Source Informatics Ltd [2000] Lloyd's Rep Med 76
Z v Finland (1998) 25 EHRR 371
Campbell v MGN [2004] 2 AC 457
W v Egdell [1990] 1 Ch 359
Jaffee v Redmond 518 US 1 (1996)
Tarasoff et al v The Regents of the University of California (1976) 17 Cal (3d) 358
Palmer v South Tees Health Authority [1999] Lloyd's Rep Med 151
R (Axon) v Secretary of State for Health [2006] QB 539
Lewis v Secretary of State for Health [2008] EWHC 2196

Chapter 5: Consent

R v Brown [1994] 1 AC 212
Laskey, Jaggard and Brown v UK (1997) 24 EHRR 39
Schloendorff v Society of New York Hospital (1914) 211 NY 125
Malette v Shulman (1990) 67 DLR (4th) 321
Gillick v West Norfolk and Wisbech Area Health Authority [1986] 1 AC 112
Prince v Massachusetts (1944) 321 US 158
R v Mobilio [1991] 1 VR 339
R v Clarence (1888) 22 QBD 23
R v Dica [2004] 1 QB 1257
Salgo v Leland Stanford Jr University Board of Trustees (1957) 154 Cal App 2d 560
Canterbury v Spence (1972) 464 2d 772
Reibl v Hughes (1980) 2 SCR 894
Rogers v Whittaker (1992) 175 CLR 479

Sidaway v Board of Governors of the Bethlem Royal Hospital and the Maudsley Hospital [1985] 1 AC 171
Pearce v United Bristol Healthcare NHS Trust [1999] PIQR P 53

Chapter 6: Clinical negligence

Donoghue v Stevenson (sub nom McAlister v Stevenson) [1932] AC 562
Caparo Industries plc v Dickman [1990] 2 AC 605
Kapfunde v Abbey National plc [1999] 2 Lloyd's Rep Med 48
Goodwill v British Pregnancy Advisory Services [1996] 2 All ER 161
Tarasoff v The Regents of the University of California (supra)
Palmer v South Tees Health Authority (supra)
Bolam v Friern Hospital Management Committee (supra)
Bolitho v City and Hackney Health Authority [1998] AC 232
Sidaway v Board of Governors of the Bethlem Royal Hospital (supra)
Canterbury v Spence (supra)
Reibl v Hughes (supra)
F v R (1983) 33 SASR 189 (FC)
Castell v De Greef (1994) (4) SA 408
Rogers v Whittaker (supra)
Chaplin v Hicks [1911] 2 KB 786
Bailey v Ministry of Defence [2009] 1 WLR 1052
McGhee v National Coal Board [1973] 1 WLR 1
Chester v Afshar [2005] 1 AC 134

Chapter 8: Resource allocation

R v Cambridge Health Authority ex p B [1995] 1 WLR 898
Airedale NHS Trust v Bland (supra)

Chapter 9: The end of life

Airedale NHS Trust v Bland (supra)
R v Cox (1992) unreported
B v An NHS Trust [2002] 2 All ER 449
Satz v Perlmutter 379 So.2d 359 (Fla.1980)
McKay v Bergstedt (1990) 801 P. 2d 617
Georgia v McAfee (1989) 259 Ga. 579 (385 SE2d 651)

Chapter 10: Organ donation and the ownership of body parts

R v Bentham [2005] 2 WLR 384
R v Kelly [1999] QB 621
Doodeward v Spence (1908) 6 CLR 406
Moore v Regents of the University of California (1990) 793 P 2d 479
Hecht v Superior Court for Los Angeles County (1993) 20 Cal Rptr 2d 275
R v Human Fertilisation and Embryology Authority ex p Blood (supra)
Evans v Amicus Healthcare: see Evans v United Kingdom (supra)
Yearworth v North Bristol NHS Trust [2010] QB 1
Diamond v Chakrabarty (1980) 447 US 303

Chapter 11: The future of medical law

Bolam v Friern Hospital Management Committee (supra)

Further reading

General

Margaret Brazier and Emma Cave, *Medicine, Patients and the Law* (London: Penguin, 2011)

Peter de Cruz, *Comparative Healthcare Law* (London: Cavendish, 2001)

Charles Foster, *Human Dignity in Bioethics and Law* (Oxford: Hart, 2011)

Andrew Grubb, Judith Laing, and Jean McHale (eds), *Principles of Medical Law*, 3rd edn (Oxford: Oxford University Press, 2010)

Jonathan Herring, *Medical Law and Ethics*, 3rd edn (Oxford: Oxford University Press, 2010)

Emily Jackson, *Medical Law: Text Cases and Materials*, 2nd edn (Oxford: Oxford University Press, 2009)

J. Kenyon Mason and Graeme T. Laurie, *Law and Medical Ethics*, 8th edn (Oxford: Oxford University Press, 2011)

Sean Pattinson, *Medical Law and Ethics*, 3rd edn (London: Sweet & Maxwell, 2011)

Chapter 1: Origins and legacies

E. Wicks (2009) 'Religion, Law and Medicine', *Medical Law Review* 17(3), 410

Chapter 2: The enforcement of medical law

See the general further reading list.

Chapter 3: Before birth

A. Alghrani and M. Brazier (2011) 'What is it? Whose is it? Repositioning the fetus in the context of research' *Cambridge Law Journal* 70: 51

Ronald Dworkin, *Life's Dominion: An Argument about Abortion and Euthanasia* (London: HarperCollins, 1993)

J. Finnis (1973) 'The rights and wrongs of abortion', *Philosophy and Public Affairs* (2) 117

Jonathan Herring, 'The Loneliness Of Status: The Legal And Moral Significance Of Birth', in F. Ebtehaj, J. Herring, M. Johnson, and M. Richards, *Birth Rites and Rights* (Oxford: Hart, 2011)

Kirsty Horsey and Hazel Biggs, *Human Fertilization and Embryology* (London: UCL Press, 2006)

Emily Jackson, *Regulating Reproduction* (Oxford: Hart, 2001)

Christopher Kaczor, *The Ethics of Abortion: Women's Rights, Human Life and the Question of Justice* (Abingdon: Routledge, 2010)

Rosamund Scott, *Rights, Duties and the Body: Law and Ethics of the Maternal–Fetal Conflict* (Oxford: Hart, 2002)

Rosamund Scott, *Choosing Possible Lives: Law and Ethics of Prenatal and Pre-implantation Genetic Diagnosis* (Oxford: Hart Publishing, 2007)

John Spencer and Antje Du Bois-Pedain (eds), *Freedom and Responsibility in Reproductive Choice* (Oxford: Hart, 2006)

Michael Tooley, Celia Wolf-Devine, Philip Devine, and Alison Jaggar, *Abortion: Three Perspectives* (Oxford: Oxford University Press, 2009)

Chapter 4: Confidentiality and privacy

Bridgit Dimond, *Legal Aspects of Patient Confidentiality* (London/Salisbury: Quay, 2010)

General Medical Council, *Good Medical Practice* (London: GMC, 2006)

General Medical Council, *Guidance on Confidentiality* (London: GMC, 2009)

Graeme Laurie, *Genetic Privacy* (Cambridge: Cambridge University Press, 2002)

William Lowrance, *Privacy, Confidentiality and Health Research* (Cambridge: Cambridge University Press, 2012)

Heather Widdows and Caroline Mullen, *The Governance of Genetic Information: Who Decides?* (Cambridge: Cambridge University Press, 2009)

Chapter 5: Consent

Christopher Johnston (ed.), *Medical Treatment: Decisions and the Law* (London: Bloomsbury, 2009)
Mary Donnelly, *Healthcare Decision-Making and the Law: Autonomy, Capacity and the Limits of Liberalism* (Cambridge: Cambridge University Press, 2010)
Alasdair Maclean, *Autonomy, Informed Consent and Medical Law: A Relational Challenge* (Cambridge: Cambridge University Press, 2009)
Sheila MacLean, *Autonomy, Consent and the Law* (Abingdon: Routledge, 2009)

Chapter 6: Clinical negligence

Lara Khoury, *Uncertain Causation in Medical Liability* (Oxford: Hart, 2006)
Marc Stauch, *The Law of Medical Negligence in England and Germany: A Comparative Analysis* (Oxford: Hart, 2008)
R. Mulheron (2010) 'Trumping *Bolam*: A Critical Legal Analysis of *Bolitho*'s "Gloss"', *Cambridge Law Journal* 69: 609

Chapter 7: Research on human subjects

Hazel Biggs, *Healthcare Research Ethics and Law: Regulation, Review and Responsibility* (Abingdon: Routledge-Cavendish, 2009)
Philip Cheung, *Public Trust in Medical Research? Ethics, Law and Accountability* (London: Radcliffe, 2007)
Ruth Macklin, *Double Standards in Medical Research in Developing Countries* (Cambridge: Cambridge University Press, 2004)
Aurora Plomer, *The Law and Ethics of Medical Research: International Bioethics and Human Rights* (Abingdon: Routledge-Cavendish, 2005)

Chapter 8: Resource allocation

Charles Camosy, *Too Expensive to Treat?—Finitude, Tragedy, and the Neonatal ICU* (Grand Rapids, MI: Eerdmans, 2010)
Y. Denier (2008) 'Mind the Gap! Three Approaches to Scarcity in Health Care', *Medicine, Health Care and Philosophy* 11: 73
Christopher Newdick, *Who Should we Treat? Rights, Rationing, and Resources in the NHS* (Oxford: Oxford University Press, 2005)

Keith Syrett, *Law, Legitimacy and the Rationing of Healthcare* (Cambridge: Cambridge University Press, 2007)

Chapter 9: The end of life

Hazel Biggs, *Euthanasia, Death with Dignity and the Law* (Oxford: Hart, 2001)
Ronald Dworkin, *Life's Dominion* (London: HarperCollins, 1993)
Jonathan Glover, *Causing Death and Saving Lives* (London: Penguin, 1990)
Richard Huxtable, *Euthanasia, Ethics and the Law: From Conflict to Compromise* (Abingdon: Routledge-Cavendish, 2007)
Richard Huxtable, *Law, Ethics and Compromise at the Limits of Life: To Treat or not to Treat* (Abingdon: Routledge-Cavendish, 2012)
Emily Jackson and John Keown, *Debating Euthanasia* (Oxford: Hart, 2011)
John Keown (ed.), *Euthanasia Examined* (Cambridge: Cambridge University Press, 1995)
John Keown (ed.), *Euthanasia, Ethics and Public Policy* (Cambridge: Cambridge University Press, 2002)
Penney Lewis, *Assisted Dying and Legal Change* (Oxford: Oxford University Press, 2007)
A. Maclean (2008) 'Advance Directives and Anticipatory Decision-Making', *Medical Law Review* 1
Sheila McLean, *Assisted Dying: Reflections on the Need to Reform* (Abingdon: Routledge, 2007)
Mary Warnock and Elisabeth Macdonald, *Easeful Death: Is there a Case for Assisted Dying?* (Oxford: Oxford University Press, 2009)

Chapter 10: Organ donation and the ownership of body parts

Richard Hardcastle, *Law and the Human Body* (Oxford: Hart, 2007)
David Price, *Human Tissue in Transplantation and Research: A Modal Legal and Ethical Framework* (Cambridge: Cambridge University Press, 2009)
Stephen Wilkinson, *Bodies for Sale: Ethics and Exploitation in the Human Body Trade* (London: Routledge, 2003)
T. M. Wilkison, *Ethics and the Acquisition of Organs* (Oxford: Oxford University Press, 2011)

"牛津通识读本"已出书目

古典哲学的趣味	福柯	地球
人生的意义	缤纷的语言学	记忆
文学理论入门	达达和超现实主义	法律
大众经济学	佛学概论	中国文学
历史之源	维特根斯坦与哲学	托克维尔
设计,无处不在	科学哲学	休谟
生活中的心理学	印度哲学祛魅	分子
政治的历史与边界	克尔凯郭尔	法国大革命
哲学的思与惑	科学革命	丝绸之路
资本主义	广告	民族主义
美国总统制	数学	科幻作品
海德格尔	叔本华	罗素
我们时代的伦理学	笛卡尔	美国政党与选举
卡夫卡是谁	基督教神学	美国最高法院
考古学的过去与未来	犹太人与犹太教	纪录片
天文学简史	现代日本	大萧条与罗斯福新政
社会学的意识	罗兰·巴特	领导力
康德	马基雅维里	无神论
尼采	全球经济史	罗马共和国
亚里士多德的世界	进化	美国国会
西方艺术新论	性存在	民主
全球化面面观	量子理论	英格兰文学
简明逻辑学	牛顿新传	现代主义
法哲学:价值与事实	国际移民	网络
政治哲学与幸福根基	哈贝马斯	自闭症
选择理论	医学伦理	德里达
后殖民主义与世界格局	黑格尔	浪漫主义

批判理论	德国文学	儿童心理学
电影	戏剧	时装
俄罗斯文学	腐败	现代拉丁美洲文学
古典文学	医事法	卢梭
大数据	癌症	隐私
洛克	植物	电影音乐
幸福	法语文学	抑郁症
免疫系统	微观经济学	传染病
银行学	湖泊	